# IP Routing Protocols

ISBN 0-13-014248-4

# Prentice Hall Series In
# Advanced Communications Technologies

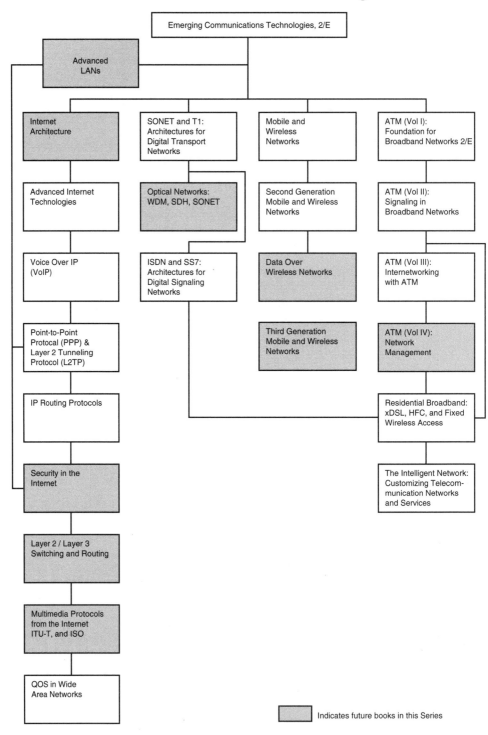

Emerging Communications Technologies, 2/E

Advanced LANs

Internet Architecture

SONET and T1: Architectures for Digital Transport Networks

Mobile and Wireless Networks

ATM (Vol I): Foundation for Broadband Networks 2/E

Advanced Internet Technologies

Optical Networks: WDM, SDH, SONET

Second Generation Mobile and Wireless Networks

ATM (Vol II): Signaling in Broadband Networks

Voice Over IP (VoIP)

ISDN and SS7: Architectures for Digital Signaling Networks

Data Over Wireless Networks

ATM (Vol III): Internetworking with ATM

Point-to-Point Protocal (PPP) & Layer 2 Tunneling Protocol (L2TP)

Third Generation Mobile and Wireless Networks

ATM (Vol IV): Network Management

IP Routing Protocols

Residential Broadband: xDSL, HFC, and Fixed Wireless Access

Security in the Internet

The Intelligent Network: Customizing Telecommunication Networks and Services

Layer 2 / Layer 3 Switching and Routing

Multimedia Protocols from the Internet ITU-T, and ISO

QOS in Wide Area Networks

Indicates future books in this Series

# IP Routing Protocols
## RIP, OSPF, BGP, PNNI, and Cisco Routing Protocols

Uyless Black

Prentice Hall PTR
Upper Saddle River, New Jersey 07458
www.phptr.com

**Library of Congress Cataloging-in-Publication Data**

Black, Uyless D.
    IP routing : RIP, OSPF, BGP, PNNI, and routing protocols  / Uyless Black.
      p.  cm.
    Includes bibliographical references and index.
    ISBN 0–13–014248–4
    1.  TCP/IP (Computer network protocol) 2.  Routers (Computer networks) I.  Title.

TK5105.585 .B535   2000
004.6′2—dc21                                       00–021908
                                                      CIP

Acquisitions editor: *Mary Franz*
Editorial assistant: *Noreen Regina*
Cover designer: *Talan Agasyan*
Cover design director: *Jerry Votta*
Buyer: *Maura Goldstaub*
Marketing manager: *Lisa Konzelmann*
Project coordinator: *Anne Trowbridge*
Compositor/Production services: *Pine Tree Composition, Inc.*

© 2000 by Uyless Black
Published by Prentice Hall PTR
Prentice-Hall, Inc.
Upper Saddle River, New Jersey 07458

Prentice Hall books are widely used by corporations and government agencies for training, marketing, and resale.

The publisher offers discounts on this book when ordered in bulk quantities. For more information contact:

        Corporate Sales Department
        Phone: 800–382–3419
        Fax: 201–236–7141
        E-mail: corpsales@prenhall.com

        Or write:

        Prentice Hall PTR
        Corp. Sales Dept.
        One Lake Street
        Upper Saddle River, New Jersey 07458

Printed in the United States of America
10  9  8  7  6  5  4  3  2  1


ISBN: 0–13–014248–4


Prentice-Hall International (UK) Limited, *London*
Prentice-Hall of Australia Pty. Limited, *Sydney*
Prentice-Hall Canada Inc., *Toronto*
Prentice-Hall Hispanoamericana, S.A., *Mexico*
Prentice-Hall of India Private Limited, *New Delhi*
Prentice-Hall of Japan, Inc., *Tokyo*
Pearson Education Asia Pte. Ltd.
Editora Prentice-Hall do Brasil, Ltda., *Rio de Janeiro*

*This book is dedicated to the folks at Pine Tree Composition. They have been with me since the beginning of this series, and have made my writing tasks much easier with their great support, patience, and editing skills. It never ceases to amaze me as to how errors continue to "stay with the book," even though the author and editors may have reread, and rechecked the material many times. Pine Tree has been a valuable cog in this series by cleaning up my grammar goofs, and gleaning out those irritating errors that spellcheckers can't find. I would especially like to thank my editor at Pine Tree, Patty Donovan, for her exceptional support to me and this series.*

The IP routing protocols are the sextants of the Internet. The chief use of the sextant is in navigation, and it enables a person to determine his or her location on earth. In so doing, the sextant provides a means for this person to discover routes, perhaps through uncharted terrain.

The chief use of the IP routing protocols is the same as the sextant: to discover routes, except these routes are through an internet terrain.

One of my favorite stories about the sextant is its use in the Lewis and Clark expedition in the early 1800s, and its contribution to the mapping of a large part of the northwestern United States. A wonderful book on this adventure is *Undaunted Courage*, by Stephen E. Ambrose.

Another of my favorite stories is my attempt to learn to use the sextant during my tour as a Communications Officer in the U.S. Navy. One of the chief bos'ns on my ship decided that I was spending too much time in the communications "shack". So, on clear days, he would respectfully ask for my presence on the bridge, and upon my arrival would teach me how to measure angular elevations of astronomical objects, all of which would lead to determine the ship's position in the South China Sea.

Even though I never mastered the sextant, I enjoyed the lessons, and I marveled at the ease with which the chief bos'n made his very accurate observations and fixes.

The sextant is more of an historical topic now than a useful tool. It has been replaced by the Global Positioning System (GPS). And I too have moved on, and the sextant is a somewhat distant memory. But, from the mid-1700s until a few decades ago, this marvelous little tool had a profound impact on the discoveries of many passages and routes throughout the world. So, it certainly deserves to grace the cover of this book.

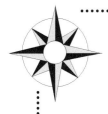

# Contents

---

**CHAPTER 4    Bridges                                                          66**

---

---

---

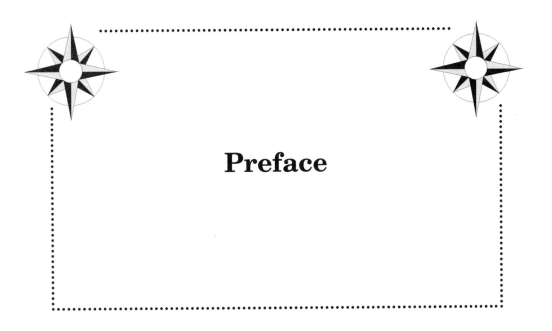

# Preface

This book is one in a series of books called, "Emerging Communications Technologies." As the name of the book implies, the focus is on how routes are discovered and used in the Internet.

The subject matter of this book is vast and my approach is to provide a system view of the topic. In consonance with the intent of this series, this general survey also has considerable detail but not to the level of detail needed to design a routing protocol, or to configure a bridge or router. For that, I leave you to your project team and the various specifications that establish the standards for routing operations.

This book is considered to be at an intermediate-to-advanced level. As such, it assumes the reader has a background in data communications.

I hope you find this book a valuable addition to your library.

## USE OF APPENDICES

The subject of internetworking and route discovery is built on many concepts, and several supporting IEEE, ISO, and Internet protocols and standards. For those readers that are familiar with these subjects, I have not encumbered the main body of the book with a description of these systems. From previous experience, I also know that a substantial number of my readers will not have full knowledge of some (perhaps all) of these supporting and underlying operations. I also know that some of the readers are well-versed in these underlying, supporting protocols.

I have provided several tutorials on these subjects and have included them in the appendices to this book. I suggest you take a look at the appendices before you start reading the book, and then study those topics in which you need more information. On occasion, I will refer to an appendix to alert you to some required background information for a subject under discussion. If appropriate, I will refer you directly to a figure or a table to enable you to do a quick check to determine if you should divert to the specific material in the appendix before proceeding further.

With this approach, I hope meet the needs of readers with various levels of experience and knowledge.

## CREDITS

Most of this book has been prepared based on my experience with routing protocols, and configuring routers. I have also relied on Cisco user manuals, and the Internet RFCs pertaining to routing protocols. I cite Cisco in some of my examples, due to Cisco's market position and the wide interest in Cisco routers.

Once again, I thank the Internet task forces and the Internet Society for their generous permission to use the Internet RFCs. Please note:

# 1

# Introduction

## INTRODUCTION

This chapter introduces internetworking and route discovery concepts, and explains why these operations are important to communications networks. The separate processes of forwarding and route advertising are defined, as well as the role of routing domains. The layered protocol model is used to clarify where the route discovery protocols are placed in relation to this model. The chapter concludes with a brief look at the routing protocols that are the subject of this book.

## WHY INTERNETWORKING?

Internetworking is the sharing of computer resources by connecting the computers through a number of communications networks. The networks can be public or private networks; they can be local or wide area networks.

Internetworking is essential to the efficient operations of communications networks for a number of reasons, all of which revolve around an idea called *packet containment*.[1] First, it is impossible to operate one

---

[1]The term *packet* is used in this book to describe the unit of traffic that is sent across a communications link from one computer to another. Other terms are used in the literature, and I refer you to Figure A-10 in Appendix A for more detailed information.

large, monolithic network throughout an enterprise or a collection of enterprises. A network distributes traffic to a selected user or to groups of users. It is unlikely each of these users wish to receive traffic from all other users in other networks. Therefore, addresses are assigned to a user or to a group of users, and packets are sent to the recipients based on these addresses.

This notion was developed and refined in telephone networks. Through the use of area codes, exchange codes, and local line numbers, a user can "select" the party to which it wishes to be connected. Therefore, traffic is restricted to a select party-pair, or a group of parties. That is, traffic is contained to a restricted "domain," and need not be sent to all parties in the network.

Second, the user of multiple networks allows these networks to be isolated from each other when needed, yet joined together, when also needed. Let's talk about the isolation aspect of internetworking. Network isolation is critical to network performance. For example, if one network fails, this failure need not place other networks in jeopardy. In addition, networks may have different security needs, and through the use of security measures, one network can be shielded from the intrusion of users on other networks.

Third, some networks are designed such that traffic sent to one user is received by all users on that network (the reader is likely familiar with this concept, a broadcast network). By partitioning these networks into single "domains," and using an internetworking unit (a switch, for example) between these broadcast networks, it is possible to contain the amount of traffic that is sent between the networks.

## WHY ROUTE DISCOVERY?

In order to connect networks together so that they may exchange information, and in order to move traffic through these networks efficiently, a method is needed whereby a specific path (a route) is found among the many nodes (routers, servers, workstations) and routes that connect two or more network users together. But it is not just a route that allows traffic to be exchanged between the users; it is the "best" route between these users.

The term *best* is defined based on what one considers important in the support of the user traffic. For a real-time video conference, best might be a route that offers the lowest and most consistent delay. For a funds transfer to a bank, best might be a route that offers encryption services.

Whatever best means, identifying a route entails a route discovery operation, the subject of this book. In its simplest terms, route discovery is the process of finding the best route between two or more nodes in an internet.[2]

## INTERNETWORKING DEFINITIONS

The term *internetworking unit* (IWU) is used to describe a machine that performs relaying (and perhaps route discovery) functions between networks.

Networks are often called subnetworks (or subnets), as shown in Figure 1–1. The term does not mean that they provide fewer functions than a conventional network. Rather, it means that the subnetworks contribute to the overall operations for internetworking. Stated another way, the subnetworks comprise an internetwork or an internet.

An internetworking unit is designed to remain transparent to the end user application. The end user application resides in the host machines connected to the networks; rarely are user applications placed in the IWU. This approach is attractive from several standpoints. The IWU need not burden itself with the application protocols. Since they are not invoked at the IWU, the IWU can dedicate itself to fewer tasks, such as managing the traffic between networks. It is not concerned with application-level functions such as database access, electronic mail, and file management.

As shown in Figure 1–1, the internetworking unit is also called by other names, such as bridge, gateway, and router, the subject of the next part of this chapter.

### Internetworking and the Protocol Stacks

Data networks were originally conceived to be fairly small systems consisting of relatively few machines. As the need for data communications services has grown, it has become necessary to connect networks together for the sharing of resources, distribution of functions, and administrative control. In addition, some LANs, by virtue of their restricted

---

[2]Internet with an uppercase I refers to the public Internet, and internet, with a lowercase i, refers to a private network.

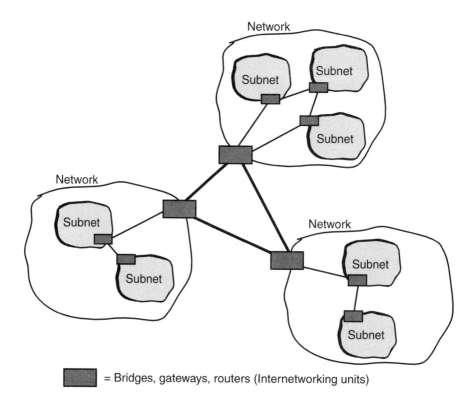

**Figure 1–1    Internetworking**

distance, often need to be connected together through other devices, such as bridges and routers.

Figure 1–2 shows the relationships of these devices vis-à-vis the layered protocol model. For those readers not familiar with layered protocols, I have provided a brief description of them in Appendix A, and Appendix B explains the addresses cited in the discussion.

The *bridge* operates at the data link layer (L_2 of the layered model). Typically, it uses media access control (MAC) addresses to perform relaying functions. The relaying functions enable the bridge to forward packets from one LAN to another.

As a general rule, a bridge is a fairly low-function device and connects networks that are homogeneous (for example, Ethernet networks). But bridges are available that internetwork different LANs, for example FDDI LANs and Ethernets. Additionally, bridges connect LANs and not wide area networks, such as Frame Relay.

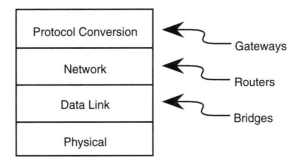

**Figure 1–2   Placement of Internetworking Operations**

A *router* operates at the network layer (L_3 of the layered model) because it uses network layer addresses (for example, an IP address) to relay packets through networks. It usually contains more capabilities than a bridge and may offer flow control mechanisms as well as interfaces to networks such as Frame Relay.

The term *gateway* is used to describe an entity (a machine or software module) which may perform packet relaying through networks, and also may act as a protocol conversion or mapping facility. For example, a gateway could relay traffic from one node to another, and also provide conversion between two different types of applications or routing protocols. I will explain the term gateway in more detail shortly.

To avoid any confusion about these terms, some people use the term internetworking unit (IWU), introduced earlier, as a generic term to describe a router, a gateway, a bridge, or anything else that performs relaying functions between networks and through networks.

## INTERNETWORKING AND THE INTERNET

Most everyone who uses the Internet knows that it has grown very rapidly in the past few years. Figure 1–3 shows the growth of the Internet routing tables, which is an indication of the overall growth of the Internet [MOY98].[3]

When the Internet was first founded, there were very few nodes and not many hosts on the network. However, as more users subscribed to

---

[3] [MOY98] Moy, John T., *OSPF: Anatomy of an Internet Routing Protocol,* Addison-Wesley, 1998.

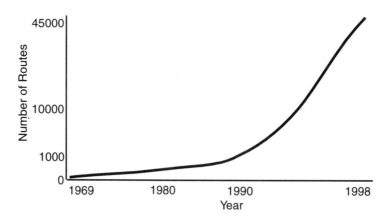

**Figure 1–3    Growth of Internet Routing Tables [MOY88]**

the Internet, and as it became a commercial network, with easy-to-use features, the number of hosts and routers increased dramatically. This rapid growth translated into the use of thousands of addresses that are loaded into routing tables. These addresses are used by the routers to make forwarding decisions on the packets that arrive at the router.

This growth and the resultant large address table places a heavy workload on the routers that use this table. Each incoming packet's destination address is compared to the entries in the table to find a match to determine the next node to which to route the packet. The large table also places a heavy workload on the route discovery protocols, since they must advertise these addresses.

This situation has not been solved, but it has been ameliorated with the use of aggregate addresses: advertising multiple IP nodes with only one IP address. We return to this subject later in this chapter.

### Connecting in the Internet

An Internet user connects to the Internet through an Internet Service Provider (ISP). In turn, the ISP connects to other ISPs through agreements called peering arrangements. These arrangements allow the ISPs to support each other in the exchange of end user traffic. This exchange of traffic occurs at "core" routers that are placed at key locations in the Internet.

Core routers are those routers at major exchange points in the Internet. ISPs are connected at these facilities, which are known as Network Access Points (NAPs), Metropolitan Area Exchanges (MAEs), or Commercial Internet Exchanges (CIXs), see Figure 1–4. The NAP's job is to exchange traffic between ISPs and other networks. NAPs must operate at link speeds of 100 Mbit/s, and thus their local networks have been implemented with FDDI (the Fiber Distributed Data Interface), 100BASE-T (Fast Ethernet at 100 Mbit/s), or 1000Base-T (Gigabit Ethernet at 1 Gbit/s). Many of them have ATM switches and SONET links to other NAPs and the larger ISPs.

Figure 1–4 also lists 11 NAPs that are currently running in the United States. Some of them are called MAEs. Some are named based on the Federal Internet Exchange (FIX), others based on the CIX. FIXs were set up by the NSF to support federal regional networks. The CIX was set up by the public Internet Service Providers.

The NAP concept was established by the National Science Foundation (NSF) when it was managing the Internet. Originally, there were four NAPs (NSF-awarded NAPs), but due to the growth of the Internet, additional NAPs have been created, as shown in Figure 1–4. If you wish more information on NAPs, the MAEs, as well as topology maps of the Internet, check www.boardwatch.com.

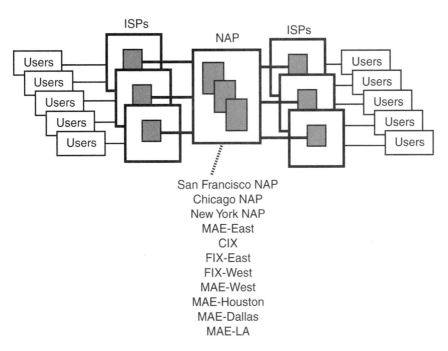

San Francisco NAP
Chicago NAP
New York NAP
MAE-East
CIX
FIX-East
FIX-West
MAE-West
MAE-Houston
MAE-Dallas
MAE-LA

**Figure 1–4   The Network Access Point (NAP) and Others**

The core routers have over 45,000 entries in their routing tables. Obviously, the manner in which the table is accessed determines to a great extent the ability of the router to support high volumes of traffic, easily tens of thousands of packets per second.

However, most routers at the edge of the Internet do not have all these entries in their routing tables. Instead, they often rely on a default entry in the table to direct their IP datagrams to a default router.

## FORWARDING AND ROUTING

Chapter 3 explains the major responsibilities of internetworking units, such as bridges and routers. For this introduction, two protocols are employed by these machines: (a) one protocol (say, protocol a) relays packets from a source user to a destination user, and (b) the other protocol (say, protocol b) finds a route for the packets to travel from the source to the destination. Unfortunately, several terms are used to describe these two types of protocols, and the terms themselves are not models of clarity. Nonetheless, we must deal with them. Figure 1–5 is used to explain these terms.

The older term to describe protocol a is routing, and the older terms to describe protocol b are route advertising, or route discovery. These latter two terms are still used in the industry.

Today, as Figure 1–5 shows, the term *routing* is now used to describe protocol b, and the term *forwarding* is used to describe protocol a. In keeping with current industry practice, the new terms are used in this book. I will use route advertising, route discovery, and routing synonymously. However, I continue to use the term *routing table* to describe the table of addresses used to forward packets through the IWU.

To summarize, two protocols are involved in the internetworking process:

- Forwarding: Using a routing table to make a forwarding decision.
- Routing: Using route advertisements to acquire the knowledge to create the routing table that the forwarding protocol uses.

The routing table need not be created with the routing protocol. In some situations, entries in the table can be manually configured, and in others, the entries are created with other protocols, such as the Address Resolution Protocol (ARP).

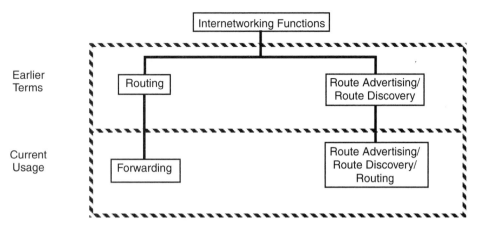

**Figure 1–5    Terms and Concepts**

## YET ANOTHER TERM: GATEWAY

Earlier discussions in this chapter introduced the term *gateway*. This term has more than one meaning; indeed, some vendors use the term in some of their commercial product names. I first came across the term when I was working with the old ARPAnet (now the Internet). It was used to describe a node in the ARPAnet that connected a user into the ARPAnet backbone. This node was called a gateway. One of the functions of the gateway node was to perform route discovery operations on behalf of a user node. These early route discovery protocols were called gateway protocols.

For many years, the term gateway protocol was used to describe what is shown in Figure 1–5 as routing advertising or route discovery. A considerable amount of literature still uses the term in this context.

But the term *gateway protocol* is also associated with an upper-layer function (see Figure 1–2) involving applications such as email and file transfer. So, an email gateway might be one that translates an organization's private email packets to Internet email packets and vice versa. A file transfer gateway may translate between two different file transfer systems, and so on.

Interestingly, some IWUs are designed to interwork different types of layer 2 or layer 3 networks. For example, in a LAN environment, it may be necessary to internetwork Ethernet networks with token ring networks. In this situation, this IWU is actually a layer 2 gateway. Yet another situation arises when different WANs must be interconnected, for example an IP-based network with an X.25 network. In this situation, this IWU is a layer 3 gateway.

To conclude this discussion, some people use the terms **router** and **gateway** synonymously. Keep in mind that the term gateway can be used in a variety of ways.

## PLACEMENT OF ROUTING PROTOCOLS IN THE PROTOCOL STACK

We have learned that route discovery can take place with layer 2 or layer 3 addresses. This section goes into more detail about the layered model and the placement of protocols in the protocol stack. Figure 1–6

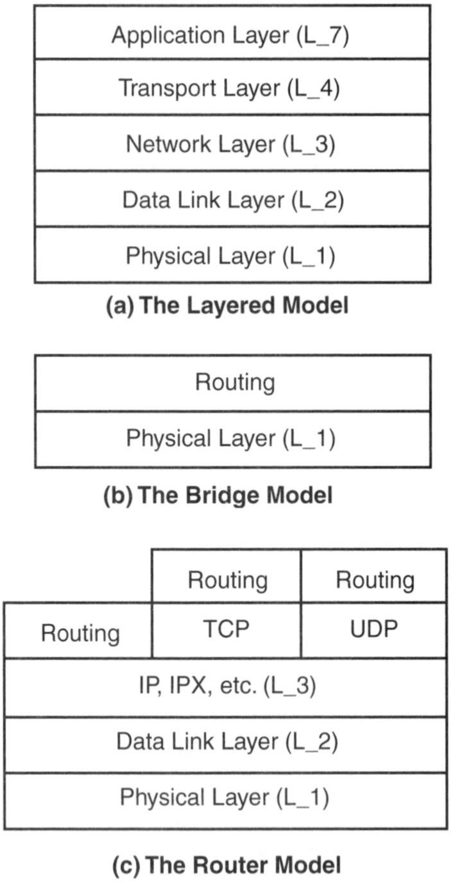

| Application Layer (L_7) |
|---|
| Transport Layer (L_4) |
| Network Layer (L_3) |
| Data Link Layer (L_2) |
| Physical Layer (L_1) |

**(a) The Layered Model**

| Routing |
|---|
| Physical Layer (L_1) |

**(b) The Bridge Model**

| | Routing | Routing |
|---|---|---|
| Routing | TCP | UDP |
| IP, IPX, etc. (L_3) | | |
| Data Link Layer (L_2) | | |
| Physical Layer (L_1) | | |

**(c) The Router Model**

**Figure 1–6   Routing Protocols and the Protocol Stack**

shows the placement of route discovery protocols in the Internet layered architecture that pertain to layer 2 or layer 3 route discovery protocols.

First, in Figure 1–6 (a), the general Internet layered model is shown. This model and the functions of the layers are described in Appendix A. Next, the bridge model is shown in Figure 1–6 (b). Recall that the bridge operates at the data link layer, with MAC addresses, and is designed to internetwork LANs.

Our focus is now on Figure 1–6 (c). The routing protocols operate in this model in three "layered positions." First, some of the protocols operate without layer 4 (TCP or UDP) and are positioned in this figure running on top of IP, IPX, etc. Second, others run over TCP, and third, others run over UDP.

## ROUTING DOMAINS

A key concept in this book is a routing domain, depicted in Figure 1–7. The routing domain is an administrative entity, and its scope depends on many factors, but they are eventually determined by the network administrator, such as an ISP. The term scope means how many networks and subnets are associated with the domain. A small domain consists of a few subnets; a large domain consists of many. The size of the routing domain is relative, but its goal is to establish boundaries for the dissemination of routing information; in effect, to realize packet containment. If the domain contains many networks, it is likely that more routing packets must be exchanged than in a domain with fewer networks.

In addition, a routing domain is useful for security administration. For example, an organization's routing domain may consist of trusted networks, in which limited security procedures are implemented. At the edges of the routing domain are firewalls that filter traffic into and out of the domain. In fact, the security policy of the routing domain may forbid the passing-through of certain types of traffic. If the traffic can indeed traverse a particular network, the network is called a pass-through network.

Another function of the routing domain for some networks is to provide accounting, billing, and revenue services. Obviously, if the network manager cannot control the routing domain and account for traffic, it is impossible to know how to charge for a service.

Figure 1–7 shows how the components may be configured inside the domain. To optimize route advertising, hierarchical routing domains are created. In this example, routing domain A (RD A) is divided into two subdomains, RD A1 and RD A2. For traffic that does not pass beyond an

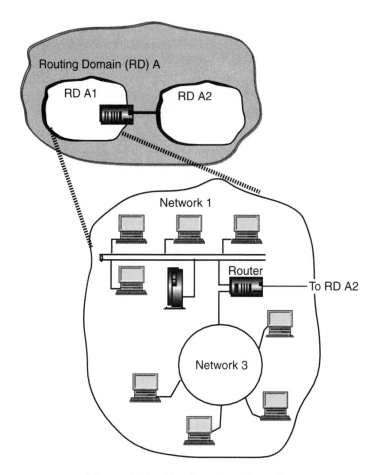

**Figure 1–7    The Routing Domain**

RD boundary, it is not necessary to know (or do route advertising) about any nodes outside the domain; once again, the idea of packet containment comes into play.

The hosts and servers attached to networks 1 and 2 in RD A1 have their presence made known to each other through route advertising packets. If they do not send or receive packets outside this domain (which is a common practice inside private enterprises), there is no need for other routing domains to know about them.

In most situations, a router acts as the conduit for passing end user traffic into and out of the domain. The router also acts as the conduit for passing route advertising information between routing domains.

In many situations, a designated router is assigned the task of route advertising for a network, and/or a routing domain, and if more than one router is attached to the network, one of them is specified as the primary router.

### Routing Domains Overcome the "Flat Network" Problem

The information that is advertised between domains is "filtered." The term *filtered* means that every advertising packet in one domain is not sent to another domain. Instead, summary or aggregated information is given to the other domains. This idea is central to the design philosophy behind hierarchical routing domains and the idea of packet containment.

The hierarchy concept obviates a flat network topology. A flat network requires each switching node to maintain a routing table of the entire topology of a routing domain or even multiple routing domains. This approach is not feasible for large internets. Thus, the routing hierarchy concept is designed to scale well for large internets.

### How a Host is Made Known to Other Domains

I just mentioned that in the Internet or in internets, a common approach is to establish hierarchies of routing domains (levels of domains). In Figure 1–8, the two routing domains explained earlier (RD A and RD B) are connected. The two routers in these domains have been configured to be domain border routers; they are responsible for the exchange of routing information on behalf of their respective routing domains.

The hierarchy in this figure is as follows: RD A is divided into two other routing domains, RD A1 and RD A2. Likewise, RD B is divided into

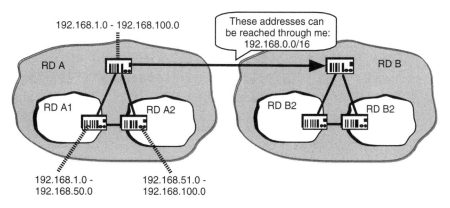

**Figure 1–8   Connecting High-level Routing Domains (RD)**

two other routing domains, RD B1 and RD B2. Each of these four "subdomains" also has a designated router (or routers) that is (are) responsible for route advertising for their respective domains.

Once again, the attractive aspect of the hierarchical approach to internetworking is the practice of using routing domains to perform summary or aggregated advertising. For example, the router at RD A can use only one route advertisement packet to advertise multiple hosts and networks within the domain.

To see how, let us assume RD A is responsible for networks with addresses in the range of 192.168.1.0 through 192.168.100.0. For this example, the third decimal digit is used to identify specific networks (as a general practice, called subnets) 1 through 100. The fourth decimal digit is used to identify the hosts attached to these networks. RD A1 is responsible for subnets 192.168.1.0 through 192.168.50.0, and RD A2 is responsible for subnets 192.168.51.0 through 192.168.100.0.

The RD A domain border router sends an advertisement packet to the RD B domain border router. The advertisement states that all IP datagrams with an IP destination address that begins with 102.168 can be sent to RD A. This information is shown in Figure 1–8 as "192.168.0.0/16."

The value of 16 is called a prefix. It is used to serve as an address mask, and the 16 signifies that the mask is 16 bits in length, that it covers the first 16 contiguous bits of the address in front of it, namely 192.168.

Let us assume that each of the 100 networks in RD A may have as many as 254 hosts attached. Therefore, this one advertisement serves the purpose of advertising 254 hosts × 100 networks = 25,400 addresses. Furthermore, the routing tables at the domain routers do not need to store 25,400 addresses, only the aggregated address and its prefix. Of course, when the IP datagram reaches its final destination subnet, then the full address (with the host number) must be used to forward the traffic to the correct host.

We must leave the subject of address aggregation and prefixes—they are subjects unto themselves. However, more information is available on this subject in Appendix B.

## MULTIPLE ROUTING PROTOCOLS

In most routing domains, more than one routing protocol is used. Several reasons exist for the use of multiple routing protocols. One reason is the simple fact that the art and science of route management continues to be improved with the resultant implementation of new protocols. Yet older systems still must use the legacy protocols.

Another reason is that some of the routing protocols have been developed by vendors, others by standards groups, and no clear "winner" has emerged among these systems. Therefore, it is not unusual for one network to support one type of routing protocol, and another network to support a different one.

There are other reasons. Networks come in many flavors, and they have different needs. For example, different route management requirements often exist inside routing domains that are different from those protocols that operate between these domains.

In some domains, it may be important to be able to calculate routes immediately and update the routing tables quickly in the event of changes. In other domains, rapid route updates may not be important, but it may be important to have address aggregation because the number of addresses in the domain are limited.

Usually, administrative routing policies within a domain are not as important as they are between domains. Typically, within the domain, the main concern is the best route. To be sure, the best route is important between domains, but that consideration may be overridden by policy concerns, say between two ISPs, and their peering arrangements with each other. Indeed, a "best" route may not be implemented between ISPs because of administrative considerations.

As a consequence of these varying needs, routing protocols are designed to handle special needs, and therefore, more than one approach is appropriate.

## DESIGN GOALS OF ROUTING PROTOCOLS

The route advertisements are used by routers and bridges to calculate routes and make entries in a routing table. The manner in which the route is calculated is based on a routing algorithm, and the algorithm is a very important part of the overall routing architecture.

The network designer and manager carefully evaluate these algorithms, and look for key aspects of their behavior. Five design goals can be established for routing algorithms [THOM98].[4] They are depicted in Figure 1–9.

---

[4][THOM98] Thomas, Thomas M II, *OSPF Network Design Solutions,* Cisco Press, Macmillan Technical Publishing, 1998

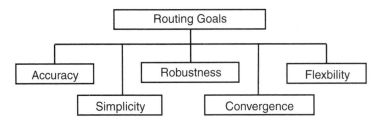

**Figure 1–9    Routing Algorithm Design Goals**

The foremost goal is accuracy. It makes little difference if the route-calculation algorithm is simple, robust, or whatever, if it does not calculate and select accurate routes according to the "best" route criteria. Of course, the best route depends on the metrics and the algorithm's use of the metrics.

Since route management is an overhead component in a bridge or router, it must not consume inordinate overhead. Insofar as possible, routing algorithms should be simple, and they should not consume a lot of memory and CPU capacity.

Routing algorithms should be robust. During periods of unusual types of traffic or large volumes of traffic, they should not fail. If they fail, it should not mean a complete loss of routing capability. Obviously the goal of robustness is one aspect of the goal of accuracy.

Another goal for the routing algorithm is rapid convergence. The term convergence in this context means the union or meeting of routing information between all routing devices in a routing domain. The idea is that once a change occurs that requires a route recalculation in the domain, the update messages and resulting recalculation of the routes is done quickly, and all nodes reach agreement (convergence) quickly.

The last goal is flexibility. A routing algorithm should accommodate different metrics; it should support default routes; it should allow a hierarchy of routing domains, it should support one or more than one path to a destination, etc.

Some routing protocols and algorithms are better than others in meeting these goals, and they are examined later in this text.


## PREVIEW OF THE ROUTING PROTOCOLS

Public and private internets have implemented a number of routing protocols, some of which have become international standards. Table 1–1 summarizes those protocols that will be explained in this book.

First, a bit of history (and not shown in Table 1–1). An early implementation of a routing protocol in the Internet was the Gateway-to-Gateway Protocol (GGP). This protocol was originally designed to be used in the ARPAnet backbone. It is not used today due to its overhead and operating restrictions. The External Gateway Protocol (EGP) replaced GGP, and for a while, was the prevalent protocol for use between networks. It overcame some of the problems of GGP, but it is no longer in use. So as a prelude to the chapters in this book, let us look briefly at the extant protocols.

The Routing Information Protocol (RIP) was designed by Xerox's Palo Alto Research Center (PARC) for use on LANs, although it is used today in many WANs. RIP had some design flaws when it was introduced into the industry. Several have been corrected by RFCs and/or vendor-specific solutions.

The Open Shortest Path First (OSPF) protocol has been designed to solve some of the problems found in RIP. OSPF is widely used in the industry. Its counterpart in the OSI protocol stack is the Intermediate

**Table 1–1    Routing Protocols**

---

*Routing Information Protocol (RIP)*

  Intended for use on broadcast LANs

  Widely used today, with several variations

*Open Shortest Path First (OSPF)*

  Designed to overcome limitations of RIP, and others

  Widely used today

*Intermediate System to Intermediate System (IS-IS)*

  Designed by Digital, and part of OSI (similar to OSPF)

*Border Gateway Protocol (BGP)*

  Overcomes some of the limitations of EGP

  Preferred protocol between ASPs

*Interdomain Routing Protocol (IDRP)*

  An OSI-based protocol

*Private Network-to-Network Interface (PNNI)*

  A newcomer

  Based on using an ATM network

*Inter-Gateway Routing Protocol (IGRP) and Enhanced IGRP (EIGRP)*

  Cisco's "RIP" with metric advertising and other improvements

---

System to Intermediate System Protocol (IS-IS). It is not used in the Internet (and not used much elsewhere), and is not discussed in this book.

The Border Gateway Protocol (BGP) performs route advertising between the routing domains in the Internet. It overcomes many of the problems of the old EGP. BGP is a prevalent protocol in the Internet and is used between the routing domains of ISPs.

The Interdomain Routing Protocol (IDRP) is an OSI-based protocol. It is not used much in North America and is not discussed in this book.

A relative newcomer to the industry is the Private Network-to-Network Interface (PNNI). It is based on using ATM in the network(s) and provides two major functions: (a) route advertising and network topology analysis, and (b) connection management (setting up and tearing ATM connections).

Cisco implements proprietary routing protocols called the Inter-Gateway Routing Protocol (IGRP), and the Enhanced IGRP (EIGRP). EIGRP has replaced IGRP in many systems. They are similar to RIP, but have several enhanced features.

## SUMMARY

Internetworking is the sharing of computer resources by connecting the computers through communications networks. These networks can be public or private networks; they can be local or wide area networks. Route discovery is the process of finding the "best" route in the internetworking (and routing) domain. Internetworking and route discovery are essential to the efficient operations of communications networks.

The internetworking unit is called a bridge, router, or a gateway. Bridges are designed to operate with LANs, and routers are designed to operate with LANs or WANs. The gateway may perform packet relaying through networks and also may act as a protocol converter.

# 2

# Internet Basics

## INTRODUCTION

Scores of books are available on the Internet and IP. We will not re-hash this information, but will use this chapter to examine those aspects of the Internet and IP that are pertinent to route discovery.

The focus of the first part of the chapter is on several protocols and routing tools that are used in conjunction with the routing protocols discussed in the following chapters. These protocols and routing tools are discussed in this order, and the reader can pick-and-choose according to your experience level: (a) Media Access Control protocols (MAC), (b) Logical Link Control (LLC) protocol, (c) routing tables, and (d) the Internet Protocol (IP). LLC should be of interest to the reader who deals with IBM-based token rings, and the data link switching protocol, subjects for Chapter 4.

The material assumes you are familiar with the subjects in the first three appendices at the back of this book.

## LAN LAYERED ARCHITECTURE

The Institute of Electrical and Electronics Engineers (IEEE) publishes several LAN standards. The IEEE LAN standards are organized as follows:

| IEEE 802.1 | High Level Interface (and MAC Bridges), and network management |
| IEEE 802.2 | Logical Link Control (LLC) |
| IEEE 802.3 | Carrier Sense Multiple Access/ Collision Detect (CSMA/CD) |
| IEEE 802.4 | Token Bus |
| IEEE 802.5 | Token Ring |
| IEEE 802.6 | Metropolitan Area Networks |
| IEEE 802.7 | Broadband LANs |
| IEEE 802.8 | Fiber Optic LANs |
| IEEE 802.9 | Integrated Data and Voice Networks |
| IEEE 802.10 | Security |
| IEEE 802.11 | Wireless Networks |

We will focus on MAC and LLC in this chapter, and MAC bridges in Chapter 4. Other literature is available on the other IEEE protocols, but a few words about some of them should prove helpful for our efforts in the next chapters.

In addition to the three basic standards of 802.3, 802.4, and 802.5 the IEEE also publishes the metropolitan area network (MAN) standard as 802.6. Another standard deals with integrated voice/data networks. It is identified with 802.9. The IEEE also sponsors standards dealing with broadband LANs under 802.7, optical fiber LANs under 802.8, and security aspects for LANs is 802.10.

The 802.1 specification contains a number of standards. Network management is published in this standard as well as the 802.1 bridge, covered in Chapter 4.

The best-known scheme for controlling a local area network on a bus structure is carrier sense multiple access with collision detection (CSMA/CD). It is based on several concepts of the ALOHA protocol, which was developed at the University of Hawaii.

The most widely used LAN implementation of CSMA/CD is found in the Ethernet specification. Xerox Corporation was instrumental in providing the research for CSMA/CD and in developing the first baseband commercial products. The broadband network aspect of CSMA/CD was developed by MITRE.

In 1980, Xerox, the Intel Corporation, and Digital Equipment Corporation (DEC) jointly published a specification for an Ethernet local network. This specification was later introduced to the IEEE 802 committees and, with several modifications, found its way into the IEEE 802.3 standard. As shown in Figure 2–1(a), Ethernet/IEEE 802.3 operate at the physical and data link layers.

The 802.1 layer in Figure 2–1(a) has a odd shape. The L-shape is meant to convey that the interfaces of this layer may occur through LLC or directly with MAC and the physical layer without passing through LLC. These interfaces are defined with OSI-based primitive calls, explained in Appendix A. The notation of "maybe" for 802.1 in this figure means that 802.1 operations may or may not be implemented.

Figure 2-1(b) shows the positions of the routing protocols in the LAN layered model, and Figure 2–1(c) shows their positions in a WAN layered model. Remember from the discussions in Chapter 1 that a routing protocol can operate: (a) at the network layer (on top of the data link layer), (b) on top of the network layer, or (c) on top of the transport layer. These placements are noted in Figures 2–1(b) and (c) with the term "Routing?", and the question mark implies that the positioning of the routing protocols vary, depending upon the specific implementation.

## INTERWORKING THE LAN AND WAN PROTOCOL STACKS

Figure 2–2 shows the relationships of the LAN and WAN protocol stacks. The salient aspect of this figure for this discussion is to note that the LAN protocols (Ethernet, in this example, at the physical and data link layers) do not operate on the point-to-point local loop. The point-to-point protocol (PPP) operates at the data link layer on this loop.

The LAN layer 1 and 2 operations are not used in the wide area network. In their place are various layer 1 operations, such as the V.90 modem, a DS 1 link, etc. For layer 2, PPP usually operates between the router and the Internet (and ISP router or access server).

## MAC OPERATIONS

This section highlights two MAC protocols, Ethernet/802.3, and the 802.5 token ring. The focus is a general description of these protocols in relation to routing. First, the Ethernet/802.3 and token ring protocols do not perform route discovery. That function is left to another protocol. Second, these protocols do not perform the table-based forwarding opera-

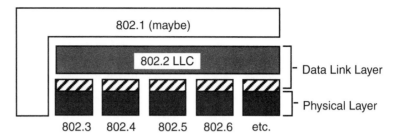

(a) The Major 802 LANs

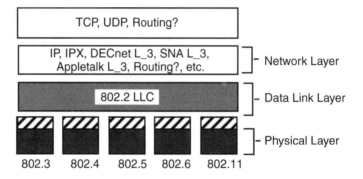

(b) Typical Protocol Stacks in a LAN

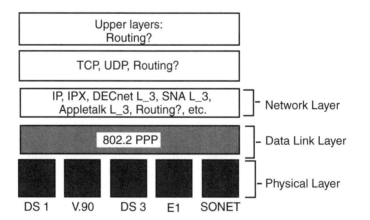

(c) Typical Protocol Stacks in a WAN and a Point-to-Point Link

Figure 2–1    Examples of Protocol Stacks

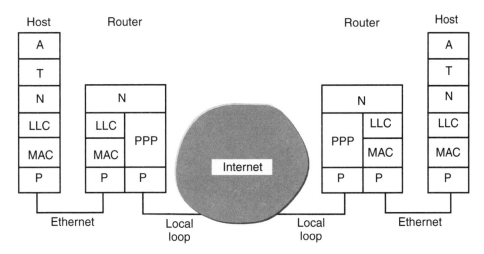

Where:
A       Application layer
LLC     Logical link control
MAC     Media access control
N       Network layer
P       Physical layer
PPP     Point-to-point protocol
T       Transport layer

**Figure 2–2   Typical Set of Protocol Stacks**

tions we have discussed earlier. Since these LANs employ a shared bus topology, it is not necessary to consult a routing table to relay a packet.

### Ethernet/802.3

Figure 2–3 depicts the Ethernet/802.3 LAN. Stations A, B, C, and D are attached to a shared hub. We assume stations A and B wish to transmit. However, station D is currently using the channel, so stations A and B "listen" and defer to the signal from station D. When the channel is idle, A and B can attempt to acquire the channel.

Because a station's transmission requires time to propagate to other stations (for example, station C to station A), station A may be unaware that a signal is on the channel. In this situation, station C could transmit its traffic even though another station has supposedly "seized" the channel (the hub). This situation is called the collision window. The collision

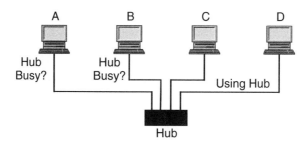

**Figure 2–3    Example of an Ethernet/802.3 Network**

window is a function of the propagation delay of the signal and the distance between the two competing stations.

Carrier sense networks are usually implemented on short distance LANs because the collision window lengthens with a longer channel. The long channel provides opportunity for more collisions and can reduce throughput in the network. Generally, a long propagation delay (the delay before a station knows another station is transmitting) coupled with short frames and high data transfer rates gives rise to a greater incidence of collisions. Longer frames can mitigate the effect of long delay, but they reduce the opportunity for competing stations to acquire the channel.

Each station is capable of transmitting and listening to the channel simultaneously. As the two signals collide, they create signal irregularities on the channel, which are sensed by the colliding stations. The stations must turn off their transmission, and through a randomized wait period, attempt to seize the channel again. The randomized wait decreases the chances of the collision reoccurring since it is unlikely that the competing stations will generate the same randomized wait time.

### 802.5 Token Ring

The token ring topology is illustrated in Figure 2–4. The stations are connected to a concentric ring through a ring interface unit (RIU). Each RIU is responsible for monitoring the packet passing through it, as well as regenerating the packet and passing it to the next station. If the address in the header of the packet indicates the data is destined for a station, the interface unit copies the data and passes the information to the user device.

If the ring is idle (that is, no user data is occupying the ring), a "free" token is passed around the ring from node-to-node. This token indicates

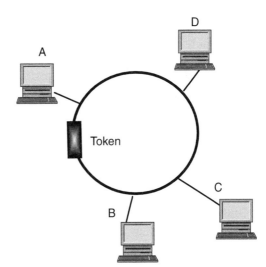

**Figure 2–4 Example of a Token Ring Network**

the ring is available and any station with data to transmit can use the token to transmit traffic. The control of the ring is passed sequentially from node-to-node around the ring.

During the period when the station has the token, it controls the ring. Upon acquiring the token (i.e., marking the token busy), the transmitting station inserts data behind the token and passes the data through the ring. As each RIU monitors the data, it checks the address in the header of the data, and passes the data to the next station.

Upon the data arriving at the transmitting station, this station makes the token free and passes it to the next station on the ring. This requirement prevents one station from monopolizing the ring. If the token passes around the ring without being used, the station can once again use the token and transmit data.

Thus, each station is guaranteed access to the network in a noncollision manner. If $n$ stations exist on the network, a station is assured of using the network every $nth$ pass of the token.

### Configuring a Priority Ring

Many token ring networks (including the 802.5 standard) use priority schemes. The object of the priority is to give each station an opportunity to reserve the use of the ring for the next transmission around the ring. As the token and data circle the ring, each node examines the token, which contains a reservation field. If a node's priority is higher than the priority number in the reservation field, it raises the reservation field number to its level, thus reserving the token on the next round. If another node does not make the reservation field higher, the station is allowed to use the token and channel on the next pass around the ring.

The station with the token is required to store the previous reservation value in a temporary storage area. Upon releasing the token, the station restores the network to its previous lowest priority request. In this manner, once the token is made free for the next round, the station with the highest reservation is allowed to seize the token.

## LOGICAL LINK CONTROL (LLC)

LLC can be implemented in a number of ways on a LAN. At its most basic function, it is used to interface the LAN functions with the user applications, typically IP. All IEEE 802 LANs require the use of LLC.

LLC can also be used for some rather elaborate connection management procedures and flow control operations. For example, one type of LLC allows the creation of connections between user stations as well as the use of positive and negative acknowledgments, sequencing, and flow control operations with sliding windows.

If these functions seem excessive for certain user applications, LLC can be configured to perform minimal levels of service. In this configuration, LLC simply provides an interface between the user application and MAC. Table 2–1 provides a summary of the major features of LLC.

At the onset of the IEEE 802 work, it was recognized that a connection-oriented system would limit the scope and power of a LAN. Consequently, two connectionless models are now specified for LLC:

**Table 2–1   Major Functions of LLC**

Interface to user application or network layer

Interface to MAC

Data transfer

Optional flow control of the user stations

Connection management

Optional traffic acknowledgments (positive or negative)

Optional sequencing of packets

- unacknowledged connectionless model
- acknowledged connectionless model

Let us consider the reason for this approach. First, many local applications do not need the data integrity provided by a connection-oriented network. As examples: (a) sensor equipment can afford to lose occasional data since the sensor readings typically occur quite frequently, and the data loss does not adversely affect the information content. (b) Inquiry-response systems, such as point-of-sale, usually perform acknowledgment at the application level. These systems do not need connection-oriented services at the lower levels.

Second, high-speed application processes cannot tolerate the overhead in establishing and disestablishing the connections. The problem is particularly severe in the LAN, with its high-speed channels and low error rates. Many LAN applications require fast setups with each other. Others require very fast communications between the user workstations.

An acknowledged connectionless service is useful for a number of reasons. Consider the operations of a LAN in a commercial bank. A data link protocol usually maintains state tables, sequence numbers, and windows for each station on the link. It would be impractical to provide this service for every station on the bank's local network. Yet, workstations like the bank's automated teller machines (ATMs) require they be polled for their transactions. The host computer must also be assured that all transactions are sent and received without errors. The data is too important to use a protocol that does not provide acknowledgments.

All 802 networks must provide unacknowledged connectionless service (type 1). Optionally, connection-oriented acknowledged service can be provided (type 2). Type 1 networks provide no ACKs, flow control, or error recovery. Type 2 networks provide connection management, ACKs, flow control, and error recovery. Type 3 networks (not used much) provide no connection setup and disconnect, but they do provide for immediate acknowledgment of data units. Most type 1 networks use a higher level protocol (i.e., TCP at the transport layer) to provide connection management functions. Table 2–2 provides a summary of this discussion.

### LLC SAPs

Appendix A introduces service access points (SAPs). Figure 2–5 shows an example of the relationship of LLC SAPs (LSAPs) in three different LAN stations. The SAPs perform the services of software ports. Their function is to identify the application entity residing above LLC. In

**Table 2–2   LLC Types and Classes**

- *Types of Operations*
    1. Connectionless
    2. Connection-oriented
    3. Acknowledged connectionless
- *Classes of Operation*
    I  Connectionless
    II  Connection-oriented & connectionless
    III  Acknowledged connectionless & connection-oriented
    IV  I, II, & III

this example, application X and Y are identified with SAP A1 and A2, respectively. In two other stations, application Q identified with SAP C1 is logically associated with application X identified with SAP A1. Additionally, application Z identified with SAP B1 is associated with application Y which uses SAP A2.

It is possible that SAP numbers could be reused at the same time in the LAN. This possibility could create ambiguity in the identification of

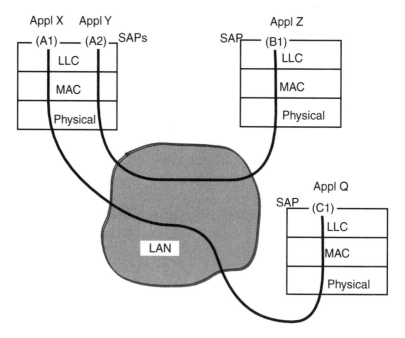

**Figure 2–5   Mapping SAPs between LAN Stations**

SAP sessions. An easy solution to this problem is to concatenate the MAC addresses with the SAP addresses. With this approach, the SAP identifiers are unique.

The IEEE provides a registration service for entities that are common in the LAN communications industry. These "well known LSAPs" identify well-known protocols that typically run on top of an IEEE 802 network. Table 2–3 shows some examples of well known LSAPs. There are other well-known LSAPs that are not included here.

### SAP Components

In accordance with the IEEE 802.2 specification, LLC is divided into several logical components. The behavior of these components is governed by state machines in regard to their external behavior: that is, how they interact with another logical component in a remote station or by a higher layer protocol residing in the same machine. Figure 2–6 shows three components defined in 802.2.

The station component handles all operations of an LLC entity. Typically, these operations pertain to all LLC activity in a LAN workstation. One station component must exist for each MAC SAP on the LAN. It handles events directed to the LLC as a whole, such as exchanging passwords, test operations, and duplicate address checking.

The SAP component processes the events for each SAP within an LLC entity. It is able to discern between the different types of LLC

**Table 2–3  Well-Known LSAPs**

| Link SAP | Description |
|----------|-------------|
| 00000000 | Null LSAP |
| 01010101 | SNAP (uses 802.2) |
| 01000010 | Bridge Spanning Tree Protocol (802.1) |
| 01000000 | Individual LLC Sublayer Management |
| 11000000 | Group LLC Sublayer Management |
| 00100000 | SNA Path Control |
| 01100000 | Internet Protocol (IP) |
| 01110000 | Proway-LAN (NW Maintenance and Initialization |
| 01110010 | EIA-RS511 (Factory Automation) |
| 01110001 | Proway-LAN |
| 01111111 | OSI Network Protocol |
| 11111111 | Global DSAP |

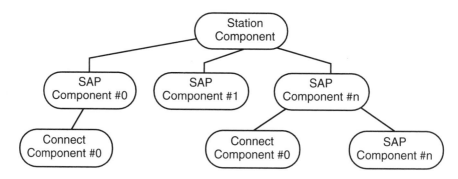

**Figure 2–6    SAPs and Connection Components**

packets, such as connectionless or connection-oriented packets. It maintains states on each SAP component such as active, inactive, and keeps a "record" of what each SAP must do upon experiencing a particular event, such as receiving a password or test packet from another workstation.

The connect components deal with the operations associated with the connection-oriented aspects of LLC. The operations include timers on transmissions, and retry values for retransmissions. They also include counters and variables to manage each connection's sequencing and acknowledgment services.

### LLC 2

LLC 2 is based on several operations of the widely-used high level data link protocol (HDLC). Since LLC 2 is connection-oriented, it requires that frames be exchanged between two entities before communications can occur. The exchange of these frames is performed through two HDLC frames: (a) the set asynchronous balanced mode extended (SABME) frame and (b) the unnumbered acknowledgment (UA) frame.

As shown in Figure 2–7, a station initiates the session establishment by sending a SABME frame to another station. This frame is encapsulated into the information (I) field of the packet. Upon receiving the SABME, the entity stores information about the sending LSAP and responds with the UA frame. During this connection setup process, both entities store information about each other, notably the SAP values. The connection setup also reserves buffers for the session, and sets a number of counters and variables that will be used later to support the ongoing communications activities. Once LLC 2 has established the data link connection, traffic can be exchanged between the two stations.

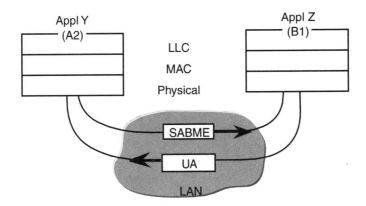

SABME = Set Asynchronous Balanced Mode Extended
   UA = Unnumbered Acknowledgment

Note: The SABME sets up the session and the UA acknowledges it

**Figure 2–7    Setting up an LLC 2 Session**

## The LLC Protocol Data Unit (PDU)

The LLC protocol data unit (PDU, another name for a packet) is shown in Figure 2–8. The LLC unit contains a destination service access point address (DSAP), source service access point address (SSAP), control field, and information field. The DSAP is an 8-bit field in which 7 bits are used for the actual SAP address. The first bit of this field is designated as the individual/group bit (I/G). When this bit is set to 0, it identifies an individual DSAP. If the bit is set to 1, it identifies a group of SAPs at a station that can receive data.

The SSAP also consists of 8 bits. Seven bits identify the source SAP; the first bit of this field is designated as the command/response bit (C/R) and is used to indicate if the PDU is an HDLC command or an HDLC response.

The HDLC-type commands and responses, established in the control field, depend on whether the LAN is type 1, 2, or 3. For type 2, the information format is used to sequence sending traffic with N(S) and to acknowledge traffic with the N(R). For sending type 1 data, the unnumbered format is used to send an HDLC unnumbered information (UI) data unit. The supervisory format is used for certain of the types to issue flow control data units as well as negative acknowledgments in the event of problems. The UI is also used for type 3 to provide a simple ACK/NAK capability. The poll/final bit (P/F) is generally implemented in accordance with conventional HDLC rules.

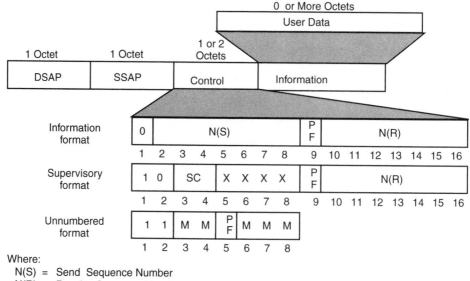

Where:
N(S) = Send Sequence Number
N(R) = Receive Sequence Number
S    = Supervisory Bits
SC   = Supervisory Code
M    = Modifier Function Bits
X    = Reserved, Set to 0

**Figure 2–8    LLC Protocol Data Unit**

## Example of LLC 2 Operations

This part of the chapter describes the LLC 2 reliable link opera-tions.[1] Figure 2–9 shows the transmission of LLC PDUs from station A to station B or from station B to station A. The notation of "I" means the LLC 2 PDU is carrying the information field. The P/F indicator is used to show if the poll/final (P/F) bit is set to 0 or 1. The N(S) and N(R) nota-tions are used to show the values of the send and receive sequence num-bers, respectively. The position of the fields in these figures do not show the order of field or bit transmission. They are drawn to show the se-quence of operations. Figure 2–9 shows the operation for a normal data transfer.

---

[1]If you have read other books in this series, you might be familiar with Figure 2–9. It has been included in other books because many link protocols use these procedures, and LLC is no exception. I include it in this book because of a LAN-based operation, called data link switching, discussed in Chapter 4.

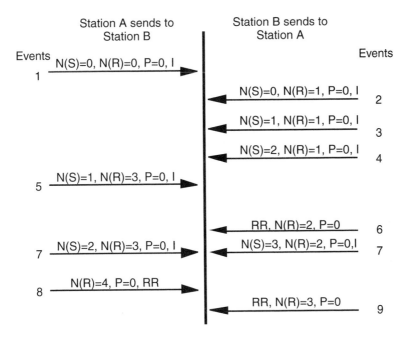

**Figure 2–9   Normal Operations**

| **Event(s)** | **Operation** |
|---|---|
| 1 | Station A sends an information PDU and sequences the frame with N(S) = 0. The N(R) = 0 means station A is expecting to receive a PDU with its field of N(S) = 0. The P bit is set to 0, which means station A does not require station B to send any non-data PDUs. |
| 2–4 | Station B sends PDUs numbered N(S) = 0 through N(S) = 2. Its N(R) field is set to 1, which acknowledges station A's PDU sent in event 1 [it had an N(S) value of 0]. |
| 5 | Station A sends an I PDU sequenced with N(S) = 1, which is the value station B expects next. Station A also sets the N(R) field to the value of 3, which inclusively acknowledges station B's previously transmitted PDUs numbered N(S) 0, 1, and 2. |
| 6 | Station B has no data to transmit. However, to prevent station A from "timing-out" and resending data, station B sends a receive ready (RR) PDU. |
| 7 | The arrows depicting the PDU flow from the two stations are aligned vertically with each other. This depiction means the two PDUs are transmitted from each station at about the |

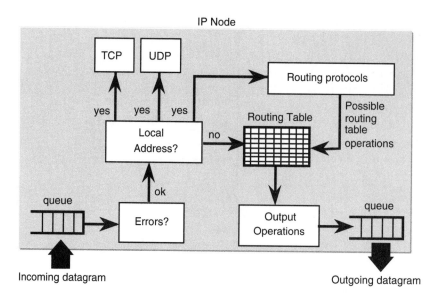

**Figure 2–10    Processing the Datagram**

same time and are exchanged almost simultaneously across the full duplex link.

8–9    Stations A and B send RR PDUs to acknowledge the PDUs transmitted in event 7.

We will return to LLC in Chapter 4 when we examine how LLC 2 is internetworked between LANs that reside between wide area networks. Now, we take a look at another Internet basic concept that is fundamental to the operations of routing protocols, the routing table. Remember that the routing table is created as a result of the information obtained by the route discovery process.

## PROCESSING THE IP DATAGRAM AND THE ROUTING TABLE

Figure 2–10 shows how a router processes an incoming IP datagram.[2] The incoming packet is stored in a queue to await processing. Once processing begins, the options field in the IP header is processed to

---

[2]See *TCP/IP Illustrated,* page 112, by W. Richard Stevens, published by Addison-Wesley. Mr. Steven's figure does not contain the error check operation, which I have added in this figure.

determine if any options are in the header (the support for this operation varies). The datagram header is checked for any modifications that may have occurred during its journey to this IP node (with a checksum field discussed later). Next, it is determined if the IP address is local; if so, the IP protocol ID field in the IP header is used to pass the bits in the data field to the next module, such as TCP, UDP, ICMP, etc.

An IP node can be configured to forward or not forward datagrams. If the node is a forwarding node, the IP destination address in the IP datagram header is matched against a routing table to calculate the next node (next hop) that is to receive the datagram. If a match in the table to the destination address is found, the datagram is forwarded to the next node. Otherwise, it is sent to a default route, or it is discarded.

If the IP protocol ID indicates that the IP traffic is a routing protocol, then the next action will be to use the information in this routing protocol packet to (possibly) make changes to the routing table.

Figure 2–11 shows an example of a routing table found in a router. Individual systems differ in the contents of the routing table, but they resemble this example. Some tables may have more entries, but most have fewer. I have included in this figure examples of entries in the table. The entries in this table are:

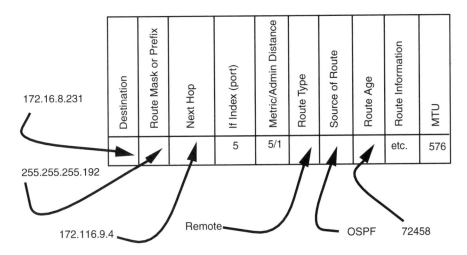

Where:
  MTU  Maximum transmission unit size (in bytes, of the L_2 I field)

**Figure 2–11   Routing Table and Examples of Entries**

- **Destination:** IP address of the destination node.
- **Route Mask or Prefix:** Mask that is used with destination address to identify bits that are used in routing. Newer systems use a prefix that accomplishes the same function. See Appendix B for information on masks and prefixes.
- **Next Hop:** IP address of the next hop in the route.
- **If Index (port):** Physical port (interface) on the router to reach the next hop address.
- **Metric/Admin distance:** "Cost" to reach the destination address, and the admin distance (a value that assesses the trustworthiness of the information).
- **Route Type:** Directly attached to router (direct), or reached through another router (remote).
- **Source of Route:** How the route was discovered (which routing protocol was used for this table entry).
- **Route Age:** In seconds, since the route was last updated.
- **Route Information:** Miscellaneous information.
- **MTU:** Maximum transmission unit size (size of L_2 data field)

## THE IP HEADER

The information in the IP datagram is used by the forwarding protocol at the router to determine the "next node." This information is contained in selected fields in the header of the IP datagram. The router uses the IP header and the routing table to "glue" together the seemingly disparate Internet. To see how, we take a look at the information in the IP header, and Figure 2–12 provides an illustration of the IP datagram. Some of the fields in the IP datagram are not relevant to our analysis, but I will describe them for the sake of giving you a complete picture of the overall IP operations.

The *version* field identifies the version of IP in use. Most protocols contain this field because some network nodes may not have the latest release available of the protocol. The current version of IP is 4.

The *header length* field contains 4 bits, which are set to a value to indicate the length of the datagram header. The length is measured in 32-bit words. Typically, a header without options contains 20 octets. Therefore, the value in the length field is usually 5.

| 0 | 1–2 | 3 | 4 | 5–6 | 7 | 8 | 9–15 | 1 5 | 1 6 | 17–22 | 2 3 | 2 4 | 25–30 | 3 1 |
|---|---|---|---|---|---|---|---|---|---|---|---|---|---|---|
| version | | | h-length | | | | type of service | | | total length | | | | |
| identifier | | | | | | | | flags | | fragment offset | | | | |
| time to live | | | | | | protocol | | | | header checksum | | | | |
| source address (32) | | | | | | | | | | | | | | |
| destination address (32) | | | | | | | | | | | | | | |
| options and padding (variable) | | | | | | | | | | | | | | |
| data (variable) | | | | | | | | | | | | | | |

Where: h-length is header length

**Figure 2–12   The IP datagram**

The *total length* field specifies the total length of the IP datagram. It is measured in octets and includes the length of the header and the data. IP subtracts the header length field from the total length field to compute the size of the data field. The maximum possible length of a datagram is 65,535 octets ($2^{16}$). Routers that service IP datagrams are required to accept any datagram that supports the maximum size of a PDU of the attached networks. Additionally, all routers must accommodate datagrams of 576 octets in total length.

Each 32-bit value is transmitted in this order: (a) bits 0–7, (b) bits 8–15, (c) bits 16–23, and (d) bits 24–31. This is known as big endian byte ordering.

The *type of service (TOS)* field can be used to identify several quality of service (QOS) functions provided for an Internet application. Transit delay, throughput, precedence, and reliability can be requested with this field.

The TOS field is illustrated in Figure 2–13. It contains five entries consisting of 8 bits. Bits 0, 1, and 2 contain a precedence value which is used to indicate the relative importance of the datagram. Values range from 0 to 7, with 0 set to indicate a *routine precedence*. The precedence field is not used in most systems, although the value of 7 is used by some implementations to indicate a network control datagram. However, the precedence field could be used to implement flow control and congestion mechanisms in a network. This would allow routers and host nodes to make decisions about the order of "throwing away" datagrams in case of congestion.

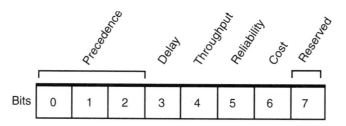

**Figure 2–13   The Type of Service (TOS) Field**

The next three bits are used for other services and are described as follows: Bit 3 is the *delay bit (D bit)*. When set to 1 this TOS requests a short delay through an internet. The aspect of delay is not defined in the standard, and it is up to the vendor to implement the service. The next bit is the *throughput bit (T bit)*. It is set to 1 to request for high throughput through an internet. Again, its specific implementation is not defined in the standard. The next bit used is the *reliability bit (R bit)*, which allows a user to request high reliability for the datagram. The last bit of interest is the *cost bit (C bit)*, which is set to request the use of a low-cost link (from the standpoint of monetary cost). The last bit is not used at this time.

The *TOS field* is not used in some vendors' implementation of IP. Nonetheless, it will be used increasingly in the future as the internet capabilities are increased. For example, it is used in the DiffServ protocol. Consequently, a user should examine this field for future work and ascertain a vendor's use or intended support of this field.

The IP protocol uses three fields in the header to control datagram fragmentation and reassembly. These fields are the *identifier, flags,* and *fragmentation offset*. They are not pertinent to this book, but a brief explanation of their operations is included here. The identifier field is used to uniquely identify all fragments from an original datagram. It is used with the source address at the receiving host to identify the fragment. The flags field contains bits to determine if the datagram may be fragmented, and if fragmented, one of the bits can be set to determine if this fragment is the last fragment of the datagram. The bit that allows or disallows fragmentation is called the "Don't Fragment" (DF) bit. The fragmentation offset field contains a value which specifies the relative position of the fragment to the original datagram. The value is initialized as 0 and is subsequently set to the proper number if/when an IP node fragments the data. The value is measured in units of 8 octets.

The *time-to-live (TTL)* parameter is used to measure the time a datagram has been in the internet. Each router in the internet is required to check this field and discard the datagram if the TTL value equals 0. An IP node is also required to decrement this field in each datagram it processes. In actual implementations, the TTL field is a number of hops value. Therefore, when a datagram proceeds through a router (hop), the value in the field is decremented by a value of one. Some implementations of IP use a time-counter in this field and decrement the value in 1-second decrements.

The time-to-live (TTL) field is used not only to prevent endless loops, it can also be used by the host to limit the lifetime that datagrams have in an internet. Be aware that if a host is acting as a "route-through" node, it must treat the TTL field by the router rules. The seminar attendee should check with the vendor to determine when a host throws away a datagram based on the TTL value.

Ideally, the TTL value could be configured and its value assigned based on observing an internet's performance. Additionally, network management information protocols such as those residing in SNMP might wish to set the TTL value for diagnostic purposes. Finally, if your vendor uses a fixed value that cannot be reconfigured, make certain that it is fixed initially to allow for your internet's growth.

The *protocol* field is used to identify the next level protocol above the IP that is to receive the datagram at the final host destination. It is similar to the EtherType field found in the Ethernet frame, but it identifies the payload in the data field of the IP datagram. The Internet standards groups have established a numbering system to identify the most widely used upper layer protocols.

The *header checksum* is used to detect an error that may have occurred in the header. Checks are not performed on the user data stream. Some critics of IP have stated that the provision for error detection in the user data should allow the receiving router to at least notify the sending host that problems have occurred. (This service is indeed provided by a companion standard to IP [the ICMP].) Whatever one's view is on the issue, the current approach keeps the checksum algorithm in IP quite simple. It does not have to operate on many octets, but it does require that a higher level protocol at the receiving host must perform some type of error check on the user data if it cares about its integrity.

The checksum is computed as follows (and this same procedure is used in TCP, UDP, ICMP, and IGMP):

- Set checksum field to 0
- Calculate 16-bit one's complement sum of the header (header is treated as a sequence of 16-bit words)

- Store 16-bit one's complement in the checksum field
- At receiver, calculate 16-bit one's complement of the header
- Receiver's checksum is all 1s if the header has not been changed

IP carries two addresses in the datagram. These are labeled *source* and *destination addresses* and remain the same value throughout the life of the datagram. These fields contain the internet addresses.

The *options* field is used to identify several additional services.[3] The options field is not used in every datagram. The majority of implementations use this field for network management and diagnostics.

## SUMMARY

This chapter has brought several protocols and concepts into the routing picture. These protocols and concepts are used in conjunction with the routing protocols to move a user's packet from one point to another. We learned that the media access control protocols (MAC) are a fundamental architecture of local area networks. And the logical link control (LLC) protocol resides above the MAC layer to enhance the "minimal" MAC operations.

We also learned that the routing tables, distributed at each node, are the glue that connects the many networks of the Internet together, and the Internet Protocol (IP) is used with the routing table at each node to decide how to handle (relay) the IP packet.

## FOLLOW-UP READING

This series has several books on the Internet and Internet protocols. Take a look at the series chart at the beginning of this book. Naturally, I recommend them highly, since I wrote them. Any of Richard Steven's and Douglas Come's texts are recommended as well.

---

[3]The option field has fallen into disuse by routers, because of the processing overhead required to support the features it identifies. The concepts of this field are well-founded, and a similar capability is found in IPv6.

# 3

# Route Discovery Principles

## INTRODUCTION

This chapter introduces the basic route discovery principles used by the routing protocols that are discussed in the following chapters. We start by expanding our understanding of routing domains by examining autonomous systems. Next, interior and exterior gateway protocols are defined, followed by an explanation of distance-vector and link state metric operations. The chapter concludes with several examples of how networks advertise addresses to each and how they rely on each other to recover from errors and failures.

## AUTONOMOUS SYSTEMS (AS)

Individual networks may be joined together by a router, which acts as a switch between the networks. The router operations are programmed to route the traffic to the proper network by examining a destination address in the packet and matching the address with entries in a routing table. Those entries indicate (one hopes) the best route to the next network or destination host.

Even though local authorities may administer these individual networks, it is common practice for a group of networks to be administered as a whole system. This group of networks is called an *autonomous system* (AS). Examples of autonomous systems are networks located on sites such as college campuses, hospital complexes, and military installations. The networks located at these sites are connected together by a router, and since these routers operate within an autonomous system, they often choose their own mechanisms for routing data. Figure 3–1 shows the layout of the autonomous system.

The local administrative authorities in the autonomous systems agree on how they provide information (advertise) to each other regarding the "reachability" of the host computers inside the autonomous systems. The advertising responsibility can be given to one router, or a number of routers may participate in the operation.

The autonomous systems are identified by autonomous system numbers. How this is accomplished is up to the administrators, (and they are assigned by the Internet), but the idea is to use different numbers to distinguish different autonomous systems. Such a numbering scheme might prove helpful if a network manager does not wish to route traffic through an autonomous system. The AS might be accisible to the manager's network, but it may be administered by a competitor, it may not have adequate or proper security services, etc. By the use of routing protocols and numbers identifying autonomous systems, the routers can determine how they reach each other and how they exchange routing information.

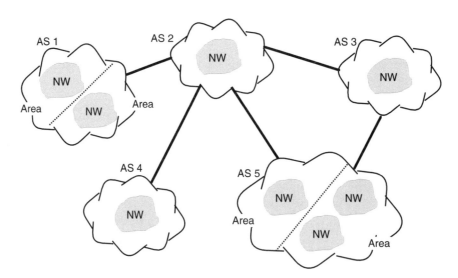

Figure 3–1 Autonomous Systems (AS), Areas, and Networks (NW)

Autonomous systems are identified with AS numbers assigned from 1 to 65,535, with 1 to 65,411 for registered Internet numbers, and 65,412 to 65,535 for private numbers.

In large autonomous systems, it is not unusual to create smaller routing domains called areas. This idea is also shown in Figure 3–1 where AS1 and AS5 are divided into areas. These areas can be serviced by one of more area border routers, just as the AS can be serviced by one or more AS border routers. As discussed in Chapter 1, the routing domain is an administrative entity, and its scope depends on the decisions of the network administrator. A small domain consists of a few subnets; a large domain consists of many.

## INTERNAL AND EXTERNAL GATEWAY PROTOCOLS

Figure 3–2 depicts internal and external gateway protocols. When ARPAnet was first implemented, it consisted of a single backbone network. With the implementation of Internet, ARPAnet then provided attached routers to local networks. A protocol, called the *Gateway-to-Gateway Protocol (GGP),* was used for these routers to inform each other about their attached local networks. Traffic passing between two local networks passed through two routers, and each router had complete routing information about the other core router. Since these routers had complete routing information, they did not need a default route.

However, things changed as the Internet grew. Therefore, the concept of a router holding complete routing information on an internet became too unwieldy.

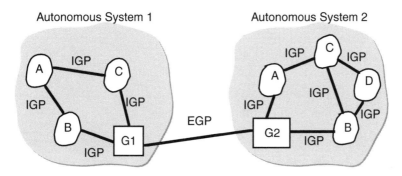

**Figure 3–2   External Gateway Protocols (EGP) and Internal Gateway Protocols (IGP)**

To approach this problem, routers were given responsibilities for only a part of an internet. In this manner, a router did not have to know about all other routers of an internet but relied on neighbor routers and/or routers in other autonomous systems to reveal their routing information. Indeed, if they had insufficient knowledge to make a routing decision, they simply chose a default route. This change gave rise to two other terms: *exterior routers* and *interior routers*. An exterior router is so named because it supports the exchange of routing information between different autonomous systems. Interior routers are so named because they belong to the same autonomous system and exchange information within the autonomous system.

## TYPES OF ROUTE ADVERTISING

There are two types of route advertising protocols used in the data communications industry: (a) distance-vector and (b) link state metric. Their operations are summarized in Table 3–1.

The distance-vector protocol is more commonly known as a minimum hop protocol, which means the protocol searches for a path between a sending and receiving node that has the fewest number of intermediate nodes (hops) between them. The term "distance" refers to number of hops, and the term vector refers to an address.

Each router calculating a best path (fewest hops) to a destination implements the minimum hop approach. If certain conditions change (such as a link failure), the router advertises this change to its neighbor(s), which results in each neighbor changing its routing table. In turn,

**Table 3–1  Types of Route Advertising**

**Distance-vector (Minimum hop)**

Route between sending and receiving machine:

  Fewest number of intermediate hops

Incremental distributed route calculation

**Link state metric**

Route between sending and receiving machine:

  Sum of path metrics with smallest value

Routes determined by a replicated database of metrics

the neighbor advertises to its neighbor until all nodes in the routing domain know about the change.

The link state metric protocol assigns a value (metric) to each link on each node in the routing domain. Each node advertises its links' metrics by sending link state advertisements (LSAs) to its neighbors. These LSAs contain the link's metric (or metrics, if advertising is done on more than one metric criteria). The path chosen between the machines is the one in which the metrics of all the links making up the path are summed to a lower value than any other contending path.

The link state approach is implemented by each router using the same copy of a database (a replicated distributed file at each router). Each router plays a part in creating this database by sending to all routers in the routing domain information on the router's active links to its local networks and to other routers. The accompanying metric becomes part of the database, which is used to compute the routes.

## STATIC ROUTES, DEFAULT ROUTES, AND STUBS

Static routes are those that are manually configured. See Figure 3–3. They are entered into the router (or bridge) tables with configuration commands. A network is not required to have any other routes than static routes.

Some implementations do not provide an alternative static route if the primary route fails. But others do, and they are effective for certain

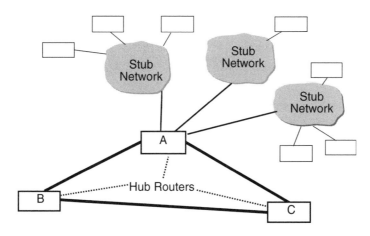

**Figure 3–3    Stubs, Static, and Default Routes**

situations. One attraction is that they do not require the running of a routing protocol, and thus do not consume resources for advertising and routing table maintenance.

Static routes are often applied to *stub* networks. A stub network is one in which traffic emanates or terminates, but traffic does not pass-through. Think of a stub network like the end-of-the-line on a subway, or a deadend street. A stub network can be entered and exited through a static route. Its exit usually points to a pre-configured router.

A *default* route is one that is used as a last resort, after the routing table has been examined and no match can be found for the destination address. It is called the gateway of last resort in some literature. Default routes to "hub routers" are often used in stub networks, once again to obviate a routing protocol.

### Configuration Ideas for Stub Routes

The stub routers do not have to learn about any dynamic IP routes. Typically, they are configured with a default route to a nonstub router, for example a router that connects as a hub to other routing domains (router A in Figure 3–3). The hub router must be configured to know which stub networks are reachable via each stub router. However, in a large domain, where there may be many hub routers, and many stub networks, the manual and static configuration tasks can become quite a chore.

Therefore, most high-end routers allow the network manager to install stub networks, and have the hub routers maintain (dynamically) the routes to the stub networks. With this arrangement, the stub router is responsible for advertising IP prefixes of the IP networks attached to the stub router's interfaces. Because prefix advertising is supported, the arrangement supports variable length subnet masks (VLSMs, see Appendix B). In turn, the hub router will send IP traffic to the stub router based on this information.

**On Demand Routing (ODR).**   The concept of allowing a stub router to advertise dynamically to a hub router is called on demand routing (ODR). Once ODR has been configured on the hub router, the next task is to install the stub networks in its IP routing table. It can also be configured to distribute this information to other routers with a routing protocol. In addition, it is possible to limit the network addresses (prefixes) the router will "learn" through ODR. This idea is called filtering ODR information, and is part of the packet containment idea discussed in Chapter 1. It helps prevent misconfigured hub routers from advertising misleading information.

## DISTANCE-VECTOR (MINIMUM HOP) PROTOCOLS

Distance-vector protocols use *distributed computation,* which means each router calculates its "best" path to a destination separately from other routers. Each router notifies its neighbors of its known best path, and at the same time, these routers also notify their neighbors of their knowledge of the best path.

So, a router obtains information from its neighbors, which may reveal a better path to a destination. In this case, the router updates its table, and also notifies its neighbors of its new choice. This process is iterative, and continues until the routes in the routing domain stabilize.

Distance-vector protocols are simple to install, maintain, and troubleshoot. They support address aggregation, and they allow a network administrator to set routing policies, if the administrator chooses to do so.

Since the advertising through a routing domain occurs in an iterative fashion, and the new route eventually snowballs through the domain, it may take a while for the best routes to be made known to all. For simple distance-vector protocols, the size of the routing domain, and the number of hops through it, are usually restricted to a small number. We will see later some examples to reinforce these points.

Figure 3–4 shows an example of how the distance-vector protocol operates. Each router (for example, R1 in this example) has stored in a routing table the "best" path to a destination address. Let us assume the destination of interest is host 1 (H1). Each router executes the distributed computation to find a route to H1. As this example, shows, R1

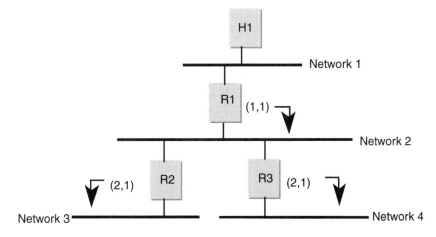

**Figure 3–4    Basics of Distance-Vector Protocols**

informs its neighbors (R2 and R3) of the path and distance to H1. The figure shows R1 sending a message out of its interface on network 2 with the values of (1,1) in the message. These two parameters are (distance, vector) with distance measured in number of hops and vector indentifying the destination address.

Routers 2 and 3 receive this information and send it on to their outgoing interfaces on networks 3 and 4. The distance value is now 2, reflecting the fact that they had to increase the distance value by 1 (one hop).

This process continues until the advertisements have been disseminated to all routers in the routing domain. That is, the process iterates until routes stabilize, a process called convergence.

### Example of Message Propagation in a Distance-Vector Routing Domain

We know that distance-vector operations rely on each neighbor informing its neighbor(s) about their knowledge of the nodes. In Figure 3–5, F informs E that it is directly attached to G on the same network or point-to-point link. Since E is aware that it is next to F, it informs C that it is one hop away from G. (Note: some protocols use 0 as directly attached; others use 1.)

C then knows that it is two hops away from G and so C informs A and D. Since A knows that it is one hop away from C, and has received an advertisement of C's two hops to G, A can make the inference that it is three hops away from G.

The advertisements of D and B also reach A. It is not unusual for a node to receive multiple advertisements about an address. A makes a comparison of the two alternative routes (one through C and one through B). Obviously A would make the choice using C, since B's advertisements would reveal that it is more hops away from G.

### Packet Containment

How can this procedure achieve packet containment? That is, what prevents the route advertisements from traversing into other networks and domains? Furthermore, what prevents the advertisements from looping through the domain, traversing the same nodes over and over again?

To answer the first question, network administrators can configure the routing protocol to send advertisements to interfaces (links) for specified networks. If an interface at a router is not specified, its interface to a network is not present in any of the advertisements. Also, the advertise-

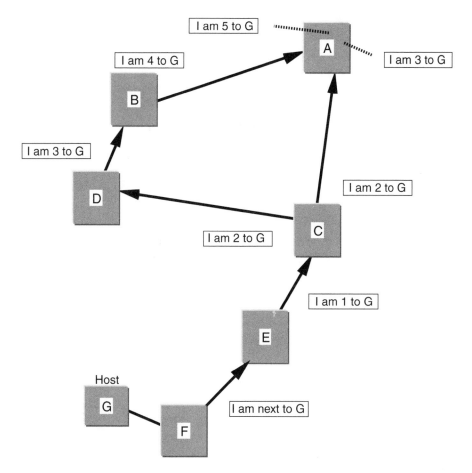

**Figure 3–5  Exchanging Hop Count Information in the Routing Domain**

ment itself can be restricted to specific interfaces. Additionally, if a mis-behaving node sends unsolicited advertisements to another domain, they are ignored.

The looping question is not as easily answered. Some networks prevent looping by configuring the physical topology without loops. This configuration certainly works, but it may not be desirable if physical loops are needed for back up (in case one path fails, the other looped path is available). Another option is to use the IP time-to-live field in the IP header to kill-off looping packets. Other methods are available using timers, age fields, and sequence numbers, and are discussed in later chapters.

## LINK STATE PROTOCOLS

The link state protocol is implemented when a router advertises the state of its local interfaces to its neighbor routers. The local interfaces are the physical links attached to the router. The neighbor router can be a router on the same subnetwork, or on the other end of a point-to-point connection. These ideas are shown in Figure 3–6.

Each link interface is assigned a value, also called a metric or a cost. In Figure 3–6, router 1 (R1) is advertising a metric of 2 for interface 1, and a metric of 5 for interface 2.

The advertisements are distributed to all routers in the routing domain. The advertisements are used by the routers to learn about the topology of the domain; that is, who is connected to whom, and at what cost.

Although not shown in Figure 3–6, router 2 (R2) and router 3 (R3) perform the same operation as router 1. Their metric on the network 2 interface will usually be 5, the same as router 1. The rules for this metric (same or different) depend on the specific routing protocol and the configuration options for the router.

The distribution of the routing information is used to create a database reflecting the topology of the domain. The information in the database is used for route calculations and the construction of a routing table.

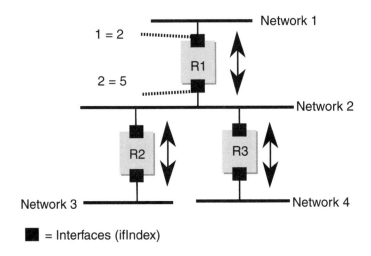

**Figure 3–6   Link State Protocols**

### Example of Message Propagation in a Link State Routing Domain

The link state metric advertisement (LSA) operations in a link state routing domain is shown in Figure 3–7. This example assumes an IP-based network, and the advertisements are encapsulated into IP datagrams.

Note that node A receives two advertisements about host G. These advertisements contain the metrics associated with each link connected to the nodes that created the advertisements.

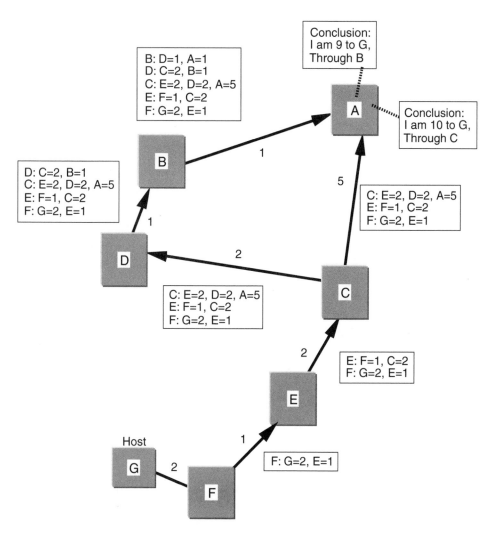

**Figure 3–7 Exchanging Information in the Link State Routing Domain**

The advertisement operations begin with node F advertising a metric of 2 on the link to G, and a metric of 1 on the link to E. The reason for node F sending the advertisement in the first place is because: (a) a new link is advertised, or (b) the metric for the link has changed. This advertisement is conveyed to node E (the advertisement is not sent back to the interface from which it was received).

The advertisements for each node are eventually sent to node A. These link state advertisements are flooded to all nodes in the routing domain. When a node receives an advertisement from its neighbor, it will examine each link state value. If the value in the advertisement is lower ("better") than the value of the last valid advertisement for the link, the node will replace the previous metric with the new metric. If a metric changes, the node will then update its routing table accordingly.

Each node is responsible for relaying the LSA it received on an incoming link to all of its outgoing links, that is, every link but the one from which is received the advertisement. This operation is called LSA repackaging, and it entails the receiving node conveying the LSA to its neighbors. The repackaging encompasses the changing of the IP addresses in the IP header. For example, the LSA from node F to node E has F and E IP addresses in the source and destination IP address fields, respectively. When the LSA is sent from node E to node C, the source and destination addresses are E and C, respectively.

The messages find their way to node A where the final link state sum is 10 on one path and 9 on the other. Consequently, if node A receives traffic destined for host G, it will relay this traffic to node B. Even though C represents the shortest path in number of hops, the path emanating from node B represents the shortest path in relation to the metric count. This situation can occur if (for example) the link between nodes C and A is congested or operating at lesser capacity than the links on the alternate path.

I recognize that in this example, it is not yet apparent how node A processes all this information to come up with a routing decision. This explanation is provided shortly.

### Packet Containment

How can this procedure achieve packet containment? It can implement the same procedures that were explained with the minimum hop operation. But the common approach is to use a combination of a sequence number, an age field, and a checksum to verify if the same advertisement has been received by a node. If so, the LSA is ignored and not relayed further. This may seem inefficient, but LSAs should not be a big part of the overall traffic pattern anyway, and if an occasional duplicate LSA is received at a node, it should not be a major overhead factor. If duplicate LSAs, those that have not silently been discarded, are creating excessive overhead, the network manager has much more serious problems than redundant LSAs. Anyway, I will explain more about packet containment of link state protocols in later chapters.


## LINK STATE PROTOCOLS AND SHORTEST PATH OPERATIONS

Many routing systems have implemented a technique, known generally as a shortest path protocol (SPF). A better term is optimum path, but the former term is now accepted. These protocols are based on well-tested techniques that have been used in the industry for a number of years. In this section, we first describe these techniques. In later chapters, we examine how bridges and routers use the SPF techniques The term *node* in this discussion is synonymous with bridge, gateway, and router.

Ideally, data communications networks are designed to route user traffic based on a variety of criteria, generally referred to as a least-cost routing or cost metrics. The name does not mean that routing is based solely on obtaining the least-cost route in the literal sense of money. Other factors are often part of a network routing algorithm, such as delay and throughput.

Even though networks vary in the use of specific least-cost criteria, three constraints must be considered: (a) delay, (b) throughput, and (c) connectivity. If delay is excessive or if throughput is too little, the network does not meet the needs of the user community. The third constraint is obvious; the network nodes and the networks must be able to reach each other; otherwise, all other least-cost criteria are irrelevant.

Figure 3–8 shows the topology or link state database that each node has for its routing domain. The nodes are labeled A, B, etc., and the solid lines between the nodes represent either (a) a communications link, or (b) a shared network. If routers are employed, remember that each router has complete information about all other routers. The bridges in a LAN operate the same way.


### Shortest Path Algorithm

Several shortest-path algorithms are used in the industry. Most of them are based on what is called algorithm A. It is used as the model for the newer internet SPF protocols and has been used for several years to

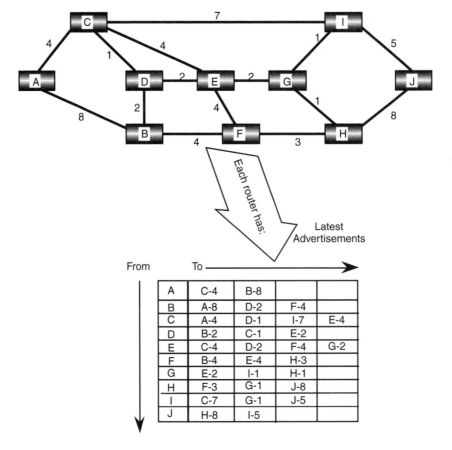

| From | To | | | |
|------|------|------|------|------|
| A | C-4 | B-8 | | |
| B | A-8 | D-2 | F-4 | |
| C | A-4 | D-1 | I-7 | E-4 |
| D | B-2 | C-1 | E-2 | |
| E | C-4 | D-2 | F-4 | G-2 |
| F | B-4 | E-4 | H-3 | |
| G | E-2 | I-1 | H-1 | |
| H | F-3 | G-1 | J-8 | |
| I | C-7 | G-1 | J-5 | |
| J | H-8 | I-5 | | |

**Figure 3–8   The Link State Database**

establish optimum designs and network topologies. The concepts discussed here are from [DIJK59][1] and [AHO74].[2]

Figure 3–9 shows an example of how algorithm A is applied, using node A as the source. Algorithm A is defined generally as:

- Least-cost criteria weights are assigned to the paths in the network.
- Each node is labeled (identified) with its least-cost criteria from the source along a known path. Initially, no paths are known, so

---

[1][DIJK59] Dijkstra, E., *Numerical Mathematics,* "A Note on Two Problems in Connection of Graphs," 1959.

[2][AHO74] Aho, A.V., et al., *The Design and Anlaysis of Computer Algorithms,* Addison-Wesley, 1974.

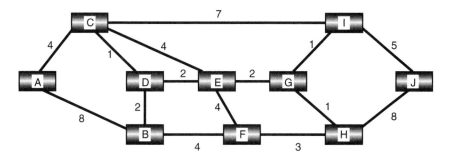

**Figure 3–9    Application of Algorithm A at Node A**

each node is labeled with infinity. However, updates to the values (once the metrics are established) is the same as an initialization.

- Each node is examined in relation to all nodes adjacent to it. (The source node is the first node considered and becomes the working node). This step is actually a one-time occurrence, wherein the source node (node A) is initialized with the costs of all its adjacent nodes. Node A's link state database entries are examined first.

- The node that is closest to the working node (smallest metric) becomes the new working node for the next iteration, and its entries in the link state database are examined, and the process from this node repeats itself until all entries in the link state database have been examined.

In Figure 3–10, A is the working node. Therefore, consulting the link state database in Figure 3–8, nodes C and B are added to a working set of nodes. Using the link metric of 4 on A's interface to C, and a link metric of 8 on A's interface to B, node A knows that it can reach these two nodes at these costs. In fact, through an initial handshake with C

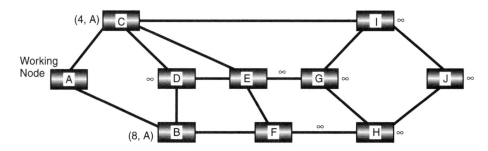

**Figure 3–10    A and Its Working Set**

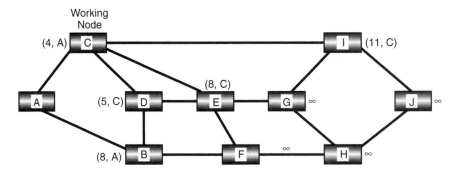

**Figure 3–11    C Becomes the Working Node**

and D (called a hello), node A discovers its adjacent neighbors (the hello is a subject of a later discussion).

After the adjacent nodes are examined, the node with a smaller metric becomes the working node. In Figure 3–11, node C becomes the working node, and its entries in the link state database are examined.

If the sum of the node's label is less than the label on an adjacent node, the adjacent node's label is changed, because a shorter path has been found to the source node. This event is shown in Figure 3–12. The selection of node D as the working node reveals that node A has a better path to node B than the path calculated in the previous step. The path from A through C, D, and then B is 7. The previous path was a direct connection from A to B with a metric of 8. One might wonder how the path through multiple nodes is better than a direct connection. It can occur. For example, the link between A and B might be a low speed point-to-point link connecting these nodes across a campus. The links (or networks) between A, C, D, and B might be high-speed LANs. If the metric represents link speed, it is easy to see why the path with more links is preferable.

Another working node is selected and the process repeats itself until all possibilities have been searched. The final labels reveal the least-cost, end-to-end path between the source and the other nodes. These nodes are considered to be within a set N as it pertains to the source node.

The following statements describe the preceding discussion [SCHW87]:[3]

---

[3][SCHW87] Schwartz, Misha. *Telecommunications Networks: Protocols, Modeling, and Anaysis.* Addison-Wesley Publishing Company, 1987.

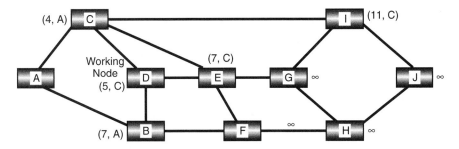

**Figure 3–12    D Becomes the Working Node**

**(1)** Let D(v) = sum of link weights on a given path
**(2)** Let c(i,j) = the cost between node i and j
**(3)** Set n = {1}
**(4)** For each node (v) not in N, set D(v) = C(1,v)
**(5)** For each step, find a node w not in N for which D(w) is a minimum; add w to set N
**(6)** Update D(v) for all nodes still not in N by:
    D(v) ← min [D(v), D(w) + c(w,v)]
**(7)** Repeat steps (4) through (6) until all nodes are in set N.

The routing topology for node A is shown in Figure 3–13. The numbers in parentheses represent the order of selection in the spanning tree.

Notice that the operation has created a spanning tree topology: (a) all nodes are connected to each other, and (b) there are no loops in the topology. Of course, the links that have been blocked (pruned) are still

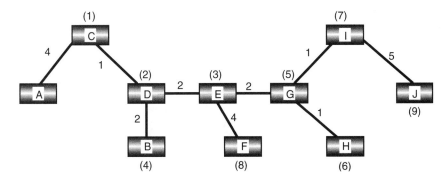

**Figure 3–13    Routing Topology for Node A**

present. They may be placed back into operation if necessary. For example, if an operational interface fails, the advertising messages will allow the routers or bridges in the routing domain to reconfigure their routing tables, and place the appropriate blocked link(s) back into operation.

As a last example of the spanning tree operation, Figure 3–14 shows the initial steps in building the tree. Notice that node B is in the tree from A at the beginning of the process. However, when node D's link

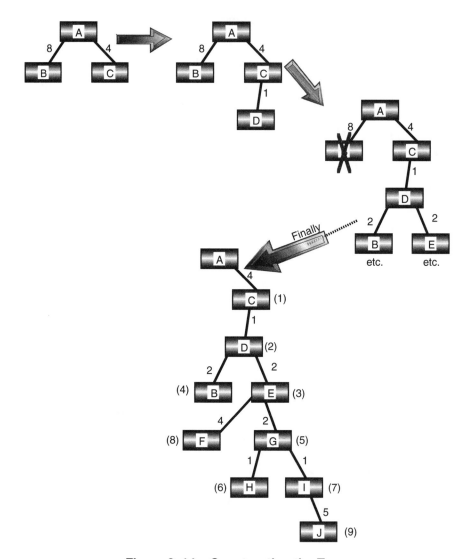

**Figure 3–14   Constructing the Tree**

states are added to the operation, node B is taken out of the path with A and placed into the path with D. The X in the figure symbolizes this operation. The bottom part of Figure 3–14 shows the final tree, with the numbers in parentheses reflecting the order the node was added to the tree.

## ROUTING BETWEEN DOMAINS

Now that we have examined how distance-vector, or link state routing protocols are used within a domain, let us expand the discussion, and see how the routing information can be propagated into another routing domain. Figure 3–15 is used for this analysis. This example is generic in that it does not illustrate any specific protocol. It uses concepts taken from several routing protocols. Two routing domains are shown, labeled RD 1 and RD 2.

Routers C and X are designated as border routers for the routing domains 1 and 2, respectively. In this figure, router C's routing information (shown on the left side of the figure) is sent to router X, which uses it to update its routing table containing reachability information pertaining to nodes A, B, C, D, E, F, and G. Router X is not concerned with how this in-

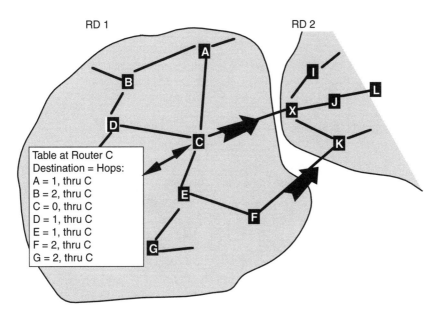

**Figure 3–15 Propagating Routing Information Across Domains**

formation was obtained by router C. It could have been obtained by an IGP method, but these internal operations remain transparent to router X.

To expand this discussion, let us assume routers F and K also exchange routing information. A routing domain is not restricted to only one border router, but an area may designate only one router for the area. Now assume in Figure 3–16 that the link or network connection is lost between E and F. Router C discovers this problem through its IGP and typically enters a metric symbolizing infinity in its routing table entry to F (16, 256, or whatever the protocol stipulates). In Figure 3–16, an "F=16, through C" message is sent to router X as shown by the arrow from C to X.

However, as seen in Figure 3–17, router X knows of a better route. Since F and K have exchanged routing information, the IGP exchange between X and K reveals that a better path than 16 exists to F. X stores in its routing table that this path is through K. It also sends an EGP message to core router C that F can be reached through X with a cost metric of 3. Since 3 is less than 16, router C updates its routing table accordingly.

One more point should be made about this example. RD 2 is acting as a pass-through network for RD 1. This means RD 2 is not emanating

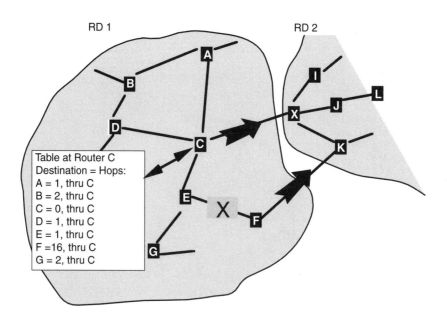

**Figure 3–16     Effect of Losing a Connection**

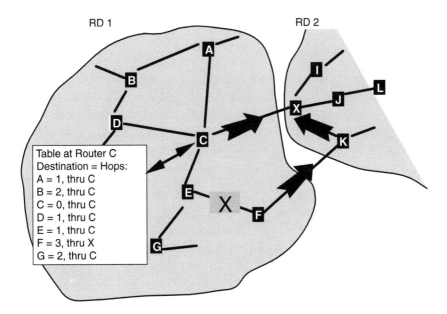

Table at Router C
Destination = Hops:
A = 1, thru C
B = 2, thru C
C = 0, thru C
D = 1, thru C
E = 1, thru C
F = 3, thru X
G = 2, thru C

Note: Be aware that this operation is not permitted in some systems

**Figure 3–17    Receiving Routing Information from Router X**

or terminating these packets, so they are coming from and going to customers other than those in RD 2's domain. RD 2 might not think this wonderful service to RD 1 is wonderful to RD 2, unless RD 2 can gain some benefit from providing this backup service. Consequently, while backup and pass-through services can be supported with most routing protocols, the network administrator may forbid it for security, traffic-load, and/or commercial reasons.

Figure 3–18 shows an example of an update message in relation to the internet topology examples discussed in previous discussions. In this figure, the networks or links between the routers have been labeled with arbitrary network IDs. Router C issues the update message in this figure to router X. The message contains a header to identify the sending node, and perhaps other fields, such as sequence numbers, time stamps, and authentication parameters. One field in the header specifies how many distances are being reported in the message; in this example the value is 3.

The data field is of interest to us here. Three distance groups are reported in the data field: 0 = networks directly attached to C (D1); 1 = networks one hop away from C (D2); and 2 = networks two hops away from C (D3).

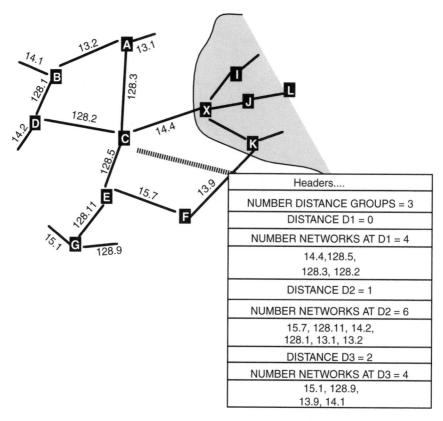

**Figure 3–18   An Update Message (Generic)**

To aid in studying this figure, abbreviated addresses are used. Four addresses are being reported at D1: 14.4, 128.5, 128.3, and 128.2. Six addresses are being reported at D2: 15.7, 128.11, 14.2, 128.1, 13.1, and 13.2. Four addresses are being reported at D3: 15.1, 128.9, 13.9, and 14.1.

Once again, this example is general and generic, and in later parts of this book, we will look at the messages of the specific routing protocols, such as RIP and OSPF.

## RELATIONSHIPS OF ROUTE DISCOVERY TO BRIDGES AND ROUTERS

Many of the operations described in this chapter are applicable to both bridges and routers. But not all. First, a bridge operates only on LANs and has no concept of autonomous systems, and network addresses. The bridge certainly can be configured to operate a spanning tree, as we shall see in Chapter 4. Routers are even more flexible, and can perform integrated routing and bridging.

### Integrated Routing and Bridging

Routers are capable of routing or bridging operations on separate interfaces in a router. A protocol, such as IP, can be routed between routed interfaces and a bridge link (or a group of links, called a bridge group). IP can also be routed between bridge groups. To provide flexibility to the network manager, packets can be:

• Switched from a bridged interface to a routed interface
• Switched from a routed interface to a bridged interface
• Switched within the same bridge group

We have learned that bridging operates at the data link layer and routing operates at the network layer. Using IP as the model, all bridged interfaces on a router belong to the same network, whereas each routed interface is a different network. To handle this situation, the router can be configured with certain interfaces set up as a bridge-group virtual interface (BVI), as shown in Figure 3–19.

The BVI does not permit bridging but does allow the bridge group to be represented to the routed interface. The attractive aspect of this approach is that the BVI gives the bridge group network addresses and masks.

Packets coming into the router from the routed interface destined for a host on the bridge group are routed to the BVI, then to the corre-

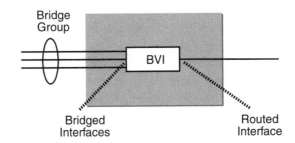

**Figure 3–19   Bridge-Group Virtual Interface (BVI)**

sponding bridge interface as bridged traffic. The BVI performs the same function for packets emanating from the bridge groups.

## OPERATING WITH MULTIPLE ROUTING PROTOCOLS

The network manager must deal with the fact that the internets may operate with multiple routing protocols. Parts of the routing domain may use RIP, and other parts may use OSPF. The reasons that multiple protocols may be used is that legacy equipment may be forced to use RIP, the internetworking of one enterprise with another may require using each other's routing procedures, and so on. Whatever the reason, using multiple routing protocols is a common occurrence.

Fortunately, routers are capable of integrating multiple routing protocols. They correlate the metrics of one protocol to another, such that the different routing protocols can understand each other. This process is called route redistribution. Cisco routers support the following combinations of route redistribution, and I refer you to [SLAT99][4] for configuration details:

- RIP and IGRP
- RIP and OSPF
- RIP and EIGRP
- RIP, OSPF, and static routes
- IGRP, EIGRP in the same AS
- IGRP, EIGRP in different ASs
- IGRP and static routes
- EIGRP and OSPF
- RIP, EIGRP, and OSPF

## KEY INTERNET ROUTING PROTOCOLS

Table 3–2 provides a summary and comparison of several of the key Internet routing protocols explained in the next chapters of the book. The legend below the table should help you while you read it.

---

[4][SLAT99] Slattery, Terry, and Burton, Bill, *Advanced IP Routing in Cisco Networks,* McGraw-Hill, 1999.

**Table 3–2   Routing Protocol Comparison Chart**

| Protocol | Type | Path | I or E | Over | Neigh | Sec | Change | Agg | Asymm |
|----------|------|------|--------|------|-------|-----|--------|-----|-------|
| RIP | D-V | Hop | IGP | UDP | No | Yes | D/F | Yes | No |
| OSPF | L-S | Metric | IGP | IP | Yes | Yes | D/P | Yes | Yes |
| BGP | D-V/ L-S | Policy | EGP | TCP | Yes | Yes | D/P | Yes | Yes |
| IGRP | L-S | Metric | IGP | IP | No | Yes | D/P | Yes | No |
| EIGRP | L-S | Metric | IGP | IP | Yes | Yes | D/P | Yes | No |
| PNNI | L-S | Metric | IGP/ EGP | ATM | Yes | No | D/P | Yes | Yes |

Legend:
Type      Type of path created:
                   D-V: Distance-vector
                   L-S: Link-state
Path      Path advertising values
I or E      IGP or EGP
Over      Runs over which protocol
Neigh      Neighbor discovery capabilities and hellos
Sec      Is security part of the protocol?
Change      Changes handled:
                   D: Dynamic
                   P: Partial advertising
                   F: Full table advertising
Agg      Address aggregation?
Asymm      Asymmetrical routing on a link (Different metric for each direction)?

## SUMMARY

Routing domains in today's Internet are called autonomous systems. Interior gateway protocols are used within the autonomous systems, and exterior gateway protocols are used between them. The protocols employ distance-vector and link state metric operations to establish the best paths for the user traffic to traverse.

## FOLLOW-UP READING

These references should be helpful as follow up reading to this chapter: (a) Lewis, Chris, *Cisco TCP/IP Routing Professional Reference*, McGraw-Hill, 1997. (b) Huitema, Christian, *Routing in the Internet*, Prentice Hall, 1995.

# 4

# Bridges

## INTRODUCTION

This chapter explains how bridges interconnect LANs. The focus is on learning and spanning tree bridges, those bridges that perform many of their operations automatically. We examine token ring bridges, also known as source routing bridges. The chapter provides examples of how the LLC protocol, configured with the type 2 option, is accommodated in a wide area internet. The chapter also explains the operations of a bridge that connects LANs on a point-to-point link to WANs, known as a half-bridge.

## WHY USE BRIDGES?

In Chapter 1, several points were made about why internetworking with routers is valuable to the communications industry. These statements apply to this chapter as well. Bridges are also important because in some networks, such as LANs, they may be a requirement to restrict the number of nodes (workstations, routers, servers, etc.) that are placed on the network media. Consequently, an enterprise may be limited in its growth potential if there is no means to connect the geographically-limited LANs together. The bridge is one tool used to connect these LANs.

Second, LANs (for example, Ethernet) are limited in the distance that the media can be strung through a building or a campus. This geographical restriction can be overcome by placing a bridge between the geographically-challenged LAN segments.

Third, as we mentioned in Chapter 1, the ability to use internetworking units, such as bridges, allows the network manager to contain the amount of traffic that is sent across the expensive network media.

Now that I have said all these wonderful things about bridges, it must also be stated that in many internetworking situations, the router is used in place of a bridge, because it has more capabilities than a bridge.

## THE MAC BRIDGE

Bridges are designed to interconnect LANs. Therefore, they use a destination MAC address (see Appendix B, Figure B–2) in determining how to relay the traffic between LANs. A bridge "pushes" the conventional network layer responsibilities of route discovery and forwarding operations into the data link layer. In effect, a bridge has no conventional network layer.

Figure 4–1 shows a multiport bridge, which accepts a frame coming in on a port from network A. The frame is examined by the MAC relay

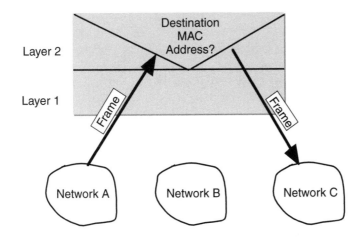

Where:
MAC   Media access control (a LAN address)

**Figure 4–1   Bridge Operations**

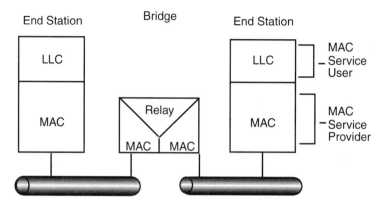

**Figure 4–2   The MAC Relay Entity**

entity and a decision is made to relay the traffic on an output port to network C.

There is no provision for data integrity in bridges (such as the acknowledgment of traffic, and the possible retransmission of erred traffic).
As a consequence, frames can be discarded if the bridge becomes congested. On the other hand, bridges are fast, and they are very easy to implement. Indeed, most bridges are self-configuring. This feature relieves
network managers of many onerous tasks, such as the ongoing management of a number of naming and network reconfiguration parameters.

## THE OTHER BRIDGE LAYERS

The IEEE internetworking entity is positioned at the MAC layer. As
shown in Figure 4–2, the relay entity is designated as a bridge. In this
example, the MAC service user is LLC and the MAC service provider is
(a) MAC and (b) the MAC relay entity.

Traffic transported across a MAC bridge need only access the MAC
layer. Except for certain network management functions, the operation
does not require the invocation of any protocol above MAC.

## TYPES OF BRIDGES

Several different types of bridges are available for internetworking
LANs. They are introduced in this section, and summarized in Table 4–1.

**Table 4-1   Types of Bridges**

Transparent basic bridge
  Places incoming frame onto all outgoing ports except original incoming port
Source routing bridge
  Relies on routing information in frame to relay the frame to an outgoing port
Transparent learning bridge
  Stores the origin of a frame (from which port) and later uses this information to relay
  frames to that port
Transparent spanning bridge
  Uses a subset of the LAN topology for a loop-free operation

### The Transparent Basic Bridge

The simplest type of bridge is called the transparent basic bridge. This bridge receives traffic coming in on each port and stores the traffic until it can be transmitted on the outgoing ports. It will not forward the traffic from the port from which it was received. The bridge does not make any conversion of the traffic. It merely extends LANs beyond what could be achieved with simple repeaters.

### Source Routing Bridge

The source routing bridge is so named because the route through the LAN internet is determined by the originator (the source) of the traffic. As shown in Figure 4-3, the routing information field (RIF), contained in the LAN frame header, contains information on the route that the traffic takes through the LAN internet.

At a minimum, routing information must identify the intermediate nodes that are required to receive and send the frame. Therefore, source routing requires that the user traffic follow a path that is determined by the routing information field.

The architecture for source routing is similar to the architecture for all bridges in that both use a MAC relay entity at the LAN node. Interfaces are also provided through primitives to the MAC relay entity and to LLC. However, the frames of the source routing protocol are different from those of other bridge frames because the source routing information must be contained within the frame.

Figure 4-4 shows the functional architecture for source routing bridges. Two primitives are invoked between the MAC entities and LLC.

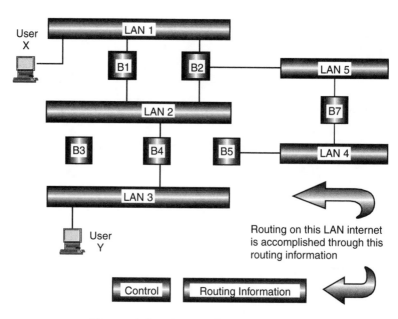

Figure 4–3    Source Routing Concept

The first primitive is the M_UNITDATA.request, and the second primitive is the M_UNITDATA.indication.

The parameters in these primitive calls must contain the information to create the frame (frame control), and the MAC addresses, and of course the routing information that is used to forward the traffic through the LAN internet. A frame check sequence value is included if frame check sequence operations are to be performed. The primitives also contain a data parameter, a user priority parameter, and a service class parameter. These latter two parameters are used only with token rings and are not found in the primitives calls for other LANs, such as Ethernet or token bus.

### The Transparent Learning Bridge

The transparent learning bridge, depicted in Figure 4–5, finds the location of user stations by examining the source and destination addresses in the frame when the frame is received at the bridge. The destination address is stored if it is not in a routing table and the frame is sent to all LANs except the LAN from which it came. In turn, the source address is stored with the direction (incoming port) from which it came.

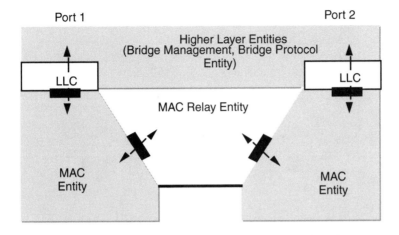

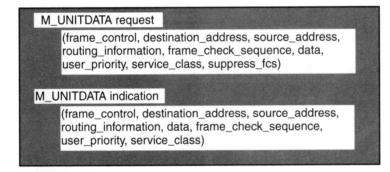

**Figure 4–4   Source Routing Layers and Primitives**

Consequently, if another frame is received in which this source address is now a destination address, it is forwarded across this port. The only restriction to the use of a transparent learning bridge is that the physical topology cannot allow loops.

The learning bridge operates with a bridge processor, which is responsible for routing traffic across its ports. The processor accesses a routing database which contains the destination ports of associated MAC addresses. When a frame arrives at an incoming port on the bridge, the bridge examines its database to determine the output port on which the frame will be relayed. If the destination address is not in the directory, the bridge processor will broadcast the frame onto all ports except the port from which the frame arrived. As mentioned earlier, the bridge processor also stores information about the source address in the frame. This information is stored in the database and contains the source port

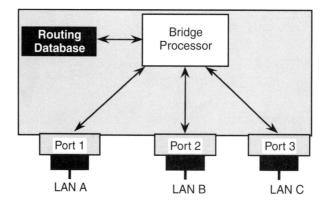

- Processor examines both source and destination addresses in frames
- Looks for destination address in routing database; if found, routes according to the database; if not found, broadcasts frame to all ports except the originating port
- Also looks for source address in the routing database; stores the direction from which it  came—on which port it arrived

**Figure 4–5    The Transparent Learning Bridge**

from which the frame arrived. This information aids the processor in determining where to route a later frame that contains (in its destination field) an address that was received earlier as a source address.

Figure 4–6 shows how a bridge processes an incoming frame in relation to its destination address (DA) and its source address (SA). The bridge is processing a frame coming in from port 1 with a DA of A and SA of B. Upon accessing its routing database, it finds that it does not have the DA of A in its database. Therefore, it broadcasts this frame out to all ports except the port from which this frame came (port 1). After it has forwarded the frame, it determines if it knows about the SA. If the SA is stored in its routing database, it will update this entry in the database by refreshing a timer which means that this address is still "timely and valid." In this example, it does not know about the SA of B. Therefore it stores in its database that B is an active station on the LAN and that, from the viewpoint of this bridge, B can be found on port 1.

In Figure 4–7, a frame arrives at the bridge on port 3 containing destination address B and source address C. The first task of the bridge is to route the frame. Therefore, it consults its routing database and determines that B can be reached through its port 1. This determination is

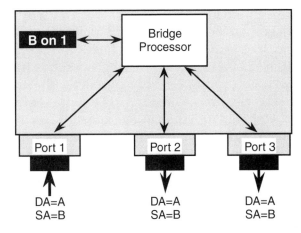

Store: B found on port 1Send frame: on ports 2 and 3

**Figure 4–6    Learning, Forwarding and Filtering Operations**

made from a previous operation in which a frame arrived on port 1 with B's address in the source address field. Since the bridge understands that address B is on port 1, it does not forward this frame to port 2. The bridge also stores in its routing database that the source address C can be reached on port 3. Additionally, it does not forward the frame to port 3 because this would send the frame backward. This latter statement is

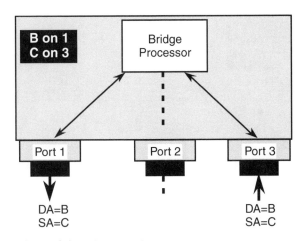

Store: C found on port 3
Send frame: on port 1

**Figure 4–7    Bridge Learns About C, Forwards to Port 1**

important because the learning bridge is based on trust. That is to say, the bridge assumes that the frame received on an incoming port has been properly delivered by the downstream bridges and LANs.

In some situations, a bridge will not forward the frame to any port. Figure 4–8 shows one example of why complete filtering is possible. A frame has arrived at the bridge on port 1. Its contents contain a DA of B and a SA of D. Once again, the bridge consults its routing database which reveals that DA B can be found on port 1. Since the frame arrived on port 1, it will not forward this frame to ports 2 and 3 nor will it send it "backward" to port 1. In addition, once it has taken care of the relaying operations, it makes certain that the SA is checked against its routing database. In this instance, the SA is D; it is not known in the database at this time, and therefore an entry to the database is added and a time is attached to the entry.

A learning bridge permits the use of multicasting and broadcasting. In Figure 4–9, a frame arrives from port 1 with a DA set to ALL (all 1s in the address field). The source address is D. The bridge processor does not update its table because D is already known as coming from port D, and the relaying process is straightforward. It need only relay the traffic to all other outgoing ports. In this example, the traffic is sent to ports 2 and 3.

Figure 4–10 provides examples of how a bridge forwards and filters frames. A frame transmitted on the LAN from station A to station B is

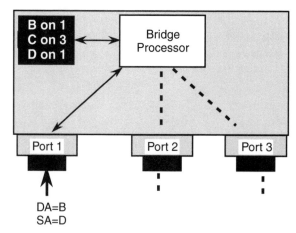

**Figure 4–8    Bridge Learns About D, but Filters**

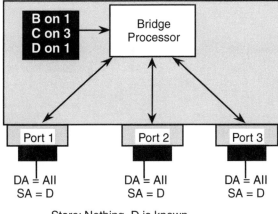

Store: Nothing, D is known
Send frame: To all ports except port 1

**Figure 4–9    Multicasting—Filtering on Incoming Port Only**

not forwarded by bridge 1. The bridge assumes the traffic was success-fully transferred on the broadcast network between A and B. Traffic des-tined from station A to station C must be forwarded by bridge 1 in order to reach station C. However, this frame is discarded (filtered) by bridge 2. Both bridges 1 and 2 must forward traffic destined from station A to sta-tion D.

Figure 4–11 shows a flowchart used by a learning bridge to (a) de-termine the destination port for a frame and (b) update the routing data-base. Upon receiving a frame from a port (in this example, port A), the bridge examines the routing database to determine if the destination

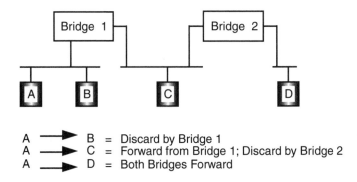

**Figure 4–10    Discarding Frames at the Bridges**

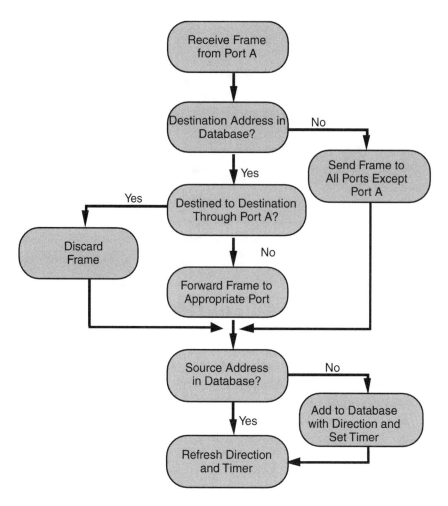

**Figure 4–11   Learning Bridge Logic**

MAC address exists. If not, the frame is broadcast to all ports except the source port (port A). If the address exists in the database, it is forwarded to the appropriate port. Otherwise, the frame is discarded.

The next step is to determine if the MAC source address that was in the frame exists in the routing database. If it does not exist, the address is added to the database with an entry revealing that it came from port A. A timer is set on this entry in order to keep the routing database up-to-date. If the database becomes full, older entries are cashed out. If the source address already exists in the database, the direction is checked, perhaps refreshed, and the timer is reset.

### The Transparent Spanning Tree Bridge

The last type of bridge is called a spanning tree (or transparent spanning) bridge. Unlike the previous examples in this explanation, the spanning tree bridge uses a subnet of the full topology to create a loop-free operation.

Figure 4–12 shows the functional logic of the IEEE 802.1 bridge. The received frame is examined by the relay entity in the following manner. The destination MAC address contained in the frame is matched against a routing database (known in some IEEE documents as the filtering database). In addition, information is stored relative to the bridge ports. This information is called port state information and reveals if a port can be used for this destination address. A port could be in a blocked state to fulfill the requirements of spanning tree operations. If the filtering database reveals an outgoing port for the frame and the port is in a forwarding state, the frame is routed across the port.

The 802.1 standard requires that the bridges' ports operate in other conditions as well. For example, a port state might be "disabled" for

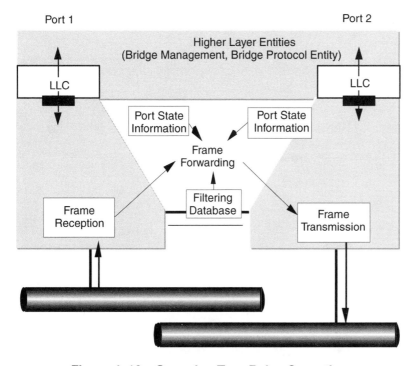

**Figure 4–12   Spanning Tree Relay Operations**

reasons of maintenance or because of malfunctions. Ports may also be temporarily unavailable if filtering databases are being changed in the bridge because of a result of changes noted during route discovery operations on the network.

### The Configuration Message

Figure 4–13 shows the format for the configuration message, also called a bridge protocol data unit (BPDU). The protocol identifier is set to 0. Also, the version identifier is 0. The message type for the configuration message is 0.

The flags field contain a topology change notification flag. It is used to inform nonroot bridges that they should age-out station entries in cache. This field also contains a topology change notification bit. It is used to inform the bridges that they do not have to inform a parent bridge that a topology change has occurred. The parent bridge will perform this task.

The root identifier contains the ID of the root, plus a 2-octet field that can be used to establish a priority for the selection of the root bridge

Octets

| | |
|---|---|
| Protocol ID | 2 |
| Version | 1 |
| BPDU type | 1 |
| Flags | 1 |
| Root identifer | 8 |
| Path cost to root | 4 |
| Bridge identifier | 8 |
| Port identifier | 2 |
| Message age | 2 |
| Max age | 2 |
| Hello time | 2 |
| Forward delay | 2 |

**Figure 4–13   802.1 Bridge Message or Protocol Data Unit (BPDU)**

and the designated bridge. The root path cost field represents the total cost from the transmitting bridge to the bridge that is listed in the root identifier field.

The bridge and port identifiers are the priority and ID of the bridge (and the reported port) that is sending the configuration message. The message age field is a time, in 1/256th of a second, since the root bridge sent its configuration message from which this message is derived. The max age field, also in 1/256th of a second, contains the time when the configuration message is no longer valid and should be deleted. The hello time field, also in 1/256th of a second, defines the time between the sending of configuration messages by the root bridge. The forward delay field, also in 1/256th of a second, is the time lapse in which a port should stay in an intermediate state (learning, listening) before moving from a blocking state to a forwarding state.

## POTENTIAL LOOPING AND BLOCKING PROBLEMS

Many LANs are internetworked with many multiport bridges, where the bridges permit a looped, nontree topology. In such a configuration, it is possible for packets to loop around through the network over and over again. Depending on how the networks and bridges are set up, it also possible for packets to be blocked by a bridge and not allowed to transit to a proper destination.

The next two sections provide examples of looping and blocking problems. I have made up these examples for the purpose of showing these potential problems; in real implementations, the bridges do not permit these operations to occur (unless the bridges have been incorrectly configured).

### Looping

As illustrated in Figure 4–14, bridges B1, B2, and B3 have two ports each for access to LAN 1 and LAN 2. This topology presents potential problems in that the three bridges could possibly forward the same copy of a frame, and continue sending the frame onto both LANs indefinitely [PERL92].[1] For example, assume a frame is sent by station ABC onto LAN 1, destined for station XYZ on LAN 2. The three bridges receive the

---

[1][PERL92] Perlman, Radia, *Interconnections: Bridges and Routers,* Addison-Wesley, 1992.

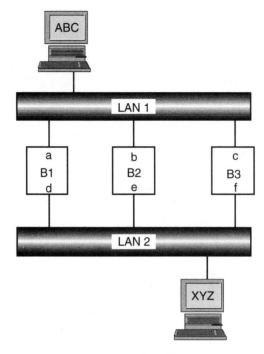

| Event | Result |
|---|---|
| 1: ABC sends packet onto LAN 1, received on ports a, b, c at bridges | Bridges note ABC is on LAN 1 and, Queue packet on ports d, e, f for LAN 2 |
| 2: Bridge 3 sends packet onto LAN 2 | Bridges 1 and 2 note ABC is on LAN 2 and, queue packet on ports a and b for LAN 1 |
| 3. Bridge 1 sends packet onto LAN 2 | Bridge 2: ABC still on LAN 2 Bridge 3: ABC has moved to LAN 2 Queue packet on ports b and C for LAN 1 |
| 4. Bridge 1 sends packet onto LAN 1 | Bridge 2: ABC moved to LAN 1 Bridge 3: ABC moved to LAN 1 Queue packet on ports e and f for LAN 2 |

**Figure 4–14   Looping Problems [PERL92]**

frame, and note the direction of the frame. B1 notes that ABC can be found on its port a, LAN 1. B2 notes that ABC can be found its port b, LAN 1. B3 notes that ABC can be found on its port c, LAN 1. The three bridges send the frame to LAN 2 across their ports d, e, and f respectively. These operations are represented by event 1 in Figure 4–14.

Three copies of the frame are now introduced onto LAN 2. For this example, let us assume that B3 sends this frame first. When this frame is processed at B1 and B2 (in event 2), they will note that ABC resides on

LAN 2, and they queue this frame back to LAN 1 on their a and b ports, respectively. Thus, a loop has started. If you follow events 3 and 4 in the table accompanying Figure 4–14, it is revealed that not only do the frames loop between the networks, they multiply: each successful frame transmittal results in yet another copy of the frame being created.

The solution to this potential problem is to prevent the bridges from forwarding the frame onto LAN 1 and to prevent the frame from being sent back to LAN 2. These preventive measures form the basis for spanning tree logic. In essence, a spanning tree protocol logically blocks certain ports such that one and only one route exists between any source and any destination.

### Blocking

Another potential problem that spanning tree algorithms solve is also illustrated in Figure 4–14, with operations at users ABC and XYZ, and B1 and B2. First, we must assume that the looping problem in the previous discussion has been solved.

User ABC sends traffic onto LAN 1 that is destined for user XYZ. The bridges note the origin of this traffic: that is, user ABC can be found on LAN 1. Next, the bridges receive each other's traffic on LAN 2. Since the source address in the frame is user ABC, the bridges assume that user ABC has relocated and is now on LAN 2. Next, assume at a later time that user XYZ sends a frame to user ABC. The bridges do not forward this frame after examining the destination address of ABC, since they assume XYZ's transmittal of this frame onto LAN 2 has reached user ABC successfully.

Clearly, these two examples of traffic flow management are not acceptable, and remedial measures are taken to prevent these operations.

## THE SPANNING TREE OPERATIONS

Before a spanning tree bridge can operate, it must first prune its topology to a nonlooping tree. In so doing, it follows several well-ordered procedures. See Figure 4–15. The first task is to determine an anchor point from which to calculate a cost through the network. This process is used to identify one bridge among all the bridges in the routing domain to be a "root." This root selection is arbitrary based on the comparison of the ID of the root, an assumed cost to the root (which is a 0 from all bridges initially because they think themselves as the root), the desig-

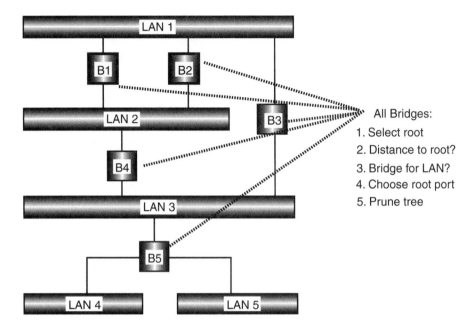

**Figure 4-15   Exchange Configuration Messages to Prune the Tree**

nated root ID, and the port ID on the root. This number concatenated from left to right is examined by each bridge when it receives messages from other bridges to determine who becomes the root bridge. Once again, this process is arbitrary, and it is not important who becomes the root as long as there is a reference point from which to calculate costs.

Next, configuration messages are exchanged between the bridges with distance values in these messages. The purpose of these exchanges is to allow the bridges to calculate the distance from themselves to the root. During this operation, each LAN will select a designated bridge on that LAN (if multiple bridges exist) to act as the bridge to the route. By examining the costs in the configuration messages, it can be determined which bridge is "closest" to the root. Upon this decision being made, this designated bridge will be assigned the job of sending messages from this LAN toward the root.

The next process involves choosing the best port from the particular bridge to the root. This process is known as "choosing the root port." Finally, after all these activities, the bridges perform the spanning tree algorithm and essentially prune out paths that could create loops by simply keeping paths open on root ports and any ports that have been designated for that bridge as the ports with the lowest cost to the root.

The configuration messages transmitted by the LAN station are used to inform other stations about the transmitting nodes knowledge of the "reachability" to these other nodes. Figure 4–16 shows the format for the configuration packet. The originator of the packet must place its MAC address in the source address field of the frame and a multicast address value in the destination address field. The SAP values are coded in accordance with specific network implementations. The information content of the frame consists of an assumed root identifier (root ID), the sending bridge ID, the identification of the port from which the message was sent (port ID), and the known cost to the perceived root.

The initial values of the root ID and the perceived cost to the root are "tentative" values in an initial configuration. As subsequent configuration messages are exchanged, these values may change.

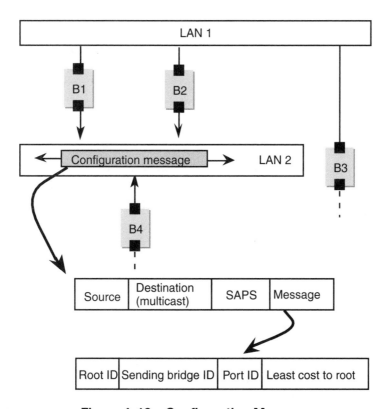

**Figure 4–16   Configuration Messages**

Each node that participates in the spanning tree operation stores the configuration messages sent to it. It uses these messages to determine the "best route" to various nodes in the network. The best route can be defined with any type of link state metric deemed appropriate by the network manager. Whatever this metric may be, it is conveyed in the configuration packet in the cost field, also known as the "path cost to root" field.

The idea behind the exchange of configuration messages is to select a root bridge for the network, calculate a shortest path to the root bridge, select a designated bridge for each network, and choose a root port from each node to the root bridge.

The "best configuration packet" is performed by comparing configuration messages received at each port to the messages that would be transmitted on that port.

The best route is one in which (a) the root ID is lower, then (b) the cost is numerically lower, then (c) the bridge ID is numerically lower, and then (d) the port ID is lower. In other words, the node looks first at the root ID, and if those values are equal it then looks at the cost field, and if those are equal it looks at the bridge ID, and so on down to the port ID. If this technique seems arbitrary to the reader, you are on target, for it is arbitrary—the idea is to find first an anchor point from which to measure (thus the need for finding a root bridge) and then to calculate the costs in relation to the anchor point. See Figure 4–17.

### The Spanning Tree Logic

The spanning tree calculation is performed (a) when the timer for a port reaches a maximum age or (b) if a received configuration message (CM) reveals that this message contains a better path than the stored configuration message.

The timer operation is illustrated in Figure 4–18(a). When the incremented timer is equal to the maximum age (MAXage), the configuration message is discarded and the bridge recalculates the root, root path cost, and root port.

The use of a configuration message is illustrated in Figure 4–18(b). When the bridge receives a configuration message on port n, it compares this message with the stored message. Two situations will lead to a recalculation: when the received CM is better than the stored CM, or the received CM has an age field smaller than the stored CM.

Figure 4–19 provides an example of how the bridge processor determines costs and roots on its ports. The bottom part of the figure shows

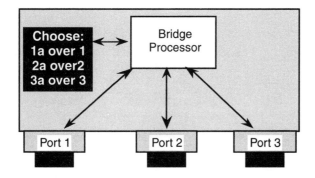

"Best" Configuration Messages:

| Message | Root ID | Send Bridge ID | Cost |
|---------|---------|----------------|------|
| 1 | 31 | 32 | 4 |
| 1a | 30 | 29 | 3 |
| 2 | 31 | 32 | 4 |
| 2a | 31 | 29 | 3 |
| 3 | 31 | 32 | 4 |
| 3a | 31 | 32 | 3 |

Note: Port ID can also be used as part of selection process

**Figure 4–17    Saving "Best" Configuration Messages**

the configuration messages that have been received on ports 1, 2, and 3. The CM on port 1 contains route ID = 10, which is smaller than the route IDs of the CMs on ports 2 and 3. Therefore, the best route is route ID = 10, and the route port is port 1.

As a result to this analysis, the bridge processor will transmit CMs with route ID = 10, sending bridge = 11, and a cost = 6. The value of 6 is used since it is one greater than the cost to the route of 5.

Since the bridge processor has ID = 11, this value is smaller than the route IDs found on ports 2 and 3, consequently it is the designated bridge on these ports and it will transmit its CMs on ports 2 and 3.

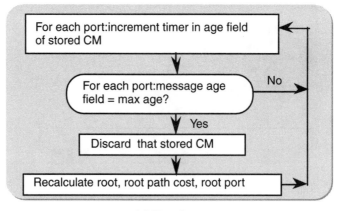

**(a) Max Age**

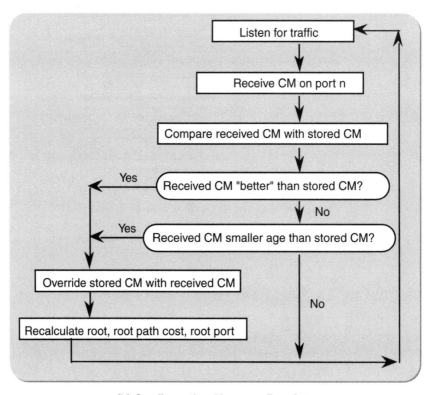

**(b) Configuration Message Receipt**

**Figure 4–18    Spanning Tree Logic**

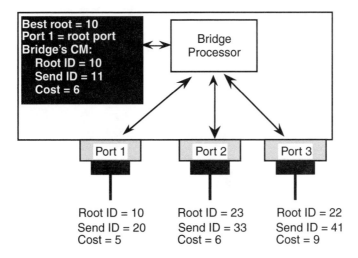

Bridge CM is "better" than CM on ports 2 and 3
Bridge is "designated bridge" on these ports
Therefore, it transmits its CMs on ports 2 and 3

**Figure 4–19   Determining the Root ID, Cost to Root, and Designated Bridge to Ports**

## The Pruned Topology

After all the exchanges of configuration messages and the selection of the root and the designated bridge for each LAN, each bridge computes the spanning tree. Figure 4–20 shows the effect of one such operation. You will notice that several of the ports have been placed in a blocking state (signified with the dashed lines). Data cannot be sent on these ports. Other ports have been placed in a forwarding state, which permits their use for user data traffic. It is also evident that the LAN internet has full connectivity (all LANs and bridges are reachable), yet no loops exist in the topology.

Table 4–2 provides a comparison of spanning tree and source routing operations. Generally speaking, most people in the industry favor the spanning tree concept over that of source routing. This table summarizes the reasons why transparent spanning tree operations are the preferred choice.

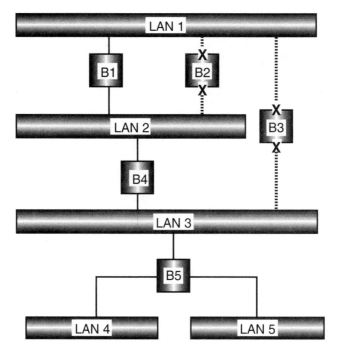

**Figure 4–20   Pruned LAN Topology**

**Table 4–2   Spanning Tree and Source Routing**

| Feature | Spanning Tree | Source Routing |
| --- | --- | --- |
| Routing | Usually, not optimal | Very efficient |
| Headers | Small | Small to very large |
| Configuration | Easy | Somewhat easy, if one is careful |
| Path discovery | Low overhead | Low to high overhead |
| End node responsibility | Very little | Considerable |
| Explicit route header | No | Yes |
| Frame size management | Restricted | No restriction |
| Performance | Fair to good | Good under transient conditions |

## INTERNETWORKING DIFFERENT LANS

Internetworking the same types of networks is a relatively simple operation. However, internetworking heterogeneous networks requires the IWU to assume additional and significant functions. Figure 4–21 shows the internetworking of an 802.3 LAN with an 802.5 LAN and lists some of the major differences that must be resolved by the IWU.

Internetworking different networks is not a trivial exercise. But the task can be accomplished if it is understood that an end user may not be able to achieve the full benefits of one or both of the internetworked protocols.

In most internetworking situations, the end user is given the capabilities of the network that exhibits the lower quality of service. This

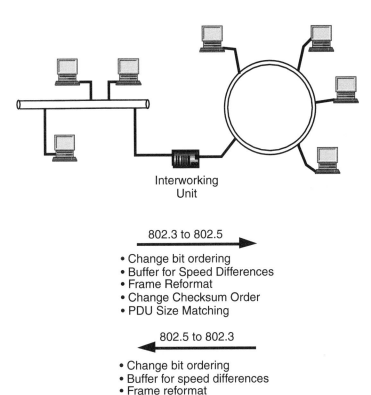

Interworking
Unit

802.3 to 802.5

• Change bit ordering
• Buffer for Speed Differences
• Frame Reformat
• Change Checksum Order
• PDU Size Matching

802.5 to 802.3

• Change bit ordering
• Buffer for speed differences
• Frame reformat
• Change checksum order
• "Map" status bits
• PDU size matching
• Absorb frame

**Figure 4–21    Internetworking CSMA/CD and Token Ring**

approach is certainly reasonable. After all, how can one expect a low function network to spontaneously raise its level of service to that of a higher quality of service network?

In any event, Figure 4–21 shows some of the major tasks that must be accomplished for internetworking 802.3 and 802.5 LANs.

### Address Mapping

One problem that must be solved is the resolution between MAC addresses. This statement seems contradictory in that one would think the use of MAC addresses between two networks would obviate any type of address resolution/mapping. Unfortunately, such is not the case. While the IEEE committees have done a laudatory job setting up efficient standards for LANs, their reluctance or inability to define the exact syntax of MAC addresses for each IEEE LAN type has complicated the internetworking of the different IEEE networks. The principal problem lies in the manner in which the bits are constructed within the address field. Certain networks place the binary low-order bits in the field first, and other networks place the high-order bits in the field first. These approaches are know as the "little endian" and "big endian" syntaxes. As examples, Ethernet, 802.3, and 802.4 transmit "little-endian," with least-significant bits first, and 802.5 and FDDI transmit "big-endian," with most-significant bits first.

### Transit Bridging

One technique to support internetworking heterogeneous LANs is known as either simple encapsulation or transit bridging. See Figure 4–22. With this approach, the router is responsible for interpreting the address of a type a network and relating that to the address of a type b network. As part of this support function, the router encapsulates the traffic of the type a network into the information field of the type b network and transports this traffic across the "transit" type b network. At the receiving router between the type a and type b networks, this router decapsulates the traffic and passes the traffic onto the type a network by placing the traffic in the type a frame.

Table 4–3 summarizes the major operations that occur in the bridging of traffic between Ethernets and token rings when translation bridging is employed. In essence, when moving traffic from a token ring to an Ethernet, the bridge must strip the routing information field (RIF), reformat the frame to the Ethernet format, and throw away the bits used by the token ring that are not used with Ethernet.

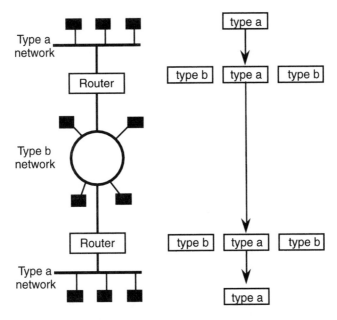

**Figure 4–22  Encapsulation/Transit Bridging**

**Table 4–3  Techniques for Bridging Traffic Between Ethernets and Token Rings: Translation Bridging**

- Token ring to Ethernet
  - Bridge caches RIF for use in sending data to source
  - Strips RIF, and reformats frame to Ethernet format
  - Throws away priority bits, token bit, monitor bit, and reservation bits
- Ethernet to token ring
  - Bridge attaches RIF (if available), else frame flooded and response to flood used for RIF
  - Inserts priority bits, token bit, monitor bit and reservation bits
  - Considerations:
    1. Loop avoidance information is not passed
    2. Does not disturb a source-route bridged network
    3. No spanning tree computations, forcing "all rings" explorer packets
    4. What about addresses in other fields (ARP, XNS, RARP)?
    5. How to handle E (error), A (address seen), and C (frame copied) bits?
       - Do nothing
       - Bridge sets C bit, but not A bit

Conversely, when relaying traffic from Ethernet to the token ring network, the bridge must attach an RIF (if this information is available) and build the token ring frame with the priority bits, the token bit, the monitor bit, and the reservation bits.

Each vendor handles translation bridging in their own fashion. Therefore, the network manager should examine how the bridge provides certain features, which are summarized at the bottom part of Table 4–3.

### Source Route Transparent Bridging (SRT)

IBM has developed a technique to allow the bridging of traffic between Ethernets and token rings. IBM calls this technique source route transparent bridging (SRT). See Figure 4–23. With this approach, a bridge can support source and nonsource routing as long as the end nodes communicate with each other with the same type of operation. Therefore, an Ethernet transparent routing structure can interwork with a token ring source routing structure.

Obviously, IBM's technique must change frame formats and eliminate RIFs and other fields when traffic is relayed from a token ring to an Ethernet, and the reverse process must be accommodated when relaying the traffic from an Ethernet to a token ring.

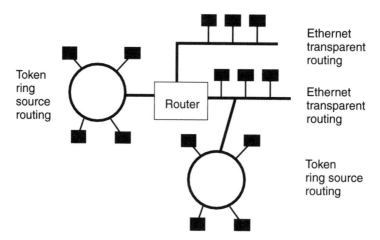

**Figure 4–23   Techniques for Bridging Traffic Between Ethernets and Token Rings: Source Route Transparent Bridging (SRT)**

## REMOTE BRIDGES

In many situations, it is not possible for LANs to interwork directly with bridges between LANs. Since many enterprises are widely distributed, the LANs must often be connected with wide area communications links. See Figure 4–24. These links connect LAN bridges as a point-to-point topology. Such a connection is called remote bridging. Some vendors, such as AppleTalk, refer to the bridges as half bridges in the sense that two bridges and the link are considered to be a single bridge.

Spanning tree operations can be applied to remote bridges. The point-to-point link is considered to be part of the spanning tree, and the bridges are obligated to forward traffic on that link to the other bridge.

That is the good news. The bad news is that the IEEE in its initial discussions on spanning tree bridges, did not define fully remote bridge operations. Therefore, vendors have taken it upon themselves to define procedures for two remote bridges to communicate with each other and determine if traffic is to be forwarded through the point-to-point link.

Another issue that should be considered is the fact that if a LAN is connected through bridges into WAN topologies, with rare exceptions, these WANs will not provide the broadcasting capability. Therefore, it may be necessary for disbursed LANs to have their bridges fully meshed in order for the bridges to communicate with each other. This fully meshed network, while expensive, allows each designated LAN bridge to communicate with the other dedicated LAN bridges.

As of this writing, the 802 committee is addressing the issue of adapting standardized procedures for remote bridge operations. Decisions being contemplated include:

- How one bridge on the point-to-point link decides or does not decide how to forward traffic

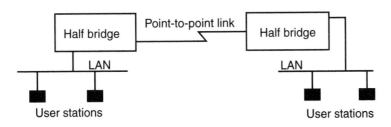

**Figure 4–24   Remote Bridges**

- How the traffic is represented from the standpoint of its syntax on the point-to-point link
- How bridges can communicate with other bridges using not only the point-to-point link method but a wide area switched network as well.

## DATA LINK SWITCHING

As shown in Figure 4–25, routers are designed to support a wide variety of communications protocols: X.25, SDLC, frame relay, TCP/IP, DECnet, IPX, AppleTalk, XNS. It also transports SNA, APPN, and NETBIOS traffic, and functions as a multiport bridge between and among token rings and Ethernets.

Many routers also provide SDLC to LLC 2 conversion, and a technique called Data Link Switching (DLS), which is used to minimize overhead by allowing the use of SNA, APPN, and NETBIOS over the same physical link, and to transport these protocols between LANs over WANs.

SNA and NETBIOS were designed for connection-oriented operations, at least at the communications layers. They do not contain sufficient information to permit the dynamic routing and rerouting found in connectionless network protocols, such as IP, CLNP, IPX, etc.

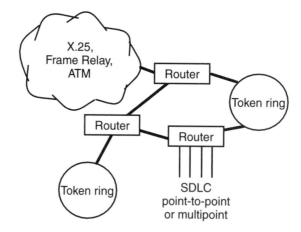

**Figure 4–25   Typical Router Internetworking Topology**

DLS has been developed to allow the transport of SNA and NET-BIOS traffic across an internet. DLS provides the following functions: First, SNA and NETBIOS traffic is transported over a multiprotocol backbone by encapsulating this traffic into the IP data field. Reliable delivery of SNA traffic is assured, and dynamic rerouting of the traffic is provided, if necessary. LLC ACK spoofing is performed on each LAN segment, and broadcast traffic control through a WAN is also provided. DLS also supports LAN and WAN congestion and flow control operations.

### DLS Configuration

Figure 4–26 shows a general configuration for DLS. The routers use spoofing (LLC termination) to minimize the impact of LLC 2 T1 timer timeouts. Spoofing also keeps the LLC2 ACKs local. DLS also terminates the IBM token ring routing information field (RIF) at the edge router, which permits the number of hops across a transport internet to be greater than the 7-hop limit that is in the RIF in some implementations. In effect, 7 hops are permitted at the local side of the WAN, and another 7 are permitted on the other side of the LAN.

The concept of a DLS circuit is also shown in this figure. It is a concatenation of the two LLC 2 sessions between the IBM devices and their respective routers, and the TCP session between the routers. This latter part of the circuit is a TPC socket between (only) the routers. This session was established when the router network was initialized.

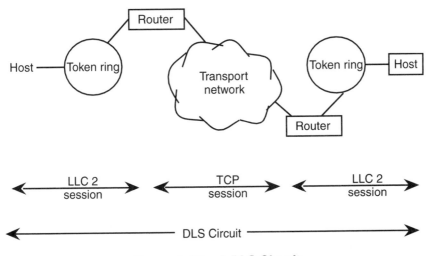

**Figure 4–26   A DLS Circuit**

For SDLC links, polling and poll response occurs locally, not over the WAN. Broadcast of search frames is controlled by the routers once the location of a target system is discovered. Finally, the switches can apply back pressure to the end systems to provide flow and congestion control.

## The DLS Specification: RFC 1795

RFC 1795 is the recognized standard for DLS [WELL95].[2] It is a detailed specification of 91 pages, so this part of the chapter provides an overview of this RFC.

The RFC defines the operations of the switch-to-switch protocol (SSP) that is used between data link switches (DLSw); that is, the routers. It defines switching at the SNA data link layer and encapsulation in TCP/IP for transport over the Internet. It also documents the frame formats and protocols for multiplexing data between the data link switches.

The DLSw in RFC 1795 can support SNA [Physical Unit (PU) 2, PU 2.1 and PU 4] systems and optionally NetBIOS systems attached to IEEE 802.2 LLC-based LANs, as well as SNA [PU 2 (primary or secondary) and PU 2.1] systems attached to IBM SDLC links. For the latter case, the SDLC attached systems are provided with a LAN appearance within the DLSw: each SDLC protocol unit is presented to SSP as a unique MAC/SAP address pair. For the token ring LAN, the DLSw appears as a source-routing bridge.

Since the DLSw is acting as a bridge, it must support the exchange of token ring traffic, notably LLC data units. Copies of the link protocol data units (LPDU) are sent between the switches in SSP messages. Retries of the LPDU are absorbed by switch that receives it. The switch that transmits the LPDU received in an SSP message to a local data link control (LLC control) will perform retries in a manner appropriate for the local DLC. In summary, DLS handles the following token ring MAC and LLC bridging operations across the WAN internet:

- Timeouts
- Acknowledgments and retries
- Flow and congestion control
- Broadcast control of search packets
- Source route bridging hop count limits

---

[2][WELL95] Wells, L, RFC 1795. "Data Link Switching: Link-to-Link Protocol," April, 1995.

## Example of DLS Operations

DLS specifies several messages for the operations between the switches. The principle messages perform the following functions, and Figure 4–27 shows the flow of these messages.

The CANUREACH, ICANREACH, and REACH_ACK message types all carry the data link ID, consisting of the MAC and LLC SAP values associated with the two end stations. The MAC and LLC identifiers are used in a token ring network to uniquely identify traffic from a host, so DLS must support the exchange of these parameters.

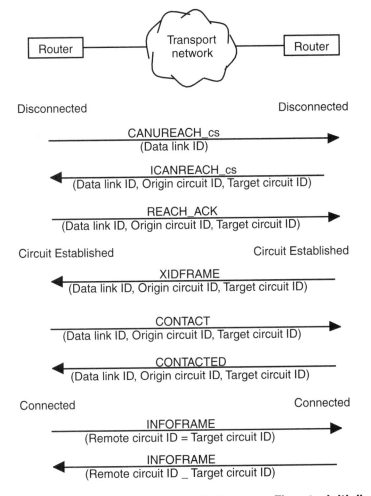

**Figure 4–27   Example of a DLS Message Flow to Initialize the DLS Circuit**

The CANUREACH and ICANREACH messages are coded as CANUREACH_ex, ICANREACH_ex (explorer messages) and CAN-UREACH_cs, ICANREACH_cs (circuit start messages). The CAN-UREACH_ex is used to find a remote MAC and LLC SAP address without establishing an SSP circuit. Upon receipt of a CANUREACH_cs message, the target DLSw starts a data link for each port, thereby obtaining a data link correlator. The purpose of the data link correlator is to provide an additional identifier for the messages and the links involved.

If the target station can be reached, an ICANREACH_cs message is returned to the originating DLSw containing a target circuit ID parameter. Upon receipt of this information, the originating DLSw starts a data link and returns the origin circuit ID to the target DLSw with the REACH_ACK message.

During the exchange of the XIDFRAME, CONTACT, and CON-TACTED messages, the pair of Circuit ID parameters is included in the message exchanges. The INFOFRAME messages are then exchanged with a header that contains only the Circuit ID associated with the remote DLSw. The Remote Data Link Correlator and the Remote DLC Port ID are set equal to the Data Link Correlator and the DLC Port ID that are associated with the origin or target Data Link Switch, depending upon the direction of the packet.

### How a Router Handles DLS

This part of our DLS analysis shows more examples of how the router implements DLS. The examples here are specific to IBM routers [TEAG92],[3] [KUBE92],[4] but other routers do about the same thing if they comply with RFC 1795.

As depicted in Figure 4–28, a new circuit is established by sending conventional explorer frames from a host to another host. The frame is broadcast or multicast to stations within an internet subnetwork. Each router relays the frame on to its outgoing ports. These frames reach the final destination, where they are analyzed for the "best" route.

---

[3][TEAG92]. "Data Link Switching on 6611," March 31, 1992, E. Teagarden, L. Bobbitt, G. Cox, J. Massara, Complex System Support, Dept. B19, Building 651, Research Triangle Park, NC.

[4][KUBE92]. IBM 6611 Performance Presentation Script, October 1992, CB Kube, IBM Washington Systems Center, Dept. JLK, Building 183, Gaithersburg, MD.

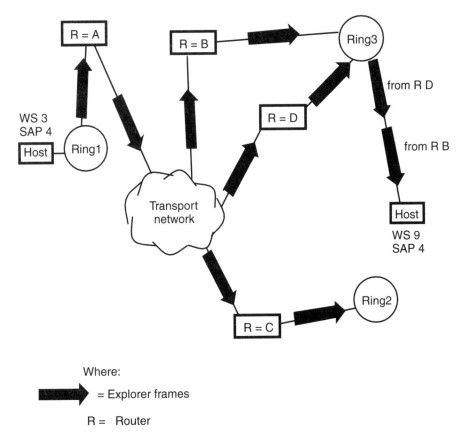

Where:

➤ = Explorer frames

R = Router

**Figure 4–28    DLS Circuit Establishment**

In Figure 4–28, the work station with a MAC address of 3 (work station is a host), and a SAP of 4 sends the explorer frame into the internet. The frame is received by router A, and forwarded to routers B, C, and D.

The explorer frame is intended for the workstation identified with a MAC address of 9 and a SAP of 4. This station receives the frame twice, one frame from router B and another frame from router D. Both of these frames contain the routes (in the RIF) that have been traversed from station 3 to station 9. The explorer frame is also sent to ring 2, but the workstation is not to be found there.

Figure 4–29 shows a simplified view of the explorer frames sent by routers B and D and received at work station 9. The S(3,4) identifies the MAC address (3) and SAP (4) of the sender. The D(9,4) identifies the MAC address (9) and SAP (4) of the intended receiver. The routing

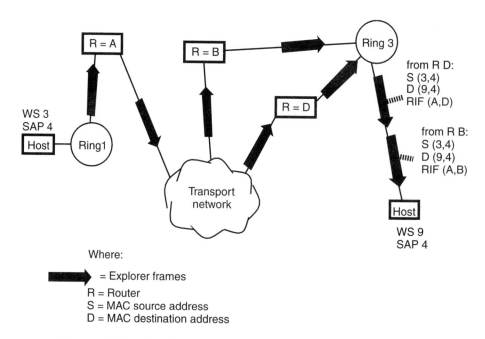

Where:

➤ = Explorer frames
R = Router
S = MAC source address
D = MAC destination address

**Figure 4–29    The Explorer Frames Received at Host 9, SAP 4**

information field (RIF) contains a record of the route that each frame has followed in its traversal through the internet. One explorer frame records the route through router B and another records the route through router D. Although the explorer frames are sent to ring 2, this ring does not interface with station 9, and is deleted from further examples.

Station 9 does not know that these frames have been sent through a wide area transport network. It views the frames as coming from one hop beyond routers B and D. This is known as a "phantom ring segment." The router, using DLS, uses source route bridging on its LAN ports for encapsulating the frames into the router. Then, the router encapsulates the SNA or NETBIOS traffic into TCP/IP for transport across the internet.

Station 9 must respond to the explorer frame by sending responses back to the originator. See Figure 4–30. A response is sent to router B and router D. These routers store information about station 3; it can be reached ("preferred") through router A. This operation obviates querying each of the routers in the internet.

In Figure 4–31, router A receives the two explorer frames and determines which one is best. In this illustration, it is assumed it receives the frame from router B first, and makes this router the preferred router to reach station 9. Router D is also noted as being capable of reaching station 9.

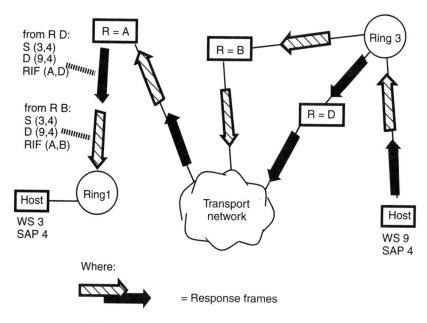

from R D:
S (3,4)
D (9,4)
RIF (A,D)

from R B:
S (3,4)
D (9,4)
RIF (A,B)

R = A

R = B

Ring 3

R = D

Host
WS 3
SAP 4

Ring1

Transport
network

Host
WS 9
SAP 4

Where:

= Response frames

**Figure 4–30   Establishment of DLS Circuit**

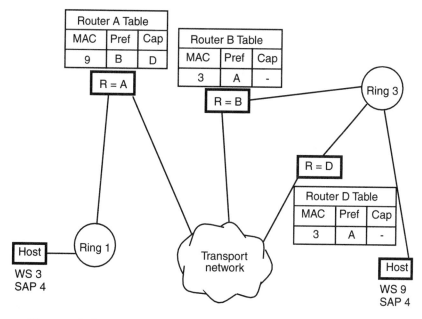

| Router A Table | | |
| --- | --- | --- |
| MAC | Pref | Cap |
| 9 | B | D |

| Router B Table | | |
| --- | --- | --- |
| MAC | Pref | Cap |
| 3 | A | - |

| Router D Table | | |
| --- | --- | --- |
| MAC | Pref | Cap |
| 3 | A | - |

R = A

R = B

Ring 3

R = D

Host
WS 3
SAP 4

Ring 1

Transport
network

Host
WS 9
SAP 4

**Figure 4–31   Effect of Circuit Establishment on Routing Tables**

A few more thoughts are pertinent to this discussion. If another station attached to ring 1 were to send an explorer frame destined for station 9 into this internet, router B intercepts this frame, because it knows a preferred route to station 9. Consequently, it sends back a response to the sending station.

After a circuit is established, traffic is managed by the router on an individual circuit basis. Flow control is provided locally (spoofing) with the conventional receive ready (RR) and receive not ready (RNR) LLC frames on each circuit.

The routers keep records on the relationship of the LLC part of the circuit to the TCP part of the circuit. Therefore, congestion problems experienced at the routers and/or within the internet can be mapped back to the LLC part of the circuit.

In effect, the end stations can be controlled, their timers satisfied, and SNA sessions will not pull themselves down (because of non-response to transmissions).

## SUMMARY

Bridges are important in data communications networks because a bridge is an efficient and cost-effective tool used to connect LANs.

LANs are limited in the distance that the media can be strung through a building or a campus of buildings. This geographical restriction can be overcome by placing a bridge between the LAN segments.

The ability to use internetworking units, such as bridges, allows the network manager to contain the amount of traffic that is sent across the expensive network media.

Data link switching is used in the token ring environment to handle topologies that use SDLC and LLC type 2. TCP serves the function of providing traffic acknowledgments between the LAN routers across the internet. Explorer frames are tunneled through the internet with the DLS protocol.

## FOLLOW-UP READING

I have cited the Perlman text earlier, and I recommend it to you for excellent descriptions of bridging and other routing operations. Of course, there is no substitute for the actual standards, and the IEEE specifications have been cited earlier in the book. For readers wishing to delve into detail about bridges and how to configure bridges, consult your vendor's user manuals. If you do not have access to these manuals, I recommend a book from the Cisco IOS Reference Library titled: *Cisco IOS Bridging and IBM Network Solutions,* by Cisco Press (available from Cisco or Macmillian Technical Publishing).

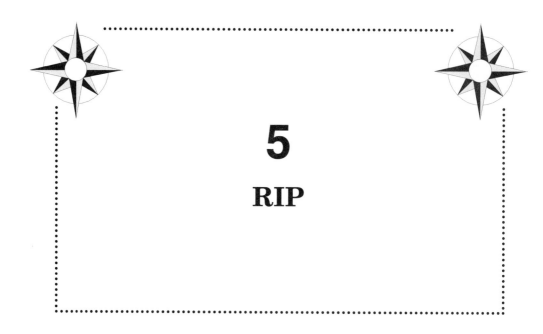

# 5
# RIP

## INTRODUCTION

This chapter explains the operations of the well known distance-vector protocol, the Routing Information Protocol (RIP). We start with a brief history of RIP, and follow with a description of RIP routing tables, and how these routing tables are created. The RIP messages are then analyzed, with examples of RIP version 1 and RIP version 2 messages. RIP advertisements are examined, and the deficiencies of the original RIP are explained, as well as measures taken to overcome some of these deficiencies. The chapter concludes with a description of the tasks used by the network manager to configure RIP operations within an autonomous system.

## DEVELOPMENT OF RIP

The Routing Information Protocol (RIP) system was developed based on research at the Xerox Palo Alto Research Center (PARC) and Xerox's PUP and XNS routing protocols. Its wide use was due to the implementation at the University of California at Berkeley (UCB) in a number of LANs. UCB also distributed RIP with its UNIX system.

RIP was designed for LANs yet is now used in some wide area networks—if for no other reason than the fact that it's there. That is, it was distributed as part of the Internet suite of protocols and was one of the first simple routing protocols that gained wide use in private internets.

RIP is classified as a vector-distance routing protocol. RIP routing decisions are based on the number of intermediate hops to the final destination. Early descriptions of this type of protocol were described by [FORD62].[1] Therefore, RIP is sometimes called a Ford-Fulkerson algorithm, or a Bellman-Ford algorithm, because R. E. Bellman devised the routing equation [BELL57].[2] RIP is published in RFC 1058.

RIP advertises only network addresses and distances (number of hops). It uses a hop count to compute the route cost, and a maximum value of 16 to indicate that an address is unreachable. A hop count of 1 is used to advertise a directly connected network.

In most systems, a router sends RIP routing information every 30 seconds. If a router does not receive an update from another router within 180 seconds, it marks the route from which no update was received as unusable. After 240 seconds, if it still has received no updates, it removes all entries from its routing table about the "absent" network.

## SCHEME FOR ROUTING UPDATES

Figure 5–1 shows the general scheme for a RIP routing update. Router A advertises the address 172.16.0.0 to routers B and C. This update occurs during time period 1. (The notation 1a means the event occurs at about the same time as event 1, and the same idea is conveyed with 2, 2a, etc.) Since A is directly attached to 176.16.0.0, it advertises a metric (hop count) of 1 to this address.

Routers B and C receive this advertisement, and compare the address and the metric with their routing tables. Assuming A had previously notified B and C about 176.16.0.0, the routing table entries at B and C for this address would be a metric of 2, with the next node identified as router A. Routers B and C add 1 to the metric value in the RIP message, and they compare this value with their table entry. In this example, the two values are 2, so the advertisement reveals no better path and no new routes are found.

---

[1][FORD62] Ford, L. R. and Fulkerson, D. R. *Flows in Networks,* Princeton University Press, Princeton NJ, 1962.

[2][BELL57] Bellman, R. E., *Dynamic Programming,* Princeton University Press, Princeton NJ, 1957.

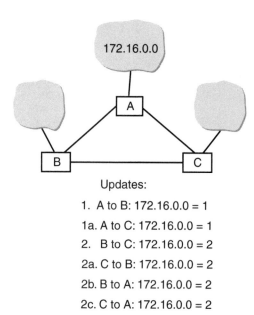

Updates:

1.  A to B: 172.16.0.0 = 1

1a. A to C: 172.16.0.0 = 1

2.  B to C: 172.16.0.0 = 2

2a. C to B: 172.16.0.0 = 2

2b. B to A: 172.16.0.0 = 2

2c. C to A: 172.16.0.0 = 2

**Figure 5–1   RIP Routing Updates**

In time period 2 and 2a, routers B and C advertise 176.16.0.0 to each other, after incrementing the metric in the message to 3. Since their routing table entries show a metric of 2, they ignore this message because it does not show a better route to 176.16.0.0.

In time period 2b and 2c, routers B and C also advertise to router A. Router A ignores these updates because its routing table has stored a better route to 172.16.0.0.

Figure 5–2 depicts a simple internet of five network segments, labeled Network 2 to 6. The focus of attention is on router 3 (R3). This router is advertising information about network 5 out of its port 2 (interface 2). The notation in the figure (2,5) is a shorthand notation used to convey that address 5 is 2 hops away from the advertising router. That is, the notation is (distance in hops, to an address); thus the term (distance, vector). R3 knows about this address because it was advertised to R3 from R5 with R5's RIP message of (1,5).

R3 sends its (2,5) message onto network 2, where it is received by R1 and R2. Now, R2 is the focus of attention (we will bring R1 into the picture shortly). R2 advertises (3,5), which is received by R4, which in turn advertises (4,5).

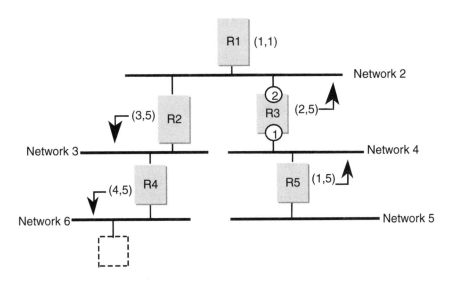

$n$ = physical port (interface) number

**RIP routing table at R3:**

| Destination | Next hop | Metric | Direct or Remote | Local or RIP | Interface |
|---|---|---|---|---|---|
| Network 2 | 0 | 1 | D | L | 2 |
| Network 3 | R2 | 2 | R | R | 2 |
| Network 4 | 0 | 1 | D | L | 1 |
| Network 5 | R5 | 2 | R | R | 1 |
| Network 6 | R2 | 3 | R | R | 2 |

**Figure 5–2   RIP Routing Table Example**

Since all routers are receiving advertisements from each other, reachability can be computed to all networks. As an example, Figure 5–2 also shows the routing table as viewed by R3.

The Destination entry in the table is an address of the destination network, as seen by R3 (in IP-based networks, an IP address). I am using generic addresses in this example for ease of reading.

The Next hop (next node) in the table is the address of the node that is to receive the traffic next. This entry is 0 in this table if there is no next hop. The Metric column states how many hops are between the advertiser of this message to the destination address. The Direct or Remote column is either D (directly attached), or R (a remote network, not directly attached). The Local or RIP column is either L (network discovered because it is local, and discovered by ARP, DHCP, etc., and discussed in Appendix C) or R (network discovered through RIP messages). The Interface column identifies the physical port at R3 on which the discovery was made.

## PROPAGATING THE UPDATES

Since RIP updates its neighbors, and these neighbors update their neighbors, and so on through the routing domain, it takes time for the updates to propagate through the domain. A router that sends its entire routing table does so every 30 seconds. Therefore, the nodes at the "end"

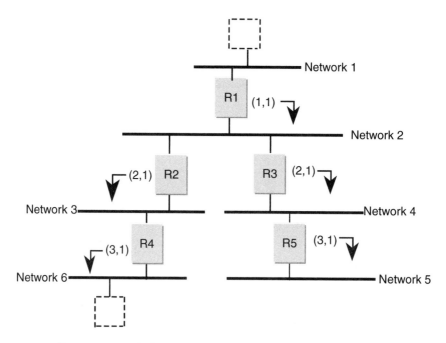

**Convergence timing to learn about network 1:**

| Time | R1 | R2 | R3 | R4 | R5 |
|------|----|----|----|----|----|
| 1 | 1 | — | — | — | — |
| 2 | 1 | 2,R1 | 2,R1 | — | — |
| 3 | 1 | 2,R1 | 2,R1 | 3,R2 | 3,R3 |

Where: n,Rx means hop count, through Rx as the next node

**Figure 5–3   Network 1 Added to Routing Domain**

of the broadcast will not find out about the change until all intervening nodes have timed-out, and sent the information to their next node.

Figure 5–3 shows an example of these events, in which network 1 is added to the routing domain. As each router receives the update from its neighbor, it checks the update fields for the IP address and its associated metric. If the metric for the address is better than the one for the same address in the routing table, the router updates its table by setting the next hop to the advertising neighbor and adding one to the metric. That is, if the metric received in the message is 2, then the routing table entry is 3, which means, "If my neighbor is 2 hops away, I am 3." This router then advertises the metric of 3 to its neighbors, and so on until all routers in the domain know about the advertised address.

Recall that the routing table has an entry called next node (or next hop). When the message is received, RIP checks the sending address of the IP datagram against the next node entry in the table. If they match, the metric in the message is checked against the metric in the table.

It is easy to see that RIP changes may take a long time to reach convergence. Later, we examine some changes made to RIP that improve upon this cumbersome operation.

## UNICAST UPDATES AND DISABLING UPDATES

RIP is designed as a broadcast protocol. But it is possible to send RIP messages to nonbroadcast nodes. This capability can be useful when connecting to another router on a point-to-point link, say from a customer router to the ISP's router.

It is also possible to disable the use of RIP on specified interfaces. In so doing, the network manager prevents RIP messages from being generated on the specified interface(s).

## RIP MESSAGES

RIP runs over UDP, so its messages are encapsulated into UDP segments and it runs on a well-known port (number 520). Two versions of RIP are available: RIP-1 and RIP-2. Figure 5–4 shows the message formats for both versions.

The command field can contain the values of 1 to 6, but 1 and 2 are the only formal (documented) values. A command code = 1 identifies a request message, and a value = 2 identifies a reply. The version field is 1 or 2 for the two versions.

The messages differ slightly. Both versions contain an address family, which is coded as a 2 for IP addresses. Next is an IP address and its metric (a hop count). These advertisement fields can be repeated 25 times. This limitation is to keep the RIP message less than 512 bytes (4 fixed bytes [command, version, 2 bytes of all zeroes] + 20 bytes × 25 repeats = 504 bytes).

For RIP-2, the unused fields in the RIP-1 message are coded as follows:

- Routing domain:            Identifier of the routing daemon associated with this message. In UNIX, this field is a process ID. By using the routing domain, a machine can run multiple, concurrent RIPs.

- Route tag:                 If RIP is used to support exterior gateway protocols (EGPs), this field contains an autonomous system number.

- Subnet mask:               Associated with the IP address in the message.

- Next hop IP address:       If this field is 0, it indicates that datagrams should be sent to the address that is sending this RIP message. Otherwise, it contains an IP address, which indicates where the datagrams should be sent.

### RIP-2 Authentication

RIP version 2 supports authentication; version 1 does not. Each RIP packet is authenticated at the receiver, if the interface has been configured to support authentication. Typically MD5 authentication is performed, although routers may have other options.

The RIP-2 packet for authentication is similar to the packet format shown in Figure 5–4. This packet is shown in Figure 5–5. The address family field is set to 0xffff, for an authentication packet. The authentication type field is set to 2 for a plain-text authentication procedure and 3 for the MD5 procedure. (Plain-text is not secure.)

The authentication information bytes contain the identifier known as the key number, and may be multiple numbers on a key chain. The

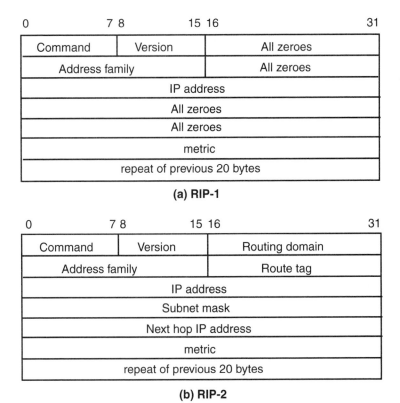

(a) RIP-1

(b) RIP-2

**Figure 5–4    Routing Information Protocol (RIP) Packets**

**Figure 5–5    RIP-2 Packet for Authentication**

user of multiple numbers permits the receiver to sequence through the keys and thus use different keys over specified times. These bytes can also contain fields that define the lifetime of the key or keys.

Each key identifier in the packet is associated with a locally stored key. The key identifier and an interface associated with the message identifies the authentication algorithm and the specific MD5 authentication key to be used for the authentication operation.

### How the Two Versions Can Be Used

RIP versions 1 and 2 can operate alone or in certain combinations with each other. The following combinations can be configured for each interface on the router:

- Send only RIP version 1 packets
- Send only RIP version 2 packets
- Send RIP version 1 and 2 packets
- Receive only RIP version 1 packets
- Receive only RIP version 2 packets
- Receive RIP version 1 and 2 packets

## CONVERGENCE PROBLEMS

RIP updates described so far are quite simple. However, this simplicity can cause some problems. One problem is the possibility of sending traffic through an inefficient path; the other is the possibility of a routing update taking a long time to reach convergence, during which the routing domain is unstable and not passing traffic efficiently and perhaps incorrectly.

To see why, we assume in Figure 5–6 that there is a failure on network 1 between host 1 (H1) and router 1 (R1). In prior advertisements, R1 informed R2 and R3 that it was the next node to get to H1. Therefore, when R1 advertises infinity (16) metric to these routers, they should be able to know that they cannot reach H1. However, if either R2 or R3 send an update to R1 *before* they receive the bad news from this router, R1 will see that the advertised metric is 2 to H1, better than R1's new metric of 16. Let's concentrate on the operations between R1 and R2.

The way RIP is constructed, R1 does not know it is the only way to H1. Instead it updates its routing table, placing a metric of 3 into its

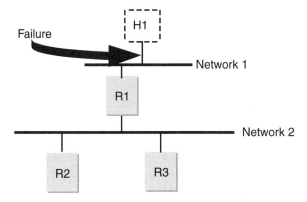

**Figure 5–6   Counting to Infinity**

table, and then, upon the next advertisement, sends a metric of 3 (to H1) to its neighbors. R1 now has its routing table "pointing" to R2 as the next node to H1.

The problem is that R1 and R2 now point to each other as the next node to H1. Therefore, when R2 receives the message from R1 with a metric of 4 to H1, it must change its table to 5. Its next advertisement to R1 is a metric of 5 to H1. Since H1's table shows R2 as the next node to H1, it changes its table to 5, and its next advertisement to R2 is a 6.

The result is a loop, and the problem will continue until the metric reaches 16, at which time, the routers will reassess the situation and converge.

During the count to infinity operation, the advertisements are looping around between the routers. As just mentioned, the looping continues until the maximum metric value of 16 is reached. At that time, H1 is indeed not reachable. The process is quite inefficient. It leads to link congestion and the possibility of losing traffic, including RIP messages.

## COUNTERACTING MEASURES

Most RIP implementations have implemented measures to counteract the count to infinity problem. One change simply eliminates the 30-second timer, and when a router has a routing update to send, it sends it immediately. Of course, this immediate update does not solve the problem, but it does speed up the time to reach convergence.

## Split Horizon

Another method is called *split horizon*. The idea behind this operation is based on the commonsense notion that it makes no sense for a router to advertise addresses though the interface from which it received the initial advertisement. In Figure 5–7, R1 would not receive advertisements from R2 or R3 about H1. That is, R2 and R3 cannot advertise H1 on their interfaces, labeled 1 in the figure. The example in Figure 5–7 shows that R2 knows not to perform the advertisement on its interface 1. This approach is effective in most situations, but it will not eliminate all problems. For example, if the physical network is a looped topology, the count-to-infinity problem still exists.

## Split Horizon with Poison Reverse

A variation to split horizon is *split horizon with poison reverse,* illustrated in Figure 5–8. Instead of R2 and R3 not sending the H1 advertisements on their interface 1, they send the metric of 16. Of course, R1 ignores this information. If only two routers are involved, split horizon with poison reverse eliminates loops.

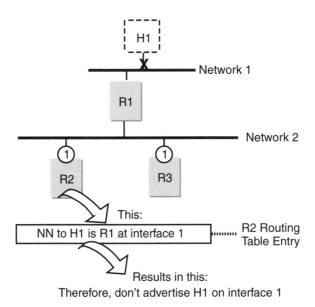

**Figure 5–7   Steps to Improve Convergence**

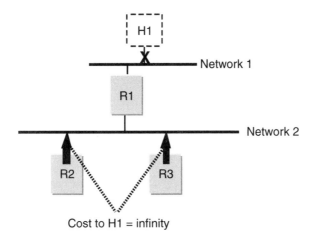

Figure 5–8   Split Horizon with Poison Reverse

## Holddown

Another distance-vector protocol enhancement is called holddown. When a route is advertised as unreachable, the advertising router refuses to accept updates for a period of time after the route has been advertised. For example, after R1 sends the message to R2 and R3 with the infinity metric for H1, it will not accept advertisements for H1 from R2 or R3.

Holddown effectively constrains forwarding loops. It is not a cure-all and does increase the time to converge. RIP does not use holddown but other distance-vector protocols do, such as Cisco's Inter-Gateway Routing Protocol (IGRP). With IGRP, when the router learns that a network is down or that a network is at a greater distance than was previously known, the route to that network is placed in holddown. During this time, the route can be advertised, but incoming advertisements about the route from any router other than the one that originally advertised the new metric is ignored.

## Disabling Split Horizon

It may not be desirable to use split horizon on serial links (non-broadcast links), such as X.25, Frame Relay, and ATM. Routers can be configured to disable split horizon if necessary.

## TIMER ADJUSTMENTS

Most high-end routers can be configured to vary the frequency of RIP routing updates and other parameters. Also, Cisco runs a set of timers for its overall on demand routing (ODR) operations for RIP. These RIP configuration parameters are available to the network manager:

- Time interval between updates (*update*): Default value for update is 30 seconds.
- Interval of time after which the route is declared invalid (*invalid*): This interval should be three times the value of *update*. This means a route becomes invalid if the route is not refreshed with the updates. This inaccessible route then enters *holddown*. It can still be used for packet forwarding. The default value for *invalid* is 180 seconds.
- Time interval during which information on better paths is suppressed (*holddown*): This value should be three times the value of *update*. When holddown expires, routes advertised by other sources are accepted, and the route is no longer inaccessible. The default value for *holddown* is 180 seconds.
- Amount of time a routing entry must remain in the routing table before it is removed from the routing table (*flush*): The interval must as least be the sum of *invalid* and *holddown*. The default value for *flush* is 240 seconds.
- Amount of time to postpone routing updates (*sleeptime*): If a router permits an immediate update (a flash update), this parameter may be configured. It should be less than *update* time. This parameter is used for Cisco's ODR operations and is not available for RIP.

### Filtering Routing Information

In order to establish control over how routing information is propagated through the router to and from the interfaces, it may be desirable to contain (filter) the routing packet flow. The router can be set up to provide the following RIP filters:

- Preventing routing updates through an interface: This operation prevents other routers on a LAN from learning about routes dynamically.

- Controlling the advertising of routes in routing updates: This operation allows the network manager to suppress routes from being advertised in the RIP updates.
- Controlling the processing of routing updates: Assuming the routes are advertised, this operation will not allow the "discovered" route to be processed.
- Filtering sources of routing information: It may happen that a more trustworthy route is found through another routing protocol. That is, some routing protocols produce more accurate information than others. It is possible to set up a router to prioritize routing information from different sources. This feature allows the network manager to select a value (an administrative distance) for an interface, thus directing the router to pick the route from the routing protocol that has the lowest administrative distance.

## CONFIGURING A RIP ROUTING DOMAIN

To configure a RIP routing domain, the routers must be configured to perform the tasks summarized in Table 5–1. This section provides an overview of each of these tasks. The specific rules for each of these tasks are documented in the router's user manuals.

**Table 5–1    RIP Configuration Tasks**

---

Enabling RIP

Allowing unicast updates for RIP

Applying offsets to routing metrics

Adjusting timers

Specifying a RIP version

Enabling RIP authentication

Disabling route summarization

Running IGRP and RIP concurrently

Disabling the validation of source IP addresses

Enabling or disabling split horizon

Configuring interpacket delay

Filtering RIP information

Key management

Variable length subnet masks (VLSM)

---

Some of these tasks are straightforward; others need more explanation. Some are somewhat tertiary to the operation of the routing domain,
and others are of primary importance. For each task explained, if I have
already discussed the operations pertaining to the task in the chapter, I
refer you to that discussion with an identification of the section header
title.

- Enabling RIP: The only task that is required to be configured. The
  result is that the router will execute RIP operations.
- Allowing unicast updates for RIP: RIP will operate as a broadcast
  protocol, unless this task is configured. With this task, the network manager can control which interfaces exchange routing information.
- Applying offsets to routing metrics: While RIP is a hop-count protocol, this task can be used to increase metrics to routes learned by
  RIP. It allows the network manager to override the RIP discoveries.
- Adjusting timers: I explained the timers and their adjustments
  earlier in this chapter in the section titled Timer Adjustments.
- Specifying a RIP version: I explained how RIP versions 1 and 2
  can be used in conjunction with each other earlier in this chapter
  in the section titled How the Two Versions Can Be Used.
- Enabling RIP authentication: RIP version 2 supports authentication. Two modes of authentication can be established: plain text
  authentication, and MD5 authentication. In order to use MD5, the
  keys must be set up and identified, and a lifetime must be stipulated for a set of keys on a "chain." Each key must be identified
  with a key ID (with this key stored locally). The key ID (and the
  interface associated with the key) uniquely identifies the specific
  authentication algorithm and the MD5 key in use.
- Disabling route summarization: Route summarization (address
  aggregation) is performed automatically by RIP version 2: Subnet
  prefixes are summarized when crossing "classful" network boundaries. If the routing domain has noncontiguous subnets, route
  summarization can be disabled.
- Running IGRP and RIP concurrently: If this task is enabled, the
  IGRP routing information overrides the RIP information, due to
  the use of IGRP's administrative distance. A minor word of caution

about running IGRP and RIP concurrently: These protocols use different update timers, which can result in one part of the routing domain believing IGRP, and another believing RIP. Convergence will occur, but this situation may affect time-sensitive applications that are attempting to set up a connection.

- Disabling the validation of source IP addresses: For security purposes, an IP source address for a RIP update message is validated against the original configuration (which address is allowed to advertise RIP on this interface). This task relaxes the "filter" on this interface, for example if you want to "talk" to an "off network" router. In effect, this task is a trapdoor into your domain, and should be implemented with care.

- Enabling or disabling split horizon: I discussed this feature earlier in this chapter, in the section titled Disabling Split Horizon.

- Configuring interpacket delay: A large RIP update (a large routing table) may require sending multiple RIP packets for this update. This task allows you to "ease" the traffic load on the receiving router by setting up an interpacket delay, that is, the emission rate of the packets to the neighbor router.

- Filtering RIP information: These operations were discussed earlier in this chapter in the section titled Filter Routing Information.

- Key management: This task was discussed earlier in this list.

- Variable length subnet masks (VLSMs): VSLMs are explained in Appendix B. VLSMs are good tools for using IP addresses effectively, but they must be implemented carefully. I refer you to RFC 1219 (and Appendix B) for VLSM guidelines.

## SUMMARY

The Routing Information Protocol (RIP) is a vector-distance routing protocol. Its routing decisions are based on the number of intermediate hops to the final destination. Its simplicity and ease of use has made it a widely used protocol. RIP was not intended to be deployed in large internets; it was not designed for internets that are physically looped. Its original version created a number of problems, principally relating to long convergence times. These problems have been corrected in the recent versions.

## FOLLOW-UP READING

RIP is well-documented in many texts, and most texts have a chapter devoted to this protocol. The texts: (a) *Routing in Communications Networks,* by Martha Steenstrup (Prentice Hall, 1995), (b) *Routing in Today's Internetworks,* by Mark Dickie (Van Nostrand, 1994), (c) *Advanced IP Routing in Cisco Networks,* by Terry Slattery and Bill Burton, McGraw-Hill, 1999, all provide good descriptions of RIP.

For the reader who wishes to delve into detail about RIP and how to configure RIP, you should consult your vendor's user manuals. If you do not have access to these manuals, I recommend a book from the Cisco IOS Reference Library titled: *Cisco IOS Solutions for Network Protocols, Volume I: IP,* by Cisco Press (available from Cisco or Macmillian Technical Publishing.)

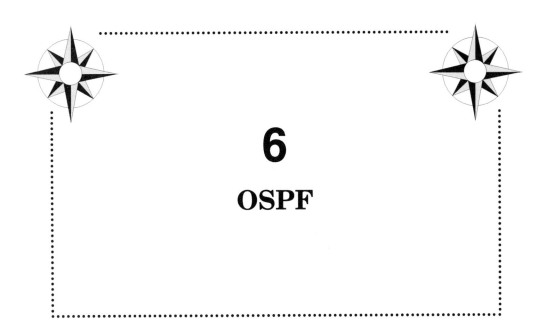

# 6
# OSPF

## INTRODUCTION

The chapter explains the operations of the widely used link state metric protocol, Open Shortest Path First (OSPF). We start with a look at the major attributes of OSPF, and follow with a discussion of the goals of the OSPF designers. The major OSPF operations are then analyzed, with examples of OSPF's advertisements, hellos, and packet containment procedures. OSPF LSA packets are examined, and we see how OSPF uses spanning tree operations to create a loop-free routing domain. The chapter concludes with a description of the tasks used by the network manager to configure OSPF operations within an autonomous system.

## ATTRIBUTES OF OSPF

OSPF protocol is an IGP. The OSPF routers are within one autonomous system. OSPF is a link state, or shortest path first protocol, in contrast to some of the earlier Internet protocols which are based on some type of Bellman-Ford approach. The protocol is tailored specifically for an internet and includes such capabilities as subnet addressing and type of service (TOS) routing.[1]

OSPF bases its route discovery decisions on addresses and link state metrics. OSPF is an adaptive protocol in that it adjusts to problems in the network (a link or node failure) and provides short convergence periods to stabilize the routing tables. It is also designed to prevent looping of traffic, which is quite important in mesh networks or in LANs where multiple routers may be available to connect different LANs.

OSPF is encapsulated into the IP datagram data field. The IP protocol ID for OSPF is 89.

## ROLE OF THE ROUTER IN OSPF

OSPF permits a router to assume several different roles in an OSPF routing domain. It can act as a designated router for an autonomous system, a designated router for an area within an autonomous system, and a designated router for a network to which multiple routers are attached. Within these routing domains, the router may send and receive several different types of LSAs. Some LSAs are for handshakes between the routers, such as a hello packet; others contain information about a node's database; still others are update packets. The approach taken in this chapter is to focus on the key routing update packets.

## DESIGN INTENT OF OSPF

The Internet working group that developed OSPF has studied many routing alternatives to get OSPF published as an operable specification. The process has taken several years, and John T. Moy who chairs the OSPF and MOSPF (multicast extensions of OSPF) Working Groups, provides an interesting and informative history of the development of OSPF [MOY98].[2] Like any complicated protocol, OSPF has gone though revi-

---

[1]TOS routing is not deployed extensively in the Internet, although it was intended in the original specifications that it be an important aspect of OSPF. Check your installation for possible TOS support.

[2]I prepared this chapter based on several RFCs (quoted at the appropriate time), my experience with Cisco router configurations, and Mr. Moy's text. I cite several sections of the Moy text in this chapter, and I recommend it to you as a followup to this general discussion.

sions in the basic design philosophy behind it. Figure 6–1 is used for this discussion.

Because of its importance in the operations of communications networks, it was (and is) subject to security mechanisms. Security is applied to OSPF messages through MD5.

In anticipation of user applications that are delay or throughput sensitive, OSPF defines a best path with metrics. The metrics can be distance, delay, security, etc. OSPF places no limit on the total path cost,

• Support security measures:

• Flexible routing metrics:

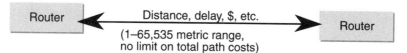

• Scalability:

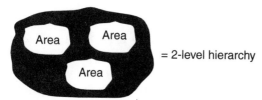

• Multiple Paths:

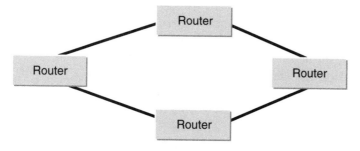

**Figure 6–1    OSPF Initial Goals**

and the metric value itself can range from 1 to 65,535. In practice, commercial implementations of OSPF calculate the metric based on the bandwidth of the link on a router interface.

One of the principal concerns of any new routing protocol is its "scalability"; that is, its ability to accommodate a large number of networks and hosts, and support the route advertising between them in an efficient manner. The approach taken by OSPF is to use a two-level hierarchy; that is, a two-level routing domain.

There exists the vexing problem of multiple paths to a destination. Older protocols did not deal with this situation very well. But the OSPF designers, recognizing the seriousness of the problem, provided solutions in the OSPF operations. OSPF provides tools to the administrator for choosing among multiple paths, and for load balancing among these paths.

Things have changed since the original publication of OSPF. I worked (as a user of the protocol) with the initial version, and I was pleased to see many improvements over protocols such as RIP. Also, I am happy to report that the revised version described in this text has improved over the first version. But the changes have improved what was a sound approach to begin with.

## DIRECTED GRAPHS

OSPF works with directed graphs, as shown in Figure 6–2(a). The graphs contain values between two points, the interfaces between two routers (their link interfaces). The values represent the weighted shortest path value with the router established as the root. Consequently, the shortest path tree from the router to any point in an internet is determined by the router performing the calculation. The calculation only reveals the next hop to the destination in the hop-to-hop forwarding process. The link state database used in the calculation is derived from the information obtained by advertisements sent by the routers to their neighbors, with periodic flooding throughout the routing domain.

The information focuses on the topology of the network(s) with a directed graph. Routers and networks form the vertices of the graph. Periodically, this information can be broadcast (flooded) to all routers in the autonomous system or area, or sent as needed, based on a change. An OSPF router computes the shortest path to the other routers in the routing domain based on the link state database. If the calculations reveal

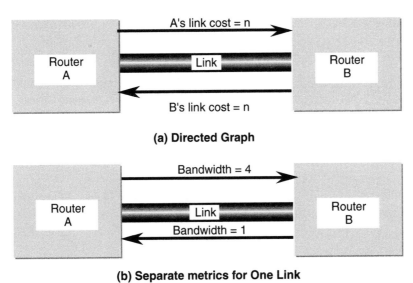

**(a) Directed Graph**

**(b) Separate metrics for One Link**

**Figure 6–2    Directed Graphs**

that two paths are of equal value, OSPF will distribute the traffic equally on these paths.

Conceptually, separate cost metrics can be computed for both directions on a link, as shown in Figure 6–2(b). However, most implementations simply use the same value for each direction on the link.

## ROUTING DECISIONS

Originally, OSPF based its routing decisions on two fields in the IP datagram: the destination IP address and the type of service (TOS). The type of service field contains several values. The values in the field that can be used by OSPF for routing are the delay, throughput, reliability, and cost fields. While the Internet Protocol and OSPF provide rules on how these fields are coded, as well as general definitions on their meaning, neither protocol dictates how the values are translated into network operations.

Thus, a network administrator was free to choose the method by which these values are employed. As OSPF found its way into commercial networks, the TOS value was not used much, and due to this very modest employment, it has fallen into disuse. Therefore, other means are now implemented to assign metrics to links and networks. We shall explore them shortly.

## OPERATING OSPF OVER DIFFERENT TYPES OF NETWORKS (MEDIA)

OSPF operates over broadcast or nonbroadcast networks. Examples of broadcast networks are Ethernet, token ring, and FDDI. Examples of nonbroadcast networks are X.25, Frame Relay, and ATM).[3] OSPF also operates over point-to-point links, in which there is no intervening network. Examples of point-to-point links are those that operate with PPP, and other variations of HDLC.

### How OSPF Supports "On-demand" Links

Dial-up lines, ISDN connections on demand, and the switched virtual call operations of X.25, Frame Relay, and ATM create an on-demand environment for OSPF. RFC 1793 was written to handle these requirements. The main idea is that OSPF will suppress some of its hello and advertising packet traffic between routers that are connected on the demand link. This approach allows the demand link to be inactive (that is, the layer 2 data link layer is not operating) but still keep its relationship with OSPF.

When the link becomes active, for example when a user makes a call on the link, OSPF will resort to its normal behavior and send its hellos and link state advertisements onto the link.

## BASIC OPERATIONS OF OSPF

OSPF's operations vary, depending upon the type of network in which it operates. Its behavior is slightly different if it is on a point-to-point network, a broadcast network, and multicast network and so on.

---

[3]The nonbroadcast networks may actually permit broadcasting and multicasting, even though they are not a shared bus, through broadcasting (or multicasting) addresses and supporting routing tables. If a "nonbroadcast" network is configured to use multicasting or broadcasting, high-end routers can be configured for OSPF to support these operations.

For this discussion (see Figure 6–3), we will examine the overall operations of OSPF that pertain to all network types.

OSPF implements a hello protocol. It is a handshaking protocol that enables the routers to learn about each other, exchange information, and later perform pings with neighbor routers to make certain the link and/or router is up.

After the hello operations have been completed, the peer routers are considered to be *merely adjacent*. This term means the routers have completed part of the synchronization, but not all of it.

Next, the routers exchange information which describes their knowledge of the routing domain. This information is called a database description and is placed in link state advertisement (LSA) messages. The database descriptions are not the entire link state database, but they contain sufficient information for the receiving router to know if its link state database is consistent with its peer's databases. If all is consistent, the neighbor is now defined as *fully adjacent*. The routers then exchange LSAs containing link state updates, eventually becoming fully adjacent.

Thereafter, periodic hellos are issued to keep peers aware of each other. Also, the LSAs that the router originated must be sent to its peers

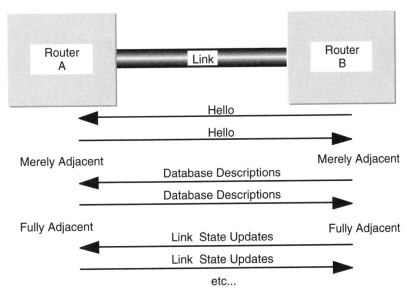

**Figure 6–3    Basic Operations of OSPF**

every thirty minutes, just to make certain all link state databases are the same.

OSPF is concerned with link state database synchronization, and much of the OSPF code is devoted to this very task.

## FLOODING ADVERTISEMENTS

Advertising is performed within the routing domain by flooding (called reliable flooding in OSPF) the LSAs to all routers. In Figure 6–4(a), router 3 has decided to send LSAs to its neighbor routers (routers 1, 2, 5, and 6). The arrows in the figure symbolize the LSA transmissions. This example is for routers connected to each other with point-to-point (nonbroadcast) links.

Remember that the cause of these updates is that router 3 wished to inform its neighbors about a change at router 3, or to refresh the LSA information. The updates are performed with LSA packets.

When these neighbors receive the LSA, they check for errors, check the LSA packet type, and make certain the LSA is a more recent than the copy in the LS database. Assuming the received LSA is new, the routers update their databases, and (a) send this LSA (bundle it up, slightly modified) out all their interfaces, except the interface from which the LSA was received. This operation is shown in Figure 6–4(b). Eventually, all routers in the routing domain receive the LSA. These routers are required to send back to the originating neighbor an acknowledgment (ACK) of the transmitted LSA—more on these ACKs shortly.

Depending on the timing in the system, some nodes might receive the LSA more than once. In Figure 6–4(b), routers 1, 2, 5, and 6 receive copies of the packet. Several fields in the LSA header will reveal that the LSA is a duplicate, and therefore not relevant.

Another point should be made here. A receiving router will not forward a single LSA to its other interfaces more than once. For example, router 2 has received the LSA from router 3 [Figure 6–4(a)], and router 1 [Figure 6–4(b)]. Router 2 knows the LSA from router 1 is a duplicate and will not process the LSA further. The two copies of the LSA router 2 sends in Figure 6–4(b) are a result of receiving that LSA in the initial advertisement shown in Figure 6–4(a).

At first glance, it might seem that flooding would create a substantial amount of overhead traffic in the routing domain. Granted, flooding can result in a node receiving more than one copy of a packet, but OSPF

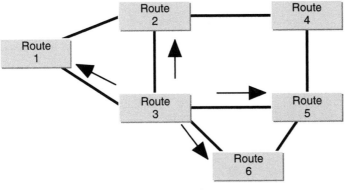

**(a) Initial advertisement**

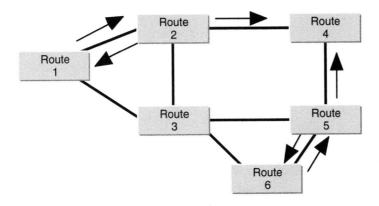

**(b) Next advertisement**

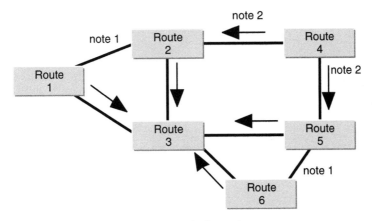

**(c) Acknowledgments**

Note 1: ACKs not required if multiple LSAs were previously sent
Note 2: Multiple copies of same LSA are not sent, but ACKs are sent

**Figure 6–4    Flooding Advertisements**

establishes several rules to mitigate against excessive copies of OSPF packets propagating into the routing domain.

We will use Figures 6–4(b) and 6–4(c) in this discussion. As before, the arrows in Figure 6–4(b) symbolize the sending of LSAs. The arrows in Figure 6–4(c) symbolize the sending of ACKs.

We just explained that a receiving router will not forward a single LSA to its other interfaces more than once. In addition, when an LSA update passes at the same time between two routers [as in Figure 6–4(b)], between routers 1 to 2 and routers 5 to 6, the routers record this event and do not send ACKs to each other, as depicted in note 1 in Figure 6–4 (c). This concept is called an implicit acknowledgment.

Note 2 of Figure 6–4(c) is used to make another point. Router 4 has received two copies of the LSA from routers 2 and 5 [shown in Figure 6–4(b)]. Figure 6–4(c) shows that router 4 is obligated to acknowledge these LSAs to both of its neighbors, but it will not send more than one copy to its other interfaces. In this example, the router has no other interfaces.

Later, we examine in more detail other rules implemented in OSPF to reduce traffic. Briefly, they are: First, an LSA can only be updated (at most) every 5 seconds. Second, a router is not allowed to accept an LSA if the copy in the database is less than 1 second old. So, if a router is configured erroneously, if its interfaces are coming up and going down in rapid succession, or otherwise experiencing problems, its neighbors will not process the spate of traffic, nor will they send the LSAs to other routers.

## OSPF AREAS

Enterprises with large systems may operate with many networks, routers, and host computers. In order to manage this vast array of communications components, it is quite possible that many LSAs must be exchanged between the routers in order to determine how to relay traffic within the autonomous system between the sending computer and the receiving computer.

The network administrator must evaluate how much routing traffic is to be sent between the routers, because this routing traffic can affect the throughput of user data. And we know that a common practice in route advertising and route discovery is to flood the advertisements to all nodes in the routing domain. While measures can be taken to reduce the amount of duplicate traffic that a node receives, it is not unusual for networks to have their routing nodes connected in such a fashion to create loops, which means that it is possible for an advertisement to be received more than one time. OSPF does a good job of packet containment and managing loops.

One approach that is used by OSPF is to divide or partition the autonomous system into smaller parts, called *areas*. This approach reduces the amount of routing traffic that is sent through the autonomous system, because the areas are isolated from each other. This practice reduces the amount of information a router must maintain about the full autonomous system. Also, it means that the overhead information transmitted between routers to maintain OSPF routing tables is substantially reduced.

A designated router, say router 3 in Figure 6–5, assumes the responsibility for informing the routers in the area about the other routers, networks and hosts residing in the autonomous system.

### Packet Containment

As a consequence of this approach, the routers within the area are not concerned about the details of the full autonomous system (the other areas). They obtain their information from a designated router, in this example, it is router 3.

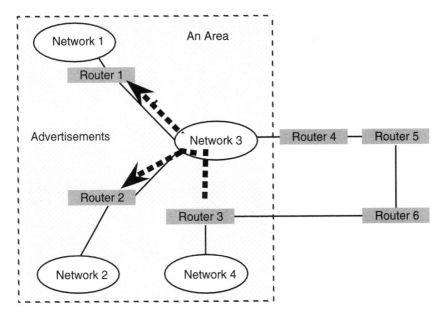

**Figure 6–5    Route Advertising Within the Area**

Assuming network 3 is a broadcast network, such as an Ethernet, OSPF uses multicasting to restrict LSA packet processing at nodes that do not need to examine certain routing packets. Assuming network 3 is a nonbroadcast network (a switched network, like Frame Relay), OSPF uses a packet "filtering" procedure to reduce the number of routing packets that are exchanged between the routers in the area. Multicasting and packet filtering are discussed later in this chapter.

### Stub Areas

In this example, networks 1, 2, and 4 are stub networks. OSPF also supports the concept of *stub areas*. The stub area is one into which routing information on external routes is not sent. Instead, the area border router generates a default route for destinations outside the area, and the routers in this stub area use this route. After all, why have all this routing information going about, when the stub area really does not act upon it anyway?

In addition, the network manager can set up the area border router to prevent it from sending summary link advertisements into the stub area. These summary link advertisements are designated as type 3 LSAs.

### Controlling and Protecting the Area

The network manager can control the area IP-addressing domain and advertisements by configuring the router with a range of addresses that are to be associated with an area. These parameters are set up for each router interface on which OSPF will operate. With this approach, one of the main goals of using areas is obtained: route summarization, address aggregation, and packet containment.

As stated in the introduction to this chapter, an area can be "protected" from unauthorized access by a rogue router (or other device) by implementing authentication procedures, typically MD5 authentication.

## VIRTUAL LINKS AND BACKBONES

OSPF requires that all areas be connected together by a backbone area (designated as area 0). Usually, a backbone is considered as a set of contiguous nodes and their interconnecting links that allow the tertiary networks (or areas) to communicate through the backbone with each other. The idea of a backbone forces a simple hub topology wherein the

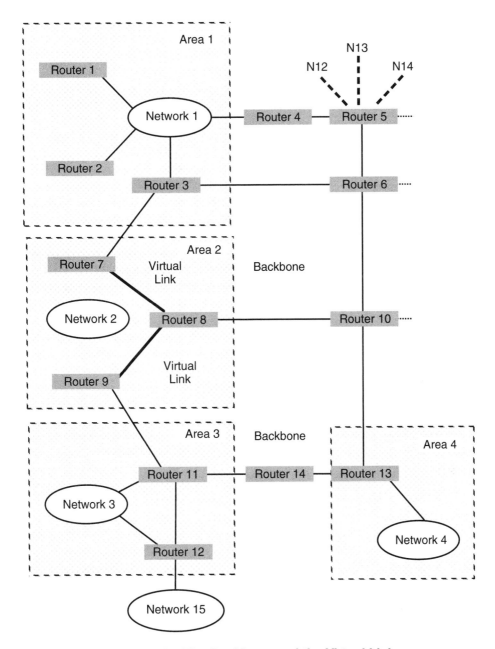

**Figure 6–6    The Backbone and the Virtual Link**

area's routing information goes through the backbone to get to another area. Conventional distance vector protocols can operate with this arrangement.

However, this arrangement might be too restrictive, since it implies that the areas attached to the backbone must be stub areas. Therefore, OSPF supports the use of *virtual links* in which routing packets can be sent through one area to another area, and not have to traverse over the backbone. The virtual links run between routers and allow summary LSA packets to be tunneled through the areas, and the arrangement maintains the simple hub and spoke topology. Figure 6–6 shows an example of the backbone and virtual link arrangement. The virtual links allow the distribution of routing information through area 2 to areas 1 and 3, an idea called tunneling.

Another attractive aspect of virtual links is that while routing information is sent in the tunnel, user traffic can still take a "better" physical path, if one exists. Moreover, the virtual links can be used to maintain connectivity between areas if the backbone fails.

The end result of this approach it that the backbone can be partitioned. It is logically connected with virtual links. As seen in Figure 6–6, router 14 is part of the backbone, but the backbone need not be physically intact.

## EXTERNAL LINKS

The networks connected outside OSPF autonomous systems are not members of this autonomous system. AS OSPF routers discover these networks through an external gateway protocol (such as BGP), and then advertise these networks within the autonomous system with external LSAs. External links are shown in Figure 6–6, with the notations N12, N13, and N14, which symbolize networks 12, 13, and 14.

## NOT SO STUBBY AREAS (NSSAs)

OSPF also supports the idea of not so stubby areas (NSSA), also shown in Figure 6–6. Areas are restricted in that they cannot receive AS external LSAs. Also, it might be desirable to allow a stubby area to pass advertising through its area, but not have to receive external LSAs from its default router. For example, in Figure 6–6, network 15 is attached to router 12, and router 12 is allowed to advertise about network 15, but need not be burdened with external advertising traffic, because router 11 provides this service.

Prior to NSSA it was not possible to run a remote site, such as network 15, to an OSPF border router, because routes from remote sites cannot be redistributed into a stub area. So, protocols like RIP handled the redistribution. NSSA permits the extension of RIP to support the remote network connection by defining the area between the OSPF "core" and the remote network as an NSSA.

## DESIGNATED ROUTER FOR A NETWORK

The value of partitioning an autonomous system into smaller and more manageable areas is especially important for an enterprise that is faced with the interconnection of a large set of networks, routers, and hosts. To illustrate, consider networks 1 and 3 and router 1 in Figure 6–7. Router 1 connects the two networks, network 1 and network 3, an Ethernet and token ring respectively.

OSPF requires that one router be assigned the *designated router* for a network. In this manner, the hosts do not have to be concerned with route advertising. In this example, router 1 assumes the responsibility for this task for network 1 and network 3. Of course, the role of the designated router for network 1 is straightforward, since router 1 is the only router connected to this network.

The assignment of a designated router is accomplished by the use of hello packets. In a subnet with multiple routers, a common practice is to configure each router with a "priority for designated router" parameter. This parameter helps in determining the designated router for the subnet. If the designated router fails, a designated backup router takes over.

As shown in Figure 6–8, R1 is the designated router and R3 is the designated backup router for a subnet, now drawn as an Ethernet and renumbered with the IP prefix of 10.1.1.0/24. The example in Figure 6–8(a) also illustrates a different network type: a broadcast network. Thus far, most of the examples have been point-to-point network types.

A process is invoked to elect a new designated backup router (R3) among the other routers. As stated earlier, each router on a subnet is assigned a router priority value, and this value is used to determine the order of selection for the designated backup router. Before proceeding further with the discussion of how OSPF operates over broadcast networks, we need to do some preliminary work.

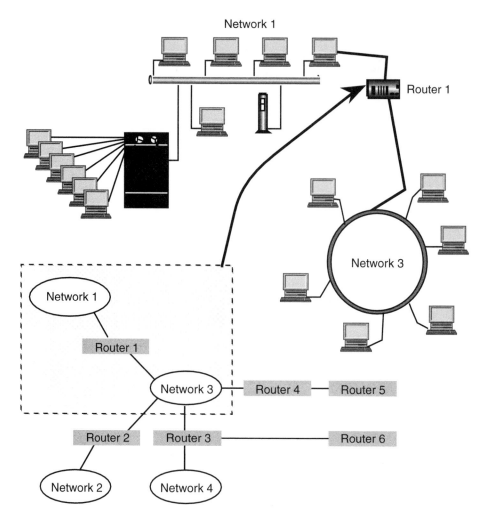

**Figure 6–7    Designated Routers**

Broadcast networks, such as Ethernet, allow the nodes on the network to receive all traffic, with the MAC address coded as all 1s. Ethernet also supports multicast, which allows the Ethernet frame to be received by a selected set of nodes on the subnet. Figure 6–8(b) shows the format for the MAC address. The low-order bit of the most significant byte is set to 1; hence, the hex format is 0x01xxxxxxxxxx. The x is a hex value.

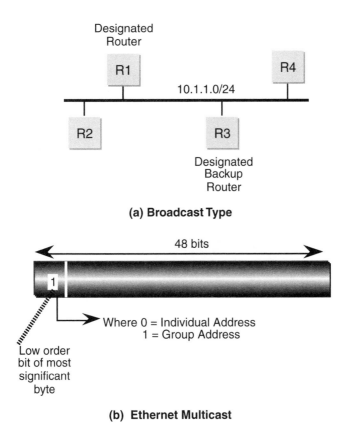

Figure 6–8   Designated Routers and Addresses

## Designated Routers and Addresses

A node can be configured to accept and process multicast addresses. This concept is important in Ethernet support of OSPF, because OSPF also uses a multicast address for some of its operations. On the Ethernet in this example, each router joins an IP multicast group. IP multicast address 224.0.0.5 has been reserved for OSPF to identify all OSPF routers on the subnet (AllSPFRouters).

In order to take advantage of Ethernet's multicasting operation, the IP multicast address is mapped with the Ethernet address, as shown in Figure 6–9. The Ethernet address is set to a multicast block of 0x01005exxxxxx. The last 24 bits of the IP address is placed into the xxxxxx of the Ethernet address, yielding the Ethernet MAC address of 0x01005e000005.

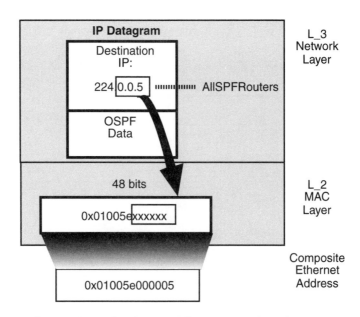

**Figure 6–9    Designated Routers and Addresses**

The ability to use L_2 and L_3 multicasting on the Ethernet allows the non-OSPF nodes to ignore the OSPF traffic. By multicasting OSPF hello packets on the subnet all OSPF routers can discover each other without the intervention of the network administrator (after the nodes have been configured with a few crafting commands).

### Neighbor Pairs

In point-to-point router topologies, a router only maintains a peer relationship with the routers connected to it on the links. Indeed, a router may only have one peer relationship. With a broadcast network (Ethernet, FDDI, token ring, etc.) a router might have a peer relationship with all routers on the network, resulting in increased overhead in hellos, LSAs, and other operations. With $n$ OSPF routers, the are $n \times (n - 1)/2$ potential peer pairs, which can translate into substantial overhead. In this example, Figure 6–10(a) shows six routers placed on a subnet. The potential peer relationships are $(6 \times (5 - 1)/2 = 15$, as depicted in Figure 6–10(b). The commonsense approach is to reduce the number of peer relationships, shown in Figure 6–11.

OSPF's use of the designated router means the other routers do not have to communicate with each other as far as exchanging hellos, down

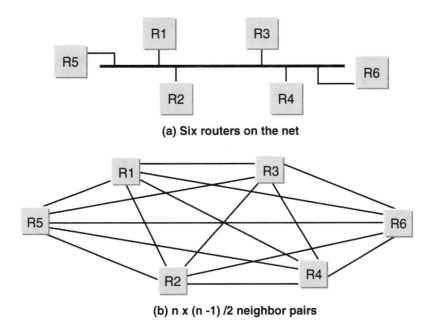

(a) Six routers on the net

(b) n x (n -1) /2 neighbor pairs

Figure 6–10    Router Neighbor Pairs

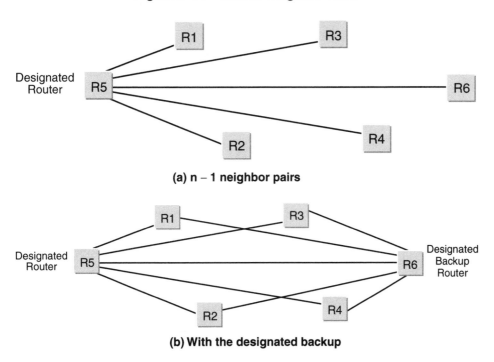

(a) n – 1 neighbor pairs

(b) With the designated backup

Figure 6–11    Router Neighbor Pairs

loading link state databases, and update LSAs. In Figure 6–11(a), the peering relationship is reduced to n –1 (or 5). R1, R2, R3, R4, and R6 keep their information updated and the databases synchronized with R5, the designated router.

This arrangement is much more efficient than a fully meshed setup, but it means the system is more vulnerable to failure. If problems occur at R5, they affect the other routers.

This is where the aforementioned designated router becomes important. As shown in Figure 6–11(b), R6 is the designated router, and all routers establish peer relationships with both R5 and R6. These other routers must synchronize their link state databases with the designated router and the backup designated router.

### Flooding Advertisements on the LAN

OSPF uses another IP multicast address to identify designated routers, including the backup router. It is AllDRouters with a value of 224.0.0.6. In Figure 6–11, R2 sends an update LSA onto the network. It has installed this LSA in its link state database, and wishes to synchronize this change with the other OSPF routers.

In event 1 in Figure 6–12, the LSA advertisement is multicasted to R5 and R6 with the AllDRouters address. The other routers ignore this message. R5 and R6 receive the information and update their databases.

In event 2, R5 floods this LSA to all the routers by placing the All-SPFRouters (224.0.0.5) in the destination address. These routers use the LSA to update their databases.

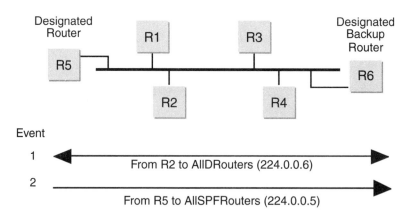

**Figure 6–12   Flooding an Advertisement**

R6 does not flood the LSA again. After all, R5 has already sent it. But R6 is acting as a watchdog over the process, and if R5 does not send the LSA within a configured interval (a few seconds), R5 will flood this LSA onto the subnet. In this manner, the chances are good that all routers will receive the update.

## ESTABLISHING LINK COSTS AND PRUNING THE TREE

We know that each output link at each router has a value assigned to it that represents a metric (or possibly, but not likely, some combination of the TOS parameters). This value can be established by the network administrator. It is technically possible to establish link costs dynamically, based on queue lengths, delays encountered at the routers, and other performance criteria. However dynamic metrics are difficult to manage, and they are not used in connectionless networks like IP or Ethernet. Connection-oriented networks, such as ATM, can use dynamic metrics very effectively because bandwidth is set up for each connection, and OSPF can be used for ongoing advertisements. Once a connection is set up, it stays on a static route (unless a problem occurs). Another user might request an identical connection a short time later, and during this time, OSPF may have found a better route. So, the second customer might have a different path.

Remember that costs are also associated with the other networks that do not belong to this autonomous system. These costs are made available through an external gateway protocol. The lower the cost, the better. This means those interfaces that advertise a low cost are more likely to be used for the relaying of traffic. But it is the sum of all link costs between any two nodes that actually determine how the traffic is routed through the internet.

By an examination of Figure 6–13, notice that there are no values associated with the output side of a network or a host.[4] A designated router that is attached to the network assumes the responsibility of generating the link state advertisements for the network. Therefore, only routers can generate link state advertisements—networks and hosts cannot advertise.

---

[4]The examples (still relevant) in this section are sourced from the original OSPF RFC, now replaced by RFC 1583.

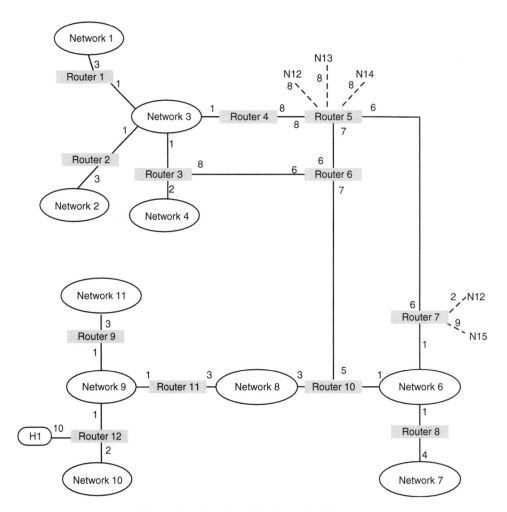

**Figure 6–13    Establishing Link Costs**

Each router contains a map of the topology of the autonomous system or area and the costs associated with all the links that make up the topology. See Figure 6–14. The router receives this information from the flooding of advertisements from the other routers. This map is the link state database discussed earlier. The database contains information about the link interfaces of the routers in the routing domain. The database is the same for all participating routers within an area. Indeed, any router can compute a route for any other router.

The autonomous system does not have to be divided into areas. If no areas exist, then the link state database is the same for all routers within

First:

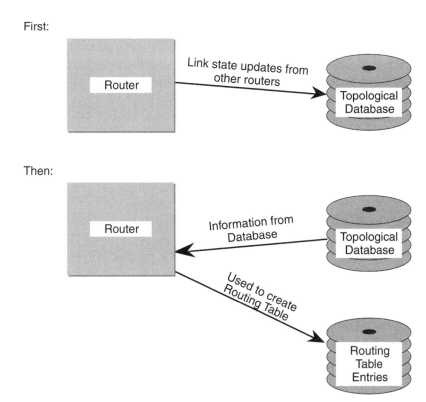

Then:

**Figure 6–14  The Link State Database and the Routing Table**

the autonomous system. [MOY98] and [MOY91][5] provide guidelines on how big areas should be. In 1991, it was about 200 routers. Today, some implementations have 350 routers, but some vendors recommend an area should not be this big, and they use a maximum number of 50.

Each router creates a routing table using the topological database. This routing table is created, based on spanning tree operations.

The routing table reflects the "pruned" tree of the network. For example, from the perspective of router 6, the network topology appears as shown in Figure 6–15.

The costs of the router links going toward router 6 are not relevant and are therefore not shown in the tree, nor reflected in the routing

---

[5][MOY91] Moy, J. *OSPF Protocol Analysis*. RFC 1245, July 1991.

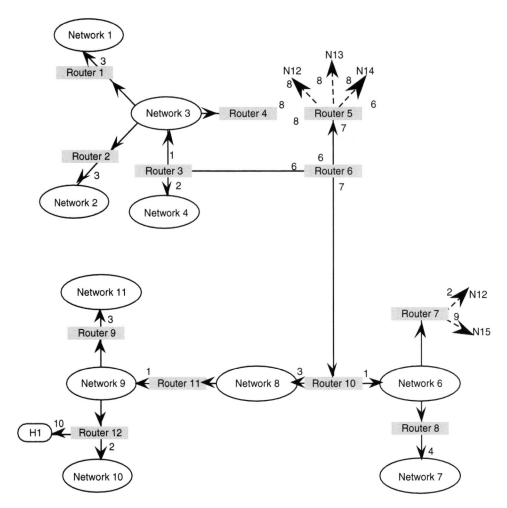

**Figure 6–15   The Pruned Tree as Viewed by Router 6**

table. Only the router links directed toward the destinations from router 6 are used by router 6 in its calculations. We learned that this concept is called a directed graph.

The routing table for router 6 lists each destination address, the next router that is to receive the traffic (the next node), and the total "distance" from router 6 to the destination. The term distance is the sum the link state costs of the output link of each router in the path to the destination.

Let's see how the table can be used to route traffic, using Table 6–1. We will assume that router 6 has received a datagram with a destination

Table 6–1    Some Entries in the Routing Table

| Destination | Next Hop | Distance |
| --- | --- | --- |
| N1 | Router 3 | 10 |
| N2 | Router 3 | 10 |
| N3 | Router 3 | 7 |
| N4 | Router 3 | 8 |
| N6 | Router 10 | 8 |
| **N7** | **Router 10** | **12** |
| N8 | Router 10 | 10 |
| N9 | Router 10 | 11 |
| N10 | Router 10 | 13 |
| N11 | Router 10 | 14 |
| N12 | Router 10 | 10 |
| N13 | Router 5 | 14 |
| N14 | Router 5 | 14 |
| N15 | Router 10 | 17 |
| Host 1 | Router 10 | 21 |
| Router 5 | Router 5 | 6 |
| Router 7 | Router 10 | 8 |

address for network 7. For our illustration, we will also assume that one spanning tree for router 6 has been calculated—the one presented in this example. The routing table reveals that the next node to receive the datagram is router 10, and that the total distance to network 7 is 12.

Looking at Figure 6–15 again, this route is chosen because the cost from router 6 to router 10 is 7 ... the cost from router 10 to router 8—going through network 6—is 1 ... and the cost from router 8 to network 7 is 4. So, 7 plus 1 plus 4 equal the total end-to-end distance from router 6 to network 7 of 12. Similar examinations of the other paths to the destinations from router 6 will sum to the total distance values in router 6's routing table.

## THE OSPF PACKETS

Figure 6–16 illustrates the 20-octet OSPF packet header. Each OSPF LSA packet is appended with this header. The fields in the header mean the following. I provide a general description here, and the many rules and details for this packet are available in the OSPF RFC.

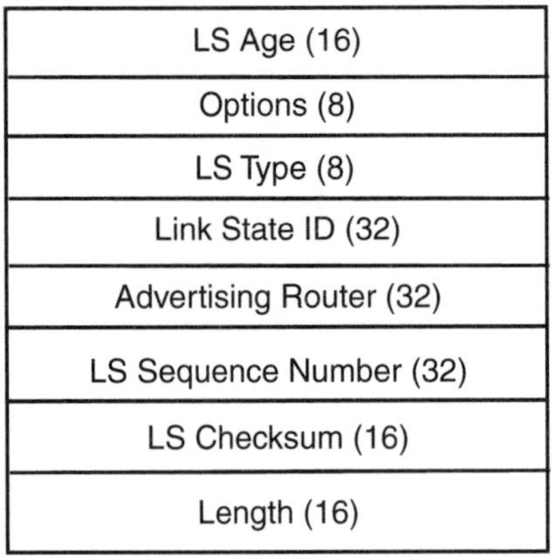

| LS Age (16) |
| :---: |
| Options (8) |
| LS Type (8) |
| Link State ID (32) |
| Advertising Router (32) |
| LS Sequence Number (32) |
| LS Checksum (16) |
| Length (16) |

Where (n) is the number of bits in each field

**Figure 6–16    The Link State Advertisement (LSA) Header**

The LS Age field shows the number of seconds from the origination of the LSA. Typically, it ranges from 0 to 30 minutes, and if the age exceeds 30 minutes, the originating router resends the LSA, and sets this field to 0 (as well as incrementing the LS Sequence Number).

The Options field is used to indicate that the LSA should be processed in a special manner. Several options have been defined.

The LS Type field identifies the type of LSA. Currently these LSA types have been defined. The rules for the use of these LSA are many and varied, and I have cited the use of some of these packets earlier in this chapter. I refer you to the RFC if you want to know more details about these LSAs. I will also comment about some of these LSAs as we proceed through the remainder of this chapter.

- Router LSA
- Network LSA
- Network-summary LSA
- Autonomous system boundary router ASBR-summary LSA
- AS-external LSA
- Group-membership LSA
- NSSA LSA
- External-attribute LSA

The Link State ID field is used to distinguish each LSA of the same LS Type that is originated by a specific router. In practice, it usually contains addressing information. For example, in a point-to-point connection, this field is the ID of the neighbor's router ID, which is usually an IP address.

The Advertising Router field contains the value of the originating router's Router ID.

The LS Sequence Number field is incremented by the LSA's originating router whenever this router wishes to update an LSA. Thus, a larger sequence number in an LSA indicates that it is more recent than an LSA with a smaller sequence number.

The Checksum is used at the receiver to check for a corrupted LSA header, and data. It is also stored in all routers' link-state databases in order to: (a) determine if two LSAs with the same sequence number are indeed identical (it also uses the age field for this check), (b) determine (periodically) if the router's hardware and software are corrupting the LSA entry in the database.

The Length field defines the length of the header and the LSA contents.

The contents of the OSPF packet fields that follow the header vary, depending on the LSA packet type, the role assigned to the router, whether the router is on a point-to-point link, or on a shared subnet, and so on. Figure 6–17 is an example of an ordinary router's LSA on a point-to-point link.

The 20-byte LSA header precedes the advertisement fields. These fields begin with the Router Type, and identify ordinary routers, border routers, etc.

The Number of Links field specifies how many links the originating router is reporting.

The Link ID value varies. For this example, which is a point-to-point connection, the field contains the neighbor router's Router ID.[6]

The Link Data field also varies, depending upon the type of advertisement. For this example, it contains the originating router's link interface number (ifIndex in the Internet and OSPF MIBs).

---

[6]This quirk of OSPF (for point-to-point links) can be confusing, but it is indeed a rule. It means the originating router advertises the neighbor's address instead of its own (yet the resultant routing table shows that the next node is actually the local router's address!). This situation has other confusing aspects. I refer you to an excellent explanation by [MOY98] John T. Moy, *OSPF: Anatomy of an Internet Routing Protocol,* Addison-Wesley, 1998.

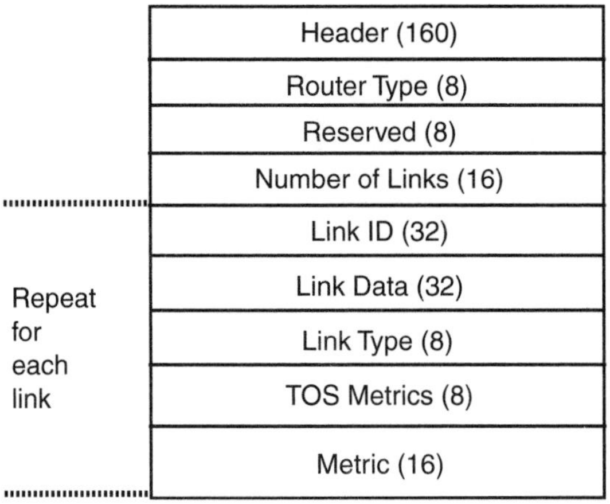

| Header (160) |
|:---:|
| Router Type (8) |
| Reserved (8) |
| Number of Links (16) |
| Link ID (32) |
| Link Data (32) |
| Link Type (8) |
| TOS Metrics (8) |
| Metric (16) |

Repeat
for
each
link

Where (n) is the number of bits in each field

**Figure 6–17    The Router Link State Advertisement (LSA)**

The Link Type field identifies the type of link, such as a point-to-point link, stub network, etc.

The TOS Metrics field is not used in the Internet, and is now omitted from the OSPF specifications. It is also omitted from the IPv6 RFCs. If you wish to use it in your private networks, check your router's rules for its implementation.

Figure 6–18 shows a link state advertisement sent by node 172.16.1.1 to five other routers in the OSPF routing domain. Two links connect this router to node 172.16.1.2 and node 172.16.1.3. The output interfaces to these nodes are ifIndex 1 and ifIndex 2 respectively. The ifIndex is the leaf entry object ID (OID) of the interfaces object group in the Internet and OSPF MIBs.

The example is created to show the major points of the LSA. I have not included the number of bits in each field and other details that are not needed for this discussion.

The header identifies the router type of 0 for a point-to-point router. The LSA advertises three links. The first two are the links to the two OSPF peers. The third link is not an actual link, but the identifier of this router's address, with the link type set to a stub. The metric for this "link" is 0.

The two links are configured with a metric of 5 for one link, and 6 for the other. The LSA fields reflect this configuration, and associate the metric with the ifIndex value, as well as the link ID.

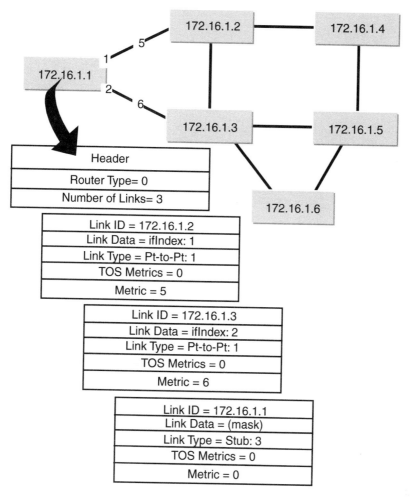

**Figure 6–18   Link State Advertisement Example**

The link ID for a point-to-point advertisement is the identifier of the peer node. In this example, it is 172.16.1.2 for one link, and 172.16.1.3 for the other link. [MOY98] has an interesting description of why the point-to-point configuration uses the peer's address, and I refer you to page 153 of his text for more details.

## Setting up the Router's OSPF Interfaces

Each router that is configured to run OSPF can be tailored to operate with a different set of parameters. However, it is important that all routers in the routing domain have comparable operating parameters. These parameters can be set up for each router in the domain:

- OSPF cost: The metric on the interface that specifies the cost of sending a packet on the interface.
- Retransmit interval: Number of seconds between LSA retransmission for adjacencies on the interface.
- Transmit delay: Estimate of the delay (in seconds) taken to send an LSA update on an interface.
- Priority: The priority number for the router, used to select the designated router for the network.
- Hello interval: The length of time, in seconds, between the sending of hello packets.
- Dead interval: The length of time, in seconds, that a neighbor has not sent a hello, before the neighbor is declared down.
- Authentication key: The password used between neighbors for simple password authentication.
- MD5 authentication: Setting up the user of MD5 for authentication.

## OTHER RFC-BASED ASPECTS OF OSPF

In a large domain, there may be hundreds of LSA entries in a database, and many LSA packets transmitted between the routers in the routing domain. On occasion, a router may go down. On other occasions, a router may wish to take a link out of operation. Moreover, the network administrator may wish to change the roles of the routers in a domain, perhaps taking one out of the role as a primary router, and placing another router in its place. Given these possibilities, it is important that capabilities exist to verify the accuracy of LSAs, and to make certain they are topical. One tool to assist in these important operations is the LS Age field, and related values stored at each router. Table 6–2 summarizes the OSPF aging and traffic control operations, as defined in the RFC specifications. You might wish to examine this table in relation to the last section in this chapter on configuring OSPF interface parameters.

Each router updates its LSAs at least once every 30 minutes. If conditions warrant, the LSA may be changed frequently. Whenever the age of the LSA reaches 30 minutes, the originating router sends out a new

**Table 6–2  Aging and Traffic Control Operations**

- LSAs sent as appropriate
- If LSA age = 30 min, LSA is resent with:

    LS Age = 0,

LS ... inc ... rou ... bas ... fro ... bas ... rou ... a ro ... tha ... face ... peri ... nor

0, and the LS Sequence Number is

not be sending any LSAs. So, other value of the age field in the LS data-, the router deletes the LSA record

n erroneous record to be in the data- in a routing calculation unless the ise the link. d (at most) every 5 seconds. Second, A if the copy in the database is less onfigured erroneously, if its inter- rapid succession, or otherwise ex- ll not process the spate of traffic, uters.

## INTERNETWORKING WITH OTHER ROUTING PROTOCOLS

It is common to run OSPF and RIP in the same autonomous system. One approach is to assign a metric of one to each interface, which provides an almost least-hop count domain. I say almost because OSPF forces a path between two routers to be OSPF-based.

RFC 1745 defines the interactions between OSPF and BGP as well as the Inter-Domain Routing Protocol (IDRP). IDRP is an ISO/OSI variation of BGP, but has not enjoyed much success in the industry.

Most high-end routers support route distribution operations, which means any IP-based routing protocol information can be redistributed into any other IP-based routing protocol. In effect, OSPF can import or export routes via RIP, IS-IS, IGRP, and EIGRP for intradomain operations. For interdomain operations, OSPF can import or export routes via BGP and even the old EGP.

## SECURITY CONSIDERATIONS

OSPF implements security operations to prevent unauthorized routers and other masquerading nodes from doing damage to a routing domain. The OSPF router can be configured to support simple password authentication in clear text, or secret key authentication, typically with the MD5 operation.

The idea of MD5 for OSPF is to make it very difficult for an attacker to generate a phony OSPF packet that would be accepted by a routing domain. A hash value is computed to authenticate the packet and MD5 is designed to prevent an attacker from appending a phony hash value to the packet. If the attacker tries to do so, the receiving router's calculations reveals that the hash value in not valid, and rejects the packet.

## CONFIGURING AN OSPF ROUTING DOMAIN

To configure an OSPF routing domain, the routers must be configured to perform the tasks summarized in Table 6–3. This section provides an overview of each of these tasks. The specific rules for each of these tasks are documented in the router's user's manuals.

Some of these tasks are straightforward; others need more explanation. Some are somewhat tertiary to the operation of the routing domain, and others are of primary importance. For each task explained, if I have already discussed the operations pertaining to the task in the chapter, I refer you to that discussion with an identification of the section header title.

- Enabling OSPF: To enable OSPF to operate on the router, this
  task specifies the range of addresses that are to be associated with

**Table 6–3    OSPF Configuration Tasks**

Enabling OSPF

Configuring OSPF interface parameters

Configuring OSPF over different physical networks

Configuring OSPF area parameters

Configuring OSPF not so stubby area (NSSA)

Configuring route summarization between OSPF areas

Configuring route summarization when redistributing routes into OSPF

Creating virtual links

Generating a default route

Configuring lookup of DNS names

Controlling default metrics

Configuring OSPF on simplex Ethernet interfaces

Configuring route calculation timers

Configuring OSPF over on-demand circuits

Logging neighbor changes

Monitoring and maintaining OSPF

the routing process, and the area IDs that are to be associated with the range of IP addresses. These parameters are set up for each interface on which OSPF will operate. This is the only task in this list that must be implemented. The others are optional.

- Configuring OSPF interface parameters: I explained this subject earlier in this chapter in the section titled Setting up the Router's OSPF Interfaces.

- Configuring OSPF over different physical networks: I explained this subject earlier in this chapter in the section titled Operating OSPF over Different Types of Networks (Media).

- Configuring OSPF area parameters: I explained this subject earlier in this chapter in the section titled OSPF Areas.

- Configuring OSPF not so stubby area (NSSA): Referring to Figure 6–6, this task allows the network manager to define an area to be a NSSA.

- Configuring route summarization between OSPF areas: If the IP addresses in an area are contiguous, route summarization permits the advertising of a single summary route to be advertised into another area by the area border router. To execute this task, the network manager configures the address range for which the summary route will be advertised.

- Configuring route summarization when redistributing routes into OSPF: Routes advertised into an OSPF domain are advertised individually in separate external LSA packets. This task instructs OSPF to advertise a single route for all the redistributed routes covered by a single network prefix.

- Creating virtual links: Referring to Figure 6–6, this task creates a virtual link between area border routers, and the virtual link must be configured in both routers. The configuration information includes the identification of the other area border router and the nonbackbone area that the two routers have in common (the transit area). Remember that virtual routes cannot be set up through stub areas.

- Generating a default route: This task is used to generate a default route into an OSPF domain. Even though a router may be an autonomous system boundary router, it does not by default generate a default route into the domain. This task will perform that function.

- Configuring lookup of DNS names: Routers have a number of commands that allow the network manager to view displays of routers. The domain name of the DNS router can be displayed with this task.

- Controlling default metrics: High-end routers allow this task to be configured based on the bandwidth of the link on each interface on the router.

- Configuring OSPF on simplex Ethernet interfaces: This task pertains to an OSPF interface on an Ethernet subnet, and permits the devices on the Ethernet segment to see each other with OSPF hello packets.

- Configuring route calculation timers: This task is used to delay the time OSPF starts a shortest path first calcuation (SPF) from its receiving an LSA that represents a topology change. It can also be used to establish the hold time between two consecutive SPF calculations.

- Configuring OSPF over on-demand circuits: I explained this subject earlier in this chapter in the section titled How OSPF Supports "On-demand" Links. The only configuration operation for this task is to enter a command that the link is a demand circuit.

However, I recommend you study the OSPF and router rules in detail if you are using on-demand links, since they entail the consideration of a wide variety of factors.

- Logging neighbor changes: Routers have extensive debugging facilities. This task can be configured if these extensive facilities are not needed, and the network manager just wants to know when an OSPF neighbor state changes.

- Monitoring and maintaining OSPF: This task provides information on a wide array of information, including the contents of IP routing tables of routers, and the link state database. It also shows information on router interfaces to neighbors, including virtual links.

## SUMMARY

OSPF is the preferred routing protocol for large interior routing domains. It uses link state metrics and spanning trees to compute the route. OSPF is very aware of its use of bandwidth vis-à-vis user traffic, and executes several procedures to reduce flooding, and the containment of its advertisement packets.

In theory, OSPF can support dynamic metrics, such as delay. In practice, its metrics are more modest and pragmatic, such as a hop-count value, and the link speed (interface bandwidth). OSPF represents the culmination of many years of research and practice on how to build a routing protocol.

## FOLLOW-UP READING

We have covered the major operations of OSPF, and I have recommended the Moy text to you. But we have only touched the surface of OSPF and related operations. For follow-up reading, you will find these references useful (they are not all-inclusive for OSPF, but represent the key standards):

Baker F. and R. Coltun, "OSPF Version 2 Management Information Base," RFC 1253, ACC, Computer Science Center, August 1991.

Moy, J., "Multicast Extensions to OSPF," RFC 1584, Proteon, Inc., March 1994.

Moy, J., ed., "OSPF Protocol Analysis," RFC 1245, Proteon, Inc., July 1991.

Moy, J., ed., "Experience with the OSPF Protocol," RFC 1245, Proteon, Inc., July 1991.

Hinden, R., "Internet Routing Protocol Standardization Criteria," RFC 1264, BBN, October 1991.

Baker, F., "IP Forwarding Table MIB," RFC 1354, ACC, July 1992.

For the reader who wishes to delve into detail about OSPF and how to configure OSPF, you should consult your vendor's user manuals. If you do not have access to these manuals, I recommend a book from the Cisco IOS Reference Library titled: *Cisco IOS Solutions for Network Protocols, Volume I: IP,* by Cisco Press (available from Cisco or Macmillian Technical Publishing). Another fine Cisco Press book about the subject is *OSPF Network Design Solutions,* by Thomas M. Thomas II. What distinguishes this book is that Thomas provides more tutorial explanations than most of the books in the Cisco library.

Another more general tutorial on OSPF is *Cisco Router OSPF Design and Implementation Guide,* by William R. Parkhurst, McGraw-Hill, 1998.

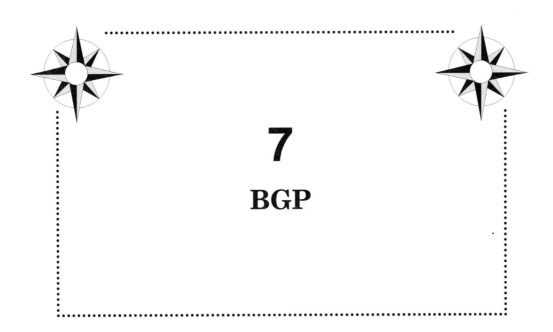

# 7

# BGP

## INTRODUCTION

The chapter explains the operations of the prominent external gateway protocol, the Border Gateway Protocol (BGP). We start with a look at the major attributes of BGP, and follow with a description of BGP advertising, and the concept of transit and nontransit autonomous systems. The major BGP operations are then analyzed, with examples of BGP's messages. The chapter concludes with a description of the tasks used by the network manager to configure BGP operations between and within autonomous systems.

## ATTRIBUTES OF BGP

The Border Gateway Protocol (BGP) is an interautonomous system protocol and is a relatively new addition to the family of routing protocols (it has seen use since 1989, but not extensively until the last few years). Today, it is the principal route advertising protocol used in the Internet for external gateway operations. Figure 7–1 shows a BGP topology, and some key terms.

BGP has a number of advantages over its predecessor, the External Gateway Protocol (EGP). First, it can operate with networks with looped topologies. Second, as a result of this advertising, a node that receives

A BGP Path Tree:

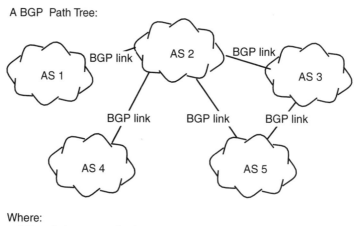

Where:
  AS    Autonomous System
  BGP   Border Gateway Protocol

**Figure 7–1    BGP AS Links and Path Tree**

more than one possible path (in advertisements) to a destination can without ambiguity, choose the best path. Third, BGP supports CIDR and address aggregation.

In addition, BGP does not care what type of intra-autonomous route discovery protocol is used, such as OSPF or RIP. It does not care if multiple intra-autonomous protocols are employed.

BGP is designed to run with a reliable transport layer protocol, such as TCP. Therefore, the BGP network manager need not be concerned about correct receipt of traffic, segmentation, etc. These potential problems are handled by the transport layer.

BGP operates by building a graph of ASs. The graph is derived from the routing information exchanged by the BGP routers in the ASs. BGP considers the entire Internet as a graph of ASs with each identified by an AS number. The graph between the ASs is also called a tree. While autonomous systems are usually connected together in a neighbor relationship, a BGP router can be configured to skip over intermediate routers in the AS path tree.

BGP also has several advantages over a conventional distance-vector protocol, such as RIP.

- BGP sends messages only if something changes, and not on a continuous basis. Obviously, this procedure keeps the overhead down on the link.
- BGP is able to select a loop-free path even though the system may contain physical loops.

- BGP stores backup paths, and in the event of failure of the primary path, it need not count-to-infinity waiting for the network routing tables to stabilize.
- Routing decisions can be based on policy considerations, and need not be based just on the fewest number of hops. This point is important for public networks, like the Internet, in which the ISPs enter into peering arrangements with each other. These arrangements can be supported with BGP routing policies.
- A BGP router enters into a relationship with another BGP router through manual configurations, and not automatically. This is also important in the Internet to support or deny peering arrangements.

## BGP NEIGHBORS

Routing protocols need to know about their neighbors, and how to exchange hellos and routing information with them. BGP is no exception, and this protocol also must consider factors beyond a hop count or a link metric. BGP must also deal with policy-based routing, since BGP may entail the transmission of traffic between different (and potentially competitive enterprises). Therefore, BGP's neighbors are very important, because they may be *external* neighbors, those belonging to another autonomous system and another enterprise.

From the technical standpoint, BGP supports two kinds of neighbors. The internal neighbor is in the same autonomous system, and the external neighbor is in a different autonomous system. As a general practice, external neighbors who are adjacent to each other a share a subnet. Internal neighbors can be non-adjacent physically; they can be located anywhere in the autonomous system.

## BGP "SPEAKERS"

BGP uses the concept of a *speaker* to advertise routing information. The speaker resides in the router. Using a common set of policies (routing agreements, described shortly), the BGP speakers arrive at an agreement as to which AS border routers will serve as exit/entry points for particular networks outside the AS. This information is communicated to the AS's internal routers, via the interior routing protocol, or with manual configurations.

Connections between BGP speakers of different ASs are called *external* links. BGP connections between BGP speakers within the same AS are called *internal* links. A peer in a different AS is referred to as an external peer, and a peer in the same AS is described as an internal peer.

## COMMUNITIES

BGP can be set up to distribute routing information on a group of destinations (networks) called communities. The idea is to be able to group destinations into these communities and apply routing policies to a community. This approach simplifies the speaker's job by aggregating routing information. It also provides a tool for the network manager to control the dissemination of routing information.

The BGP community operation offers considerable flexibility. For example, a destination can belong to multiple communities, and the AS network manager can define the community to which a destination belongs. Given that one belongs or does not belong to a community, BGP will or will not support the distribution of routing information.

The communities operation is a powerful aspect of BGP-capable routers. Once again, we see how BGP is quite different from the other routing protocols discussed so far in this book: Policy-based "metrics" are fundamental to BGP, whereas link-based metrics are fundamental to the IGP routing protocols, such as RIP, and OSPF.

## BGP ADVERTISING

BGP need not adhere to a minimum hop approach. Figure 7–2 shows why. Routers 1 to 10 are BGP routers that connect ASs 1 to 5 together. The topology forms a loop between AS 2, AS 3, and AS 5. Under the older distance-vector protocols, a break in the topology, say between router 1 and router 2, would invoke the count to infinity procedure between routers 4, 5, 6, 7, 9, and 10, as well as between router 3 and 8.

BGP knows better. It has discovered that the prefix 192.169.0.0/16 is reachable through AS 1. AS 2 knows that it is in the path to the address, so it would reject any message that had AS 2 in the advertisement.

Furthermore, let us assume that the link between routers 4 and 9 fails. In this situation, AS 5 knows of another path to AS 1, and can make an immediate recovery. However, keep in mind that AS 5, because of policy decisions, may be prevented from using a path, regardless of the number of hops to the desired destination.

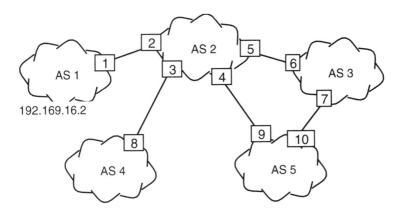

**Figure 7–2    BGP Advertising**

As a result of the advertising, here is what AS 5 learns about 192.169.0.0/16:

- AS 1 advertises:     192.169.0.0/16     AS 1
- AS 2 advertises:     192.169.0.0/16     AS 1     AS 2
- AS 3 advertises      192.169.0.0/16     AS 1     AS 2     AS 3
- AS 5 sees:           192.169.0.0/16     AS 1     AS 2
- AS 5 also sees:      192.169.0.0/16     AS 1     AS 2     AS 3

## CONFIGURATIONS WITH CUSTOMER

Like other routing protocols, BGP uses the concept of a stub. The stub is a network that does not pass-through traffic; it acts as a source and sink for the traffic (it sends or receives traffic). In Figure 7–3, the customer network is a stub.

It has been noted in this book that an External Gateway Protocol (EGP) is designed to operate between autonomous systems (AS), and an internal gateway protocol operates within an autonomous system (AS). But what about the operations between an AS (say, an ISP) and a customer? Three methods are used to support this interface, shown in Figure 7–3 [HALA97].[1]

---

[1][HALA97] Halabi, Bassam, *Internet Routing Architectures,* Cisco Press, New Riders Publishing, 1997.

In Figure 7–3(a), BGP is deployed between the customer and the service provider (an ISP that is assigned an AS number). In this situation, BGP is called the external BGP (EBGP). It is so-named because BGP can operate between ASs or within an AS. As discussed later, an internal BGP (IBGP) is used to tunnel a user's traffic through a transit (pass-through) AS. For this operation, the provider gives the customer a private AS number (65,412–65,535), but uses the provider's AS number for its operations beyond the provider-customer interface.

In Figure 7–3(b), an IGP is deployed between the customer and the service provider. In this situation, the customer uses RIP, OSPF, etc. to advertise its addresses to the service provider. This operation is set up by agreements between the two parties. As examples, conventional prefix advertising may be performed, or the customer may use the ISP's address space, and the two may use the Network Address Translation (NAT, see Appendix C) protocol for the non-global address-to-global address translation.

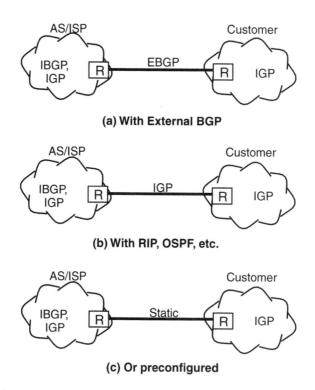

**Figure 7–3   Configurations with Customer [HALA97]**

In Figure 7–3(c), the customer has static (preconfigured) routes to the provider. After all, the customer's network is a stub, and there is only one way into and out of the stub. This interface can also be supported by NAT.

## BGP POLICY-BASED ARCHITECTURE

As stated earlier, one of the unique aspects of BGP is its policy-based architecture. RFC 1655 describes this architecture, and this part of the chapter provides a summary of RFC 1655's description of this aspect of BGP.

BGP provides the capability for enforcing policies based on various routing preferences and constraints, such as economic, security, or political considerations. Policies are not directly encoded in the protocol. Rather, policies are provided to BGP in the form of configuration information, explained in the last section of this chapter.

The BGP routers are capable of allowing the network manager (the AS administration) to perform "policy configuration" tasks when a policy is created or changed. These changes affect the path selection at the router, as well as the redistribution of routing in the BGP domain.

Of course, efficient traffic management is important, and BGP can control the following aspects of traffic forwarding at the router:

- An AS can minimize the number of transit ASs. (Shorter AS paths can be preferred over longer ones.)
- If an AS determines that two or more AS paths can be used to reach a given destination, the AS can use a variety of means to decide which of the candidate AS paths it will use. The quality of an AS can be measured by such things as link speed, capacity, and congestion tendencies. Information about these qualities might be determined by means other than BGP, such a router's administrative metrics.
- Preference of internal routes over external routes.

### Advertise What Is Used

BGP must adhere to this important rule: An AS advertises to its neighboring ASs only those routes that it uses. This rule reflects the "hop-by-hop" routing paradigm generally used by an internet.

## PATH SELECTION WITH BGP

A BGP speaker evaluates different paths to a destination network from its border gateways at that network, selects the best one, applies relevant policy constraints, and then advertises it to all of its BGP neighbors. A complication in Inter-AS routing does arise from the lack of a universally agreed-upon metric among ASs that can be used to evaluate external paths. Each AS may have its own set of criteria for path evaluation.

Anyway, the BGP speaker builds a routing database consisting of the set of all feasible paths and the list of networks reachable through each path. In actual BGP implementations, the criteria for assigning degree of preferences to a path is specified in configuration tasks. These tasks include configuring BGP neighbors, setting up administrative weights for a path to a neighbor, restricting routing information to and from neighbors, setting up aggregate addresses, etc. These tasks are defined in the last section of this chapter.

## SELECTING A PATH

There are two primary sources of information on how to select a BGP path. I include both in this section. The first is provided by RFC 1655. I quote directly:

> The process of assigning a degree of preference to a path can be based on several sources of information:
> 1. Information explicitly present in the full AS path.
> 2. A combination of information that can be derived from the full AS path and information outside the scope of BGP (e.g., policy routing constraints provided as configuration information).
>
> Possible criteria for assigning a degree of preference to a path are:
> - AS count. Paths with a smaller AS count are generally better.
> - Policy considerations. BGP supports policy-based routing based on the controlled distribution of routing information. A BGP speaker may be aware of some policy constraints (both within and outside of its own AS) and do appropriate path selection. Paths that do not comply with policy requirements are not considered further.
> - Presence or absence of a certain AS or ASs in the path. By means of information outside the scope of BGP, an AS may know some performance characteristics (e.g., bandwidth, MTU, intra-AS diameter) of certain ASs and may try to avoid or prefer them.
> - Path origin. A path learned entirely from BGP (i.e., whose endpoint is internal to the last AS on the path) is generally better than one for which part of the path was learned via EGP or some other means.

- AS path subsets. An AS path that is a subset of a longer AS path to the same destination should be preferred over the longer path. Any problem in the shorter path (such as an outage) will also be a problem in the longer path.
- Link dynamics. Stable paths should be preferred over unstable ones. Note that this criterion must be used in a very careful way to avoid causing unnecessary route fluctuation. Generally, any criteria that depend on dynamic information might cause routing instability and should be treated very carefully.

For the second source, the Cisco approach is to set up the router with a set of factory defaults. These defaults can be overridden by a configuration task called BGP administrative weights. This weight is a number used to control the path selection process, and can number from 0 to 65,535. Default paths are 32,768, and other paths have 0. To instruct a router to "prefer" one neighbor over another, the weight must be higher than all routes learned by that router. Here are Cisco's rules [CISC98a]:[2]

- If the next hop is inaccessible, do not consider it.
- Consider larger BGP administrative weights first.
- If the routers have the same weight, consider the route with the higher preference.
- If the routers have the same local preference, prefer the route that the local router originated.
- If no route was originated, prefer the shorter autonomous system path.
- If all paths are of the same autonomous system path length, prefer the lowest origin code (IGP < EGP < INCOMPLETE). The origin indicates the protocol that originated the routing update. BGP considers three origin types, and prefers them in this order: IGP, then EGP, and then INCOMPLETE. The latter type is one in which BGP received a routing packet by redistribution, and these routes may have originated from anywhere.
- If origin codes are the same and all the paths are from the same autonomous system, prefer the path with the lowest Multi Exit Discriminator (MED) metric. A missing metric is treated as zero. The MED is used to give a preference into an autonomous system that has multiple entry points.

[2][CISC98a] *Cisco IOS Solutions for Network Protocols, Volume I: IP,* Macmillan Technical Publishing, 1998.

- If the MEDs are the same, prefer external paths over internal paths.
- If IGP synchronization is disabled, and only internal paths remain, prefer the path through the closest neighbor. IGP synchronization is an operation that has BGP wait for an IGP to send routing information before advertising transit routes to other autonomous systems.
- Prefer the path with the lowest IP address value for the BGP router ID.

## BGP ROUTING MODEL

Figure 7–4 shows the BGP routing model, based on Cisco's operation [HALA97]. A BGP routing table is kept separate from the IP routing table. The BGP table is used to determine how the router passes routing information to the router's peers. The IP routing table is populated by: (a) routes within the autonomous system, and (b) routes advertised by other autonomous systems. The IP routing table is used for the final routing.

The input policy engine is the first major process in the router to do route analysis. It contains filtering software that examines address prefixes, AS path information, and BGP attribute information to make its decisions. It can change path attributes as well. This affects the next operation, the decision process, that determines the route taken to the next

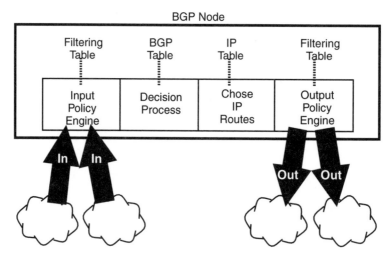

**Figure 7–4    BGP Routing Model [HALA97]**

node. For example, the input policy engine can change attributes that affect the choice of routes.

I mentioned attributes in the previous paragraph. Attributes are parameters that are associated with routes. They are used by BGP to select routes. We have more to say about attributes later, but for now, simply consider them as the metrics we have discussed in previous chapters.

The decision process is used to determine the route to be taken to the destination. These routes have been filtered through the input policy engine. If more than one route is available to the destination, the attributes for the routes are examined, and the "best" route is chosen.

These best routes are placed in the IP routing table, and they are advertised to this router's BGP peers.

The output policy engine is the same as the input policy engine except it is applied on the output interface, and it includes routes that are generated at this local node. It also performs the important function of not passing routes learned from internal nodes to other internal nodes. That operation is left to an IGP.

Finally, the output is the advertisements sent to this router's BGP neighbors (peers).

### Interactions with IGPs

If the AS passes routing information between other autonomous systems, the AS must be consistent about the information it provides these systems. For example, if BGP advertises a route before all the routers in the AS learn about the route from the AS IGP, these routers might receive traffic for which they have no routing table entry. To prevent this situation, BGP provides a process called BGP (or IGP) synchronization, and BGP waits until the IGP has propagated routing information across the AS.

Of course, if the AS is not going to be a transit AS, it is not necessary to set up the synchronization operations. In addition, the network manager must be careful how route redistribution is implemented. For example, if BGP is used to redistribute routes into the IGP, it may happen that these routes are then redistributed back to BGP.

## NONTRANSIT AND TRANSIT ASs

An AS need not originate and terminate all traffic that flows through it. This AS is a *multihomed* transit network. The term multihomed means that the AS has more than one interface to other ASs. The term transit means the traffic has a source or destination address outside the AS. The term nontransit means that the AS does not permit traffic not destined for the AS (or not originated in the AS) to pass through it.

Some intranet routing domains permit transit operations, and some do not. The decision to permit transit traffic to pass through an organization's AS is based on the organization's routing policy.

Figure 7–5 shows an example of a multihomed non-transit AS, which is AS 1, and ISP A. AS 1 advertises addresses for NW1 and NW2 to AS 2 and AS 3. AS 2 and AS 3 advertise NW3, NW4 and NW5, NW6 respectively to AS 1.

AS 1 does not relay the respective advertisements of AS 2 and AS 3 any farther than its own AS. Consequently, AS 2 and AS 3 do not know they can reach each other through AS 1, and will not relay traffic to AS 1 for the networks that reside in these two autonomous systems.

Figure 7–6 shows a transit multihomed AS. This AS relays traffic through it; that is, traffic that does not originate nor terminate in the AS. The figure also shows two other aspects of multihomed transit ASs. The BGP operation that exchanges advertisements between the autonomous systems is called an external BGP, or EBGP. The routers that operate at

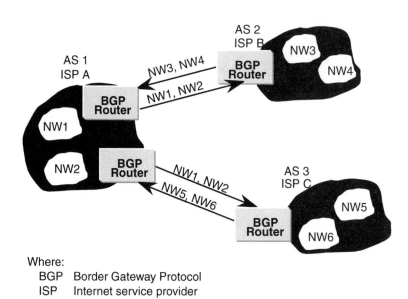

Where:
  BGP   Border Gateway Protocol
  ISP   Internet service provider
  NW    Network

**Figure 7–5  Multihomed Non-Transit Autonomous System (AS)**

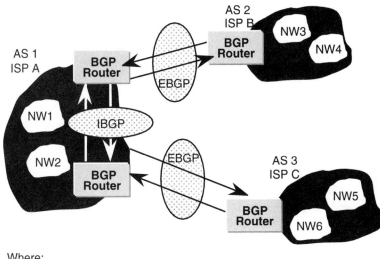

Where:
  BGP     Border Gateway Protocol
  EBGP   External BGP
  IBGP   Internal BGP
  ISP     Internet service provider
  NW    Network

**Figure 7–6   Multihomed Transit Autonomous System (AS)**

this interface are called BGP border routers. The advertisements are also carried through AS 1 to allow AS 2 and AS 3 to inform each other about their networks. This BGP operation is called an internal BGP, or IBGP. The routers that exchange this information are called transit routers.

To continue the discussion on multihomed transit autonomous systems, Figure 7–7 shows how the route advertisements are conveyed by AS 1 to AS 2 and AS 3. The fact that AS 1 is advertising on behalf of AS 2 and AS 3 means that AS 1 agrees to be a transit network for AS 2 and AS 3.

The transit routers in AS 1 may also be connected to non-transit routers in the autonomous system. The non-transit routers need not be configured with BGP, but can use an internal gateway protocol (IGP) such as OSPF.

### Fully Meshed IBGP Speakers and Avoiding Routing Loops

BGP requires that all IBGP speakers in the routing domain be fully meshed. Figure 7–8 shows the operations for this requirement. Router 1 is an external speaker and sends routing information into this

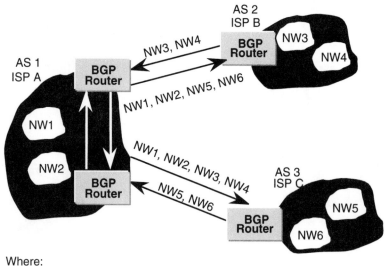

Where:
BGP     Border Gateway Protocol
EBGP    External BGP
IBGP    Internal BGP
ISP     Internet service provider
NW      Network

**Figure 7–7     Multihomed Transit Autonomous System (AS)**

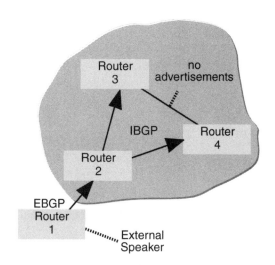

**Figure 7–8     Fully Meshed IBGP Speakers**

autonomous system via router 2. In turn, router 2 is obligated to advertise this information to routers 3 and 4.

To avoid routing information loops, routers 3 and 4 do not pass this information to each other. The rule to avoid this potential loop is that routers do not pass routes learned from internal BGP neighbors to other internal BGP neighbors.

Thus, router 2 in this example must mesh with all other internal routers in order to pass them the routing information. This approach works well enough for small routing domains, but for large systems, it places a big burden on (in this example) router 2. It might have to support scores of IBGP neighbor routers, and in large domains, the sessions to the other routers number over 100.

This problem is partially solved with two approaches discussed in the next two sections of this chapter: (a) routing domain confederations, and (c) route reflectors.

## ROUTING DOMAIN CONFEDERATIONS

As large enterprises, such as ISPs, become even larger, one autonomous system can become unwieldy. The IBGP configurations can become quite complex, and a router may have to support many internal BGP sessions. One method to deal with this problem is to "divide and conquer," break the AS down into smaller parts.

An autonomous system can be divided into multiple autonomous systems, and grouped into a single confederation. To the outside, this partitioning is transparent, and the divided ASs appear as one autonomous system. Figure 7–9 shows the idea of the routing domain configuration.

Each of the autonomous systems is fully meshed within itself and has connections to the other ASs in the confederation. The peers in the different autonomous systems have EBGP sessions, but they exchange routing information as IBGP peers, and the conventional rules for IBGP are in effect. Several key router configuration parameters are used to enable one IBGP to be used within the confederation (these parameters are next-hop, MED, and local preference, and they are explained in the last section of this chapter).

Notice that EBGP is operating between the ASs in the confederation. This configuration is needed because each AS uses a unique AS number, and thus the EBGP routing packets are used.

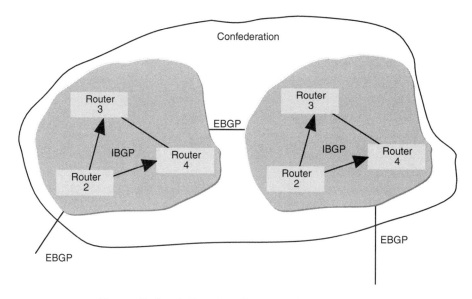

**Figure 7–9    A Routing Domain Confederation**

## ROUTE REFLECTORS

Another approach to combat the scaling problem is to configure the routers to support a route reflector. This operation means that all IBGP speakers do not have to be fully meshed. The approach is depicted in Figure 7–10. Router 2 is configured to be a route reflector, and assumes the responsibility for passing the routing information to a set (or one) of IBGP neighbors. When router 2 receives the routing information from router 1, it advertises the information to router 3. Router 3 then "reflects" the routing information to router 4. Thus, IBGP sessions between router 2 and router 4 are unnecessary.

This simple example may not show the savings in routing sessions through the use of the router reflector. But consider that router 2 might have IBGP sessions with hundreds of other routers, and the reflector helps reduce the overhead of these many sessions. To see why, we need some more information. Internal BGP peers of the route reflector are divided into: (a) client peers, and (b) nonclient peers. The route reflector forms an association with its client peers called a cluster, and these routers do not have to be fully meshed with each other. They do *not* communicate with IBGP speakers that are outside the cluster.

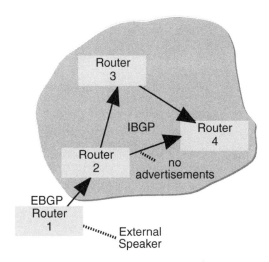

**Figure 7-10   The Route Reflector**

To demonstrate the reflector operations, consider that when a route reflector receives routing information, it performs the following operations:

- It advertises the external BGP information to all clients and nonclient peers.
- Any information from a nonclient peer is advertised to all clients.
- A route from a client is advertised to all clients and nonclient peers, which means the clients do not have to be fully meshed.

## BGP MESSAGES

BGP uses four different types of messages for its operations. They are described in this section. First, each message is proceeded by a header shown in Figure 7-11. The marker field contains a value that the receiver of the message can predict. If the type of the message is OPEN, or if the authentication code used in the OPEN message of the connection is zero, then the marker must be all ones. Otherwise, the value of the marker can be predicted by a computation specified as part of the authentication mechanism used. The marker is used to detect loss of synchronization between a pair of BGP peers, and to authenticate incoming BGP messages.

| 0 | 9–15 | 1 5 | 1 6 | 17–22 | 2 3 | 2 4 | 25–30 | 3 1 |
|---|------|-----|-----|-------|-----|-----|-------|-----|

Marker

| Length | Type | Not used |
|--------|------|----------|

**Figure 7–11  The BGP Message Header**

The length field indicates the length of the entire message, and the type field is coded to indicate the type of message, such as OPEN, UPDATE, etc.

### OPEN

The OPEN message is used to establish neighbors (BGP peers). This operation occurs before any advertising can take place. It is an initial handshake message between the BGP routers. If the OPEN message is received at the other router, it responds with a KEEPALIVE message. Once this handshake occurs, the BGP neighbors can exchange UPDATE, KEEPALIVE, and NOTIFICATION messages. The OPEN message is shown in Figure 7–12.

The first part of the message contains the version number of BGP, and the autonomous system number of the sender. The next field is the hold time, which indicates the number of seconds that the sender proposes for the value of the hold timer. The hold timer indicates the length of time the BGP neighbors should consider the sender's information valid.

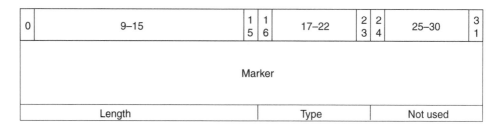

| 0 | 9–15 | 1 5 | 1 6 | 17–22 | 2 3 | 2 4 | 25–30 | 3 1 |
|---|------|-----|-----|-------|-----|-----|-------|-----|
| Version | My Autonomous System | | | | | | Hold Time | |
| Hold Time (cont.) | Auth. Code | | BGP Identifier | | | | | |
| BGP Identifier (cont.) | Authentication Data | | | | | | | |
| Authentication Data (cont.) | | | | | | | | |

**Figure 7–12  The OPEN Message**

The next field is the BGP identifier, and it is the identifier of the BGP sender. This value is determined during the handshake operations between the BGP peers, and is the same value for every local interface and every BGP peer.

The last two fields in the packet are the authentication code and authentication data. The code field indicates the authentication procedure used for the BGP session, and the authentication data field depends on the code field.

### UPDATE

The UPDATE message, illustrated in Figure 7–13, is used to exchange addresses and routing information. It advertises one route to a BGP peer, and it may also withdraw multiple "unfeasible" routes from service. This message contains three major fields, and two length fields. The withdrawn routes field contains a list of IP address prefixes of the routes that have been withdrawn for service. The path attribute field is a list of path attributes, coded as: attribute type (explained shortly), attribute length, and attribute value. The network reachability field contains a list of IP address prefixes that the BGP router knows about and can reach.

A couple of comments are important here about the BGP UPDATE message. First, an UPDATE message can advertise at most one route, which may be described by several path attributes. Second, an UPDATE message can list multiple routes to be withdrawn from service.

### NOTIFICATION

This message is used when an error occurs, or a peer connection is closed. It contains a number of error codes (such as timer expired, etc.), that are described in RFC 1655.

| Unfeasible Routes Length (2 octets) |
| :---: |
| Withdrawn Routes (variable) |
| Total Path Attribute Length (2 octets) |
| Path Attributes (variable) |
| Network Layer Reachability Information (variable) |

**Figure 7–13   The UPDATE Message**

**KEEPALIVE**

The KEEPALIVE messages are used between peers to make sure the peers are up-and-running, and the link to them is operational. The KEEPALIVE message consists of only the BGP message header. KEEPALIVE messages are exchanged between peers often enough as not to cause the hold timer to expire.

**PATH ATTRIBUTES**

A key aspect to BGP is the idea of path attributes, which are contained in the update messages, along with network addresses of the advertised networks. Several attributes are defined; here is a summary of the major attributes (others are defined in RFC 1655):

| | |
|---|---|
| • ORIGIN | Defines the origin of the path information. It describes the origin as an IGP, EGP, or an origin of some other means. |
| • AS_PATH | Lists the ASs that have been traversed to reach the advertised networks. |
| • NEXT_HOP | Contains the IP address of the border router that is to be used as the next hop to reach the networks listed in an UPDATE message. |
| • MULTI_EXIT_DISC | Used on external (inter-AS) links to discriminate among multiple exit or entry points to the same neighboring AS. |
| • LOCAL_PREF | A degree of preference of a BGP speaker for each external route. |
| • ATOMIC_AGGREGATE | If a BGP speaker selects a less specific route then the local system can attach this attribute to the route when propagating it to other BGP speakers. |
| • UNREACHABLE | Notification that a previously advertised route has become unreachable. |

## CONTROLLED DISTRIBUTION OF ROUTING TO ENFORCE TRANSIT POLICIES

BGP enforces its transit policies by the controlled distribution of routing information. A router is set up to support these policies by using one of three methods (a) using IP addresses as a control mechanism, (b) using the AS_PATH attribute, and (c) using the communities attribute. These methods have been explained in earlier parts of this chapter. More information is provided in the last section of this chapter, dealing with router configurations.

## CONFIGURING A BGP ROUTING DOMAIN

To configure a BGP routing domain, the routers must be configured to perform the tasks summarized in Tables 7–1 and 7–2. This section provides an overview of each of these tasks. The specific rules for each of these tasks are documented in the router's user's manuals.

Some of these tasks are straightforward; others need more explanation. Some are somewhat tertiary to the operation of the routing domain, and others are of primary importance. For each task explained, if I have already discussed the operations pertaining to the task in the chapter, I refer you to that discussion with an identification of the section header title.

**Table 7–1   BGP Basic Configuration Tasks**

Enabling BGP
Configuring BGP neighbors
Configuring BGP soft reconfiguration
Resetting BGP connections
Configuring BGP interactions with IGPs
Configuring BPG administrative weights
Configuring BGP route filtering by neighbor
Configuring BGP path filtering by neighbor
Disabling next-hop processing on BGP updates
Configuring the BGP version
Setting the network weight
Configuring the multi exit discriminator metric

**Table 7–2    BGP Advanced Configuration Tasks**

Using route maps to modify updates

Resetting EBGP connections immediately upon link failure

Configuring aggregate addresses

Disabling automatic summarization upon link failure

Configuring BGP community filtering

Configuring a routing domain confederation

Configuring a route reflector

Configuring neighbor options

Configuring BGP peer groups

Indicating backdoor routes

Modifying parameters while updating the IP routing table

Setting administrative distance

Adjusting BGP timers

Changing the local preference value

Selecting a path based on MEDs from other autonomous systems

Configuring route dampening

BGP is a bit different regarding configuration tasks. The tasks are organized as basic and advanced tasks, and are set up to give the network manager options on how elaborate (and complex) the BGP operations will be. At a minimum, the first three basic tasks in Table 7–1 must be configured. The other tasks are optional.

As we did with RIP and OSPF, we conclude the chapter by explaining the router configuration tasks. We start with the basic tasks listed in Table 7–1, followed by the advanced tasks listed in Table 7–2.

The basic tasks are as follows:

- Enabling BGP: This task enables the BGP routing mode, which also allows the entering of other configuration tasks. Part of this process is the identification of the networks that are local to this autonomous system. One of the configuration commands in this task allows IGP routes to be placed into the BGP table.

- Configuring BGP neighbors: This task identifies the neighbor BGP routers with IP addresses and AS numbers. I explained this subject earlier in this chapter in the section titled BGP Neighbors. Obviously, if a neighbor is not entered, it cannot take part in the BGP operations.

- Configuring BGP soft reconfiguration: This task allows policies to be configured, and activated without clearing a BGP session, a nice feature for allowing the network manager to configure policies without affecting ongoing sessions. It is performed on a per-neighbor basis in one of two ways: (a) inbound soft configuration: used to generate inbound updates from a neighbor, and (b) outbound soft configuration: used to send a set of updates to a neighbor.

- Resetting BGP connections: However, BGP neighbors must be reset if the network manager enters a configuration change, such as a filter, timer, version, distance, and so on. These tasks must be performed if the changes are to take effect.

- Configuring BGP interactions with IGPs: I explained this subject earlier in this chapter in the section titled Interactions with IGPs.

- Configuring BPG administrative weights: I explained this subject earlier in this chapter in the section titled Selecting a Path.

- Configuring BGP route filtering by neighbor: This task is used to restrict (filter) the BGP routing updates to and from specific neighbors. This filter is applied to network numbers, and not autonomous systems.

- Configuring BGP path filtering by neighbor: This filter applies to incoming and outgoing updates based on BGP autonomous system paths.

- Disabling next-hop processing on BGP updates: Appendix D contains information on non-broadcast networks, and the Next Hop Resolution Protocol. This task pertains to these types of networks. It is used to disable next-hop processing for BGP updates to a neighbor. It may be useful in ATM, Frame Relay, or X.25 networks when BGP neighbors do not have direct access to all neighbors on the same IP subnet. This command has the effect of the router advertising itself as the next hop for the specified neighbor. The result is that other routers will forward to it packets for that address.

- Configuring the BGP version: BGP sessions default to version 4. This task allows a negotiation to an earlier BGP version.

- Setting the network weight: The task sets a weight for a network, which of course affects the best path selection process.

- Configuring the multi exit discriminator metric: The MED is used to give a preference into an autonomous system that has multiple entry points. This task gives a "hint" to external neighbors about preferred paths.

The advanced tasks are as follows:

- Using route maps to modify updates: A route map is a method to filter routing updates or inbound or outbound packets. The "map" can be applied on a per-neighbor basis. Only the routes that pass the route map are sent or accepted. The filtering is applied on (a) autonomous system path, (b) community, and (c) network numbers. The idea of a community is to be able to group destinations into "communities" and apply routing policies to a community. I explained the communities idea earlier in this chapter in the section titled Communities.

- Resetting EBGP connections immediately upon link failure: When a link between external routers goes down, BGP does not reset this link immediately. It is not BGP's primary concern to achieve routing convergence. But if it is important to react quickly to a link interface failure, this task enacts a fast reset operation.

- Configuring aggregate addresses: Appendix B explains the use of address aggregation. This task is used to aggregate addresses in order to reduce the size of routing tables.

- Disabling automatic summarization or network numbers: If network summarization is not desired, this task disables the operation.

- Configuring BGP community filtering: Based on an identified community, this task is used to control the distribution of routing information. Three predefined communities can be configured: (a) internet: advertise the route to the Internet community; (b) no-export: do not advertise the route to EBGP peers, and (c) no-advertise: do not advertise the route to any peer (internal or external).

- Configuring a routing domain confederation: I explained the routing domain confederation idea earlier in this chapter in the section titled Routing Domain Confederations.

- Configuring a route reflector: I explained the route reflector idea earlier in this chapter in the section titled Route Reflectors.

- Configuring neighbor options: This task allows the network manager to specify an access list of BGP neighbors (a peer group). The result is that it sets up the router to accept neighbors based on this access list. A good way to think about this operation is that it is a check on whether a potential neighbor can even gain access (and communicate with) the router. But it also "tailors" options for a peer group, so it is a very useful tool for establishing BGP routing policies. Examples of these options include: (a) specification of the neighbor, (b) how the COMMUNITIES attribute is sent to the neighbor, (c) addressing prefixes used with the neighbor, (d) invocation of MD5, (e) filtering with access lists, (f) disabling of next-hop processing, (g) application of a route map to incoming or outgoing routes, and so on.

- Configuring BGP peer groups: This task sets up a BGP neighbor to be a member of a BGP peer group.

- Indicating backdoor routes: This task is used to indicate to a border router which networks are reachable. A backdoor network is treated as a local network, except it is not advertised. This configuration informs the border router which networks it should use.

- Modifying parameters while updating the IP routing table: When a BGP route is put into the routing table, the MED parameter is converted in a route metric, the BGP next hop is used as the next hop for the route, and the tag is not set. This task can be used to set up the metric and tag information.

- Setting administrative distance: This task assigns an administrative distance to a BGP route.

- Adjusting BGP timers: This task is used to adjust keep alive and hold time timers. The keep alive timer is used to control the sending of KEEPALIVE packets to check on a neighbor. The hold timer is advertised to the neighbors and indicates the length of time they should consider the sender valid.

- Changing the local preference value: This task allows the network manager to define a path as more or less preferable than other paths.

- Selecting a path based on MEDs from other autonomous systems: By default, MED comparisons are done only for paths that belong to the same autonomous system. This task is used to allow a comparison of MEDs among paths irrespective of the autonomous system.

- Configuring route dampening: A flapping route is an unstable route, one that continually changes between being available and unavailable. It is desirable to reduce or eliminate flapping, but another system may be experiencing frequent transient problems with links. This task reduces this flapping problem.

## SUMMARY

The Border Gateway Protocol (BGP) is an interautonomous system protocol and is the principal route advertising protocol used in the Internet for external gateway operations. BGP is different from the routing protocols that have been explained thus far in this book in that routing decisions can be based on policy considerations, and need not be based just on the fewest number of hops, or link metrics.

BGP has a set of mechanisms to enable the network manager of a routing domain (in this case, an autonomous system) to control to whom traffic is sent, and from whom traffic is received, thus the idea of packet containment. This "to-from" capability exists to a limited extent in OSPF, but BGP uses policies to enforce its to-from filters.

## FOLLOW-UP READING

I have cited the Halabi text and recommend it highly. Indeed, I have referenced this book also in the Appendices. In addition to the BGP RFC 1654, these RFCs also have information on BGP and associated operations. RFC 1655 provided information on the use of BGP in the Internet, and we have covered many of the points made in this RFC. RFC 1656 is a short document about conclusions on running BGP in the Internet. RFC 1657 provides information on managed objects for BGP, when running SNMP as the network management protocol.

For the reader who wishes to delve into detail about BGP and how to configure BGP, you should consult your vendor's user manuals. If you do not have access to these manuals, I recommend a book from the Cisco IOS Reference Library titled: *Cisco IOS Solutions for Network Protocols, Volume I: IP,* by Cisco Press (available from Cisco or Macmillian Technical Publishing).

This text has a good explanation of BGP, and is an overall excellent book on routing protocols:

*Advanced IP Routing in Cisco Networks,* by Terry Slattery and Bill Burton, McGraw-Hill, 1999.

In addition this list of "older" references about exterior routing protocols may be of historical interest to you.

Mills, D., "Exterior Gateway Protocol Formal Specification," STD 18, RFC 904, BBN, April 1984.

Rekhter, Y., "EGP and Policy Based Routing in the New NSFNET Backbone," RFC 1092, T.J. Watson Research Center, February 1989.

Braun, H-W., "The NSFNET Routing Architecture," RFC 1093, MERIT/NSFNET Project, February 1989.

"Information Processing Systems—Telecommunications and Information Exchange between Systems—Protocol for Exchange of Interdomain Routeing Information among Intermediate Systems to Support Forwarding of ISO 8473 PDUs," ISO/IEC IS10747, 1993.

Fuller, V., Li, T., Yu, J., and Varadhan, K. "Classless Inter-Domain Routing (CIDR): An Address Assignment and Aggregation Strategy," RFC 1519, BARRNet, cisco, MERIT, OARnet, September 1993.

# 8

# Cisco Routing Protocols

## INTRODUCTION

This chapter explains the routing protocols that have been developed by Cisco. They are proprietary protocols, but they have much in common with the routing protocols explained in earlier chapters in this book. Therefore, we should be able to deal with these protocols with a shorter narration. The focus of attention is on two protocols: (a) the Inter-Gateway Routing Protocol (IGRP), and its replacement, the Enhanced IGRP (EIGRP).

## IGRP AND EIGRP

As just stated, the IGRP and the EIGRP are routing protocols developed by Cisco and EIGRP has replaced IGRP in many systems. Table 8–1 summarizes the major attributes of these protocols, and will be a convenient reference as we proceed through this discussion.

## IGRP

Let us start with IGRP. First, it is similar to RIP in that it is a distance-vector protocol. However, IGRP uses more elaborate metrics than a simple hop count. IGRP advertises three types of routes, as shown in Figure 8–1.

**Table 8–1    Inter-Gateway Routing Protocol (IGRP) and Enhanced IGRP (EIGRP)**

- Proprietary protocols from Cisco
- Distance vector protocols with metrics based on:
  Fixed delay between nodes (D)
  Bandwidth (B)
  Traffic load (L)
  Error rate on the path: reliability (R)
  Count of the hops on the path to the destination (H)
  The path's MTU

- Support load balancing across multiple paths to a destination
- Use triggered updates, split horizon, and holddown
- EIGRP also has:
  CIDR prefixes
  Better methods for convergence
  Hellos
  Reliable transport mechanisms
  Alternate routes

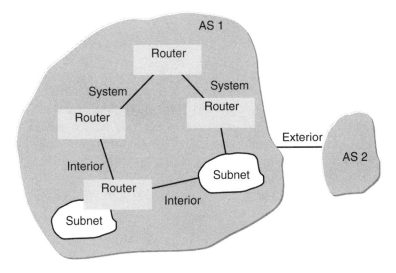

**Figure 8–1    Types of Routes**

*Interior* routes are routes between subnets in a network attached to a router. The network must be subnetted, otherwise, IGRP will not advertise the interior routes. *System* routes are routes within an autonomous system. System routes do not include subnet information. Exterior routes are routes to networks outside the autonomous system and are called a gateway of last resort. IGRP provides a list of exterior routes and the router chooses a gateway of last resort from this list. This route is chosen only if the router cannot find a better route, and the destination is not on a connected network.

IGRP uses these metrics in computing routes. They are:

- Delay between nodes (D): Route delay in tens of microseconds. It can range from 0 to a multiple of 30.1 nanoseconds with a maximum size of 4,294,967,040 nanoseconds.
- Bandwidth (B): Minimum bandwidth of the route in kbit/s
- Traffic load (L): Effective bandwidth of the route, with values ranging from 0 to 255, and 255 means 100% loading.
- Error rate on the path: reliability (R): Likelihood of a successful packet transmission expressed as 0 (no reliability) to 255 (100% reliability).
- Count of the hops on the path to the destination (H): Maximum hop is 255, with a default of 100.
- The path's MTU: The minimum maximum transmission unit (MTU) size of the route in bytes, from 0 to what the layer 2 protocol on the link allows.

IGRP runs directly over IP, as IP protocol 88. It selects a path to a destination with the lowest summed metric. If two paths are equal, the path is chosen that has the lowest delay (D). Or if two paths differ only in their bandwidth (B), the path with the higher bandwidth is chosen. Like RIP, IGRP does not have any message support except updates (no hellos, no pings, etc.).

IGRP sends its routing table every 90 seconds. However, in the event of a change, a triggered update is sent (and the entire table is in the update). A route is declared inaccessible if it does not receive an update from the first router in the route within three update periods. After seven update periods, the route is removed from the routing table. In addition, IGRP uses split horizon, and hold down.

### Metrics

IGRP uses a set of values to compute routes, which were just listed. An algorithm is applied to the values using coefficients K1, K2, K3, K4, and K5 as follows. The idea is to compute one metric for the link:

$$\text{Metric} = (K1 * \text{Bandwidth}) + (K2 * \text{Bandwidth}) / (256 - \text{Load})) + (K3 * \text{Delay})$$

If K5 is not equal to 0, an additional calculation is added to the metric:

$$\text{Metric} = \text{Metric} + (K5 / (\text{Reliability} + K4))$$

Where defaults are: K1 =1, K2 = 0, K3 = 1, K4 = 0, K5 = 0

Neither a hop count or MTU is used to calculate the metric. The MTU is examined by the router to make decisions about possibly invoking the IP fragmentation routine to fragment the packet into an acceptable size for the link. If the IP header has the "do not fragment" bit set to 1; the router might look for an link that supports the MTU size.

Even though the hop count is not in the metric calculation, it is an important piece of information because if it has increased, it means there has been a change in the network, and it can also be used to sniff-out a loop in the routing domain.

## EIGRP

EIGRP has all the features of IGRP, and supports route aggregation with CIDR prefixes. It also has improved operations to ensure loop-free paths during network changes. It also adds Hello messages, sequencing, and reliable transport operations.

Cisco routers use an administrative distance to assign a rating to routing information. Each method of route discovery is assigned a value, which identifies each specific method. The range of values is 0 to 255, with the smaller numbers being more trusted route discovery methods.

Table 8–2 shows the administrative default distances for the various methods of finding a route. Most of the entries pertain to routing protocols, the others are about manually configured static routes, and routes found by ARP and other configuration protocols.

**Table 8–2   Administrative Distance**

| Routing Information Source | Default Distance |
| --- | --- |
| Connected interface | 0 |
| Static route | 1 |
| Enhanced IGRP summary route | 5 |
| External Border Gateway Protocol (EBGP) | 20 |
| Internal Enhanced Inter-Gateway Routing Protocol (IGRP) | 90 |
| Inter-Gateway Routing Protocol (IGRP) | 100 |
| Open shortest path first (OSPF) | 110 |
| Intermediate System to Intermediate System (IS-IS) | 115 |
| Routing Information Protocol (RIP) | 120 |
| External Gateway Protocol (EGP) | 140 |
| Internal BGP | 200 |
| Unknown/untrusted | 255 |

If multiple routes exist to a destination, and they are discovered by different protocols, the route is selected that has a lower administrative distance. In a diverse internet, routes may be found from multiple sources; so the administrative distance is an effective mechanism for assuring the optimum route.

In addition, it may happen that the more trustworthy route (the primary route) fails. If this situation occurs, the other route (or routes) can be selected on a rational basis. This table shows the Cisco configurations for administrative distances. I have sourced this table from [SLAT99].[1]

## Bandwidth Consumption

When a topology change occurs in the EIGRP routing domain, the router that notices the change check its neighbors to find an alternate route. The query is sent through the domain until a route is found around the failure. During these times, it is conceivable that routing traffic could consume a significant part of the bandwidth in the network. By default, EIGRP will not consume more than 50% of the bandwidth, and this consumption can be further reduced by a configuration command discussed in the next section.

---

[1][SLAT99] Slattery, Terry, and Burton, Bill, *Advanced IP Routing in Cisco Networks,* McGraw-Hill, 1999.

## CONFIGURING THE IGRP ROUTING DOMAIN

To configure an IGRP routing domain, the routers must be configured to perform the tasks summarized in Table 8–3. This section provides an overview of each of these tasks. The specific rules for each of these tasks are documented in the router's user's manuals.

Some of these tasks are straight-forward; others need more explanation. Some are somewhat tertiary to the operation of the routing domain, and others are of primary importance. For each task explained, if I have already discussed the operations pertaining to the task in the chapter, I refer you to that discussion with an identification of the section header title.

- Creating the IGRP routing process: This task is the only mandatory task that must be configured for enabling IGRP.
- Applying offsets to routing metrics: The purpose of this task is to increase incoming and outgoing metrics to routes learned by IGRP.
- Allowing unicast updates for IGRP: IGRP was conceived as a broadcast protocol, and this task allows it to operate with non-broadcast networks. See Appendix D for more information on this topic.
- Defining unequal-cost load balancing: Load balancing is a common practice in data networks to increase throughput and reliability. It entails using more than one path to a destination. This task is used to implement load balancing, and allows the use of up to four

**Table 8–3   IGBP Configuration Tasks**

Creating the IGRP routing process

Applying offsets to routing metrics

Allowing unicast updates for IGRP

Defining unequal-cost load balancing

Controlling traffic distribution

Adjusting the IGRP metric weights

Adjusting timers

Disabling holddown

Enforcing a maximum network diameter (number of hops)

Enabling or disabling split horizon

paths for a given destination network. The term unequal-cost refers to the fact that the paths can have unequal metrics and IGRP will distribute the traffic among the routes.

- Controlling traffic distribution: This task modifies the previous task in that it allows low metric routes to be avoided completely.

- Adjusting the IGRP metric weights: The IGRP metric can be adjusted for each link, if desired. This task allows the network manager to override the IGRP default metrics. This task allows changing of the K1, K2, K3, K4, and K5 variables that are used in the metric computation discussed earlier in this chapter in the section titled Metrics. As a general rule, do not alter these values unless you have a compelling reason to do so.

- Adjusting timers: The timers used with IGRP are similar to those for RIP, and like RIP these timers can be adjusted. I refer you to Chapter 4, and the section titled Timer Adjustments for more information on timers.

- Disabling holddown: Holddown was covered in Chapter 5, see the section title Holddown. If routing loops are not a problem in a network, the operation should be disabled.

- Enforcing a maximum network diameter (number of hops): IGRP defaults to a maximum network diameter of 100 hops. This parameter can be overridden with any value of up to 255 hops. (If your packet is going through more than 100 hops, you have serious problems).

- Enabling or disabling split horizon: I refer you to Chapter 5, see the section titled Disabling Split Horizon. In addition, Appendix D will be helpful.

## CONFIGURING THE EIGRP ROUTING DOMAIN

To configure an EIGRP routing domain, the routers must be configured to perform the tasks summarized in Table 8–4. This section provides an overview of each of these tasks. The specific rules for each of these tasks are documented in the router's user's manuals.

Some of these tasks are straightforward; others need more explanation. Some are somewhat tertiary to the operation of the routing domain, and others are of primary importance. For each task explained, if I have already discussed the operations pertaining to the task in the chapter, I refer you to that discussion with an identification of the section header title.

**Table 8–4    EIGBP Configuration Tasks**

Enabling IP enhanced IGRP

Transitioning from IGRP to Enhanced IGRP

Logging Enhanced IGRP neighbor adjacency changes

Configuring the percentage of link bandwidth used

Adjusting the IP enhanced IGRP metric weights

Applying offsets to routing metrics

Disabling route summarization

Configuring summary aggregate addresses

Configuring Enhanced IGRP route authentication

Configuring Enhanced IGRP protocol-independent parameters

Disabling split horizon

- Enabling IP enhanced IGRP: This (the only mandatory task) creates the EIGRP routing process. It entails associating the EIGRP with an autonomous system and a network number.
- Transitioning from IGRP to Enhanced IGRP: This task is configured for a routing domain in which a transition is being made from IGRP to EIGRP. Transition routers are designated on which both IGRP and EIGRP operations are configured.
- Logging Enhanced IGRP neighbor adjacency changes: This task is used to monitor the stability of the routing system. It logs neighbor adjacency changes.
- Configuring the percentage of link bandwidth used: Cisco manuals state that EIGRP consumes a maximum of 50% of a link's bandwidth. This task changes the link level of bandwidth utilization. This topic is discussed in this chapter, see the section titled Bandwidth Consumption.
- Adjusting the IP enhanced IGRP metric weights: This task allows the network manager to adjust the K1, K2, K3, K4, and K5 variables that are used in the metric computation discussed earlier in this chapter in the section titled Metrics. As stated earlier, do not alter these values unless you have a compelling reason to do so (and know the consequences).
- Applying offsets to routing metrics: This task increases incoming and outgoing metrics to routes learned by EIGRP, and provides a local mechanism for increasing a metric.

- Disabling route summarization: This task disables a default operation of summarizing subnet routes into network routes.
- Configuring summary aggregate addresses: This task is used to aggregate addresses on a specified interface, so if there are more specific routes in the routing table, they will be advertised with the aggregated address.
- Configuring Enhanced IGRP route authentication: EIGRP supports MD5 authentication. In order to use MD5, the keys must be set up, and identified, and a lifetime must be stipulated for a set of keys on a "chain." Each key must be identified with a key ID (with this key stored locally). The key ID (and the interface associated with the key) uniquely identifies the specific authentication algorithm and the MD5 key in use.
- Configuring Enhanced IGRP protocol-independent parameters: I refer you to Chapter 5, see the section titled Disabling Split Horizon. In addition, Appendix D will be helpful.

## SUMMARY

The IGRP and the EIGRP are routing protocols developed by Cisco. IGRP is based on RIP, and was developed to supplant or enhance the RIP operations. Both IGRP and EGRIP offer substantial advantages over RIP. EIGRP has replaced IGRP in many systems.

## FOLLOW-UP READING

Most routing protocol books have information on Cisco's routing protocols. For the reader who wishes to delve into detail about the Cisco protocols and how to configure them, you should consult your vendor's user manuals. If you do not have access to these manuals, I recommend a book from the Cisco IOS Reference Library titled: *Cisco IOS Solutions for Network Protocols, Volume I: IP,* by Cisco Press (available from Cisco or Macmillian Technical Publishing).

This text has a good explanation of the Cisco protocols, and is an overall excellent book on routing protocols. It was cited in earlier chapters: *Advanced IP Routing in Cisco Networks,* by Terry Slattery, and Bill Burton, McGraw-Hill, 1999.

# 9

# PNNI

## INTRODUCTION

This chapter examines the Private Network-Network Interface (PNNI), a protocol published by the ATM Forum. We learn the reason PNNI was developed as well as the PNNI operations. Two aspects of PNNI are described. One deals with route advertising and the other deals with signaling. The former is the main focus of this chapter since this book concentrates on routing protocols.

PNNI is a book unto itself (383 pages). The approach in this chapter is to provide an overview of the protocol, as defined in the ATM Forum's specification [ATMF96],[1] and recommend you obtain this material if you are going to implement and/or maintain a PNNI routing domain.

Other chapters in this book devoted to a specific routing protocol include a section on configuration parameters. This chapter does not have this section, because PNNI is not yet defined for implementations on routers.

---

[1][ATMF96]. Private Network-Network Interface Specification Version 1.0 (PNNI 1.0), ATM Forum Technical Committee document number af-pnni-0055.000, March, 1996.

## RATIONALE FOR PNNI

One can reasonably ask why yet another set of specifications is required to define another protocol in the ATM environment. Indeed, for the ATM network manager, or the user of the ATM equipment, the proliferation of new specifications creates more complexity in a network.

But PNNI is published for a very good reason. The ITU-T is the "authoritative" standards body for ATM, but does not concern itself with the operations of private networks. (From the ITU-T perspective, the Internet is considered to be a private network.) Additionally, the ITU-T does not concern itself with the distribution of routing information, route discovery nor topology analysis (except for some of the newer SS7 protocols). These operations have been left to the implementation of individual telecommunications administrations.

This approach is not the case with PNNI. The PNNI philosophy is that these important considerations cannot be left to individual implementations. For full internetworking to occur between ATM-based switches, there must be standards involved to define how addressing and routing information is distributed between switches in an ATM network.

As mentioned, PNNI consists of two parts. The first part defines a protocol to exchange routing information for route discovery. It defines the operations for the distribution of topology and routing information between ATM switches. It allows the switches to compute paths through a routing domain. PNNI will automatically configure the routing domain if the routing domain address structure reflects the domain topology.

### The Power of PNNI

A key concept of PNNI is that the ATM/PNNI nodes must not only know about routing addresses, and have the ability to make routing decisions on these addresses, they must also be able to support a call request from a network user based on that user's ATM quality of service requirements, such as high peak cell rate, minimum cell burst size, and so on. This aspect of PNNI goes far beyond any of the other routing protocols we have discussed in this book.

## THE PNNI REFERENCE MODEL

Figure 9–1 illustrates the reference model for PNNI. On the network side, it is divided into three major areas of cell stream, NNI signaling, and the topology protocol. On the user side, it is divided into the cell

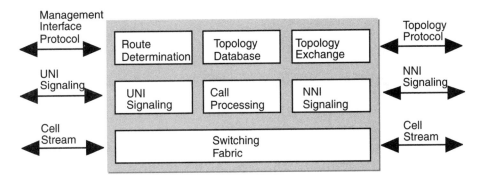

**Figure 9–1    The PNNI Reference Model**

stream, UNI signaling, and the management interface protocol. These operations are further divided into the components shown in the figure. The switching fabric is based on a cell technology switching elements. The call processing modules and signaling modules are based on the Q Series specifications, and the topology exchange, topology database, and route determination functions are based on shortest path route discovery technology, the subject of this chapter.

The PNNI protocol stack is depicted in Figure 9–2. It is almost identical to the NNI signaling stack defined by other ATM standards. One difference pertains to the PNNI call control and PNNI protocol control.

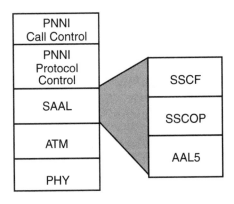

Where:

AAL       ATM adaptation layer
SAAL      Signaling ATM adaptation layer
SSCF      Service specific coordination function
SSCOP     Service specific connection oriented protocol

**Figure 9–2    The PNNI Protocol Stack**

The call control layer is responsible for processing the signaling packets. It operates with state machines for the incoming and outgoing calls. The PNNI protocol control layer rests below the call control layer and thus provides services to call control, such a routes for the ATM connections. The layers below these two layers are based on the ITU-T Q.2xxx specifications.

## THE SIGNALING ATM ADAPTATION LAYER (SAAL)

The overall functions of the SAAL can be summarized as follows. SAAL is responsible for the correct transfer of data on a point-to-point ATM connection. One of its primary functions is to relieve the user from any concern for data errors, loss, duplications, or insertions that may occur on the link.

SAAL provides a link monitoring service and "proves" that links are stable and error-free enough to be used (with alignment procedures that deal with testing the link). It can also take a link out of service if it becomes unreliable.

SAAL also provides for flow control procedures and employs mechanisms to insure that two ATM nodes do not create congestion problems with each other.

The sublayers of SAAL contribute to these overall functions. Let us take a brief look at them, before we move to the main part of the chapter.

### Functions of Service Specific Coordination Function (SSCF)

SSCF acts as a "go-between" for PNNI protocol control and the service specific connection oriented protocol (SSCOP). As such, it maps primitives from PNNI protocol control to the required SSCOP signals and vice versa. In essence, it passes signals back-and-forth between SSCOP and PNNI protocol control. As such, it does not send much information (packets) to its peer entity in the receiving node, but relies on SSCOP to convey its information in the SSCOP packets. Notwithstanding, it has other responsibilities as well. They are summarized here:

*Flow control:* SSCF notifies the user about levels of congestion (or if no congestion exists) in order to prevent cell loss. It also regulates its flow of packets to the lower layers to prevent congestion at the other end.

*Link status:* SSCF maintains information (local state variables) about the status of the link, such as "aligned ready," "out of service," etc.

Using this information, it may generate primitives to SSCOP to aid in managing the link.

*Alignment procedures:* SSCF maintains the information (state variables) about all the alignment procedures that are taking place when a link is brought into service or taken out of service.

### Functions of SSCOP

Why is another lower layer protocol needed to support a routing protocol? The answer is that older protocols, while well-designed and powerful in their functions, contain some operations and fields that are not needed in an ATM-based system. Some of the older link protocols have also been found to be deficient in how they handle certain sequencing, flow control, and acknowledgment operations on the signaling link. Therefore, the ATM standards groups decided that a new protocol was needed.

SSCOP keeps all PNNI packets in sequential order that flow across the link, and it also provides for retransmission of erred traffic. To make certain the communicating nodes are operational, each node executes a "keep alive" procedure with its neighbor node. SSCOP also contains a procedure that allows the local user to look at the SSCOP queue for purposes of determining the status of messages. The SSCOP also provides a number of status reporting operations.

## ATM ADDRESSES

PNNI uses the 20-octet ATM address for route advertising and address aggregation. The address format is shown in Figure 9–3. This address can have prefixes applied to it, and the prefix can vary in length, depending upon the network configuration.

The specific rules for using the initial domain part (IDP) and the domain specific part (DSP) fields are defined in the basic ATM standards, and are not pertinent to our analysis. Nor are the other fields; the end

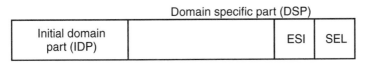

**Figure 9–3   The ATM Address Format for PNNI**

system identifier (ESI) is required, and the selector (SEL) is not used by PNNI. It has local significance only.

A 19-octet address is very large (152 bits), but once again, prefixes can be used, and actual summaries of routes in PNNI should be shorter. Later discussions in this chapter expand the discussion on address prefixes.

## THE PHYSICAL NETWORK

PNNI operates over an ATM network, as shown in Figure 9–4. This topology is a network of lowest-level nodes in which data passes through these nodes to user nodes, called end systems. The end systems are not shown in this figure. The circles symbolize ATM nodes and the lines between the nodes symbolize communications links. End systems are identified by the 19 most significant octets of the ATM end system address, so as stated earlier, the selector octet is not used by PNNI.

PNNI uses the term port to describe the interface on the link at the node. The links, such as DS3 or SDH/SONET links must be duplex (supporting two-way simultaneous transmissions), but the bidirectional traffic flow may be different in each direction, thereby supporting asymmetrical bandwidth. Each physical link is identifed by two sets of parameters containing a port ID, and a node ID.

PNNI supports alternate routing, thus allowing the diversion of traffic to a new path if an attempt to set up a connection to a previously

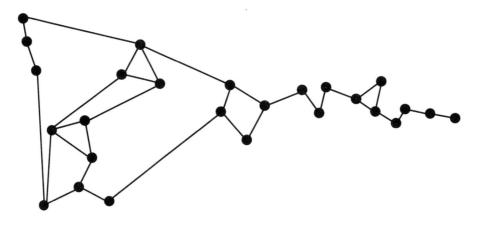

● Where circles are switches and lines are communications links

**Figure 9–4   The PNNI Physical Network**

selected path fails. The routing is performed with a designated transit list (DTL). This list contains a list of nodes and (as an option) link IDs that specify the complete path through the physical network (the routing domain) between the end systems.

Each link in the PNNI routing domain is associated with a link attribute, a value that is similar to the term link metric we have used in previous chapters. However PNNI makes a distinction between link attribute and link metric. The link attribute is a parameter that is considered *individually* to determine whether a specific link is desirable for carrying a connection. The link metric is a parameter that represents a combination of all the links in the end-to-end path, and is used to determine whether the path is desirable for the connection.

PNNI goes a step farther in determining a route. It also uses nodal attributes and nodal metrics. The nodal attribute is a parameter that is considered *individually* to determine if a node is desirable for carrying a connection. The nodal metric is a combination of all the nodes in the end-to-end path, and is used to determine whether the path is desirable for the connection.

Like other routing protocols, PNNI performs route computations to determine the routes through the routing domain. It might use the Dijkstra algorithm for this computation.

## PNNI HIERARCHY AND THE LOWEST HIERARCHICAL LEVEL

The PNNI architecture is based on a hierarchical structure. Nodes are associated with a level in a hierarchy and nodes that belong to the same hierarchy are in the same peer group. An example of the PNNI hierarchy is provided in Figure 9–5. The routing hierarchy is now divided into two hierarchies; that is, peer groups. For this example, the two groups are called peer group A and peer group B.

The peer group is a set of nodes that are grouped together to create a routing hierarchy. And here, we introduce the concepts of a logical node, a logical group node, and a logical link. First, a logical group node is an abstraction of a peer group as a single point for one level of a PNNI routing hierarchy. The term logical node is the lowest-level node and is used in PNNI synonymously with logical group node.

A logical link is an abstraction of the connection between two logical nodes. The logical link includes the physical links between the logical nodes, as well as the ATM virtual path connections.

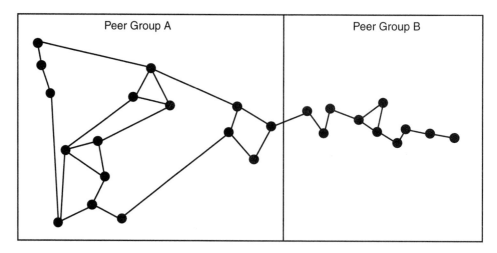

**Figure 9–5   The Lowest Hierarchical Level and Two Peer Groups**

## THE HIERARCHY IN MORE DETAIL

All the nodes in the PNNI routing domain store *topology state parameters* (which are known as link state parameters in other route discovery protocols). This information is used in making routing decisions and also is used to accumulate the values to determine the shortest path based on the link metrics. Of course, certain types of topology state information such as delay and bandwidth may change. On the other hand, other information such as security may remain static. PNNI makes no distinction between dynamic or static parameters when it advertises routes between nodes.

I explained earlier that the nodes at the same hierarchical level are known as a peer group. All nodes in a peer group exchange topology information with each other. Topology information is based on these concepts:

- Topology state parameter: A link parameter or a nodal parameter.
- Topology attribute: A link attribute or a nodal attribute.
- Topology database: A database that describes the complete PNNI routing domain.
- Topology aggregation: Summarizing and compressing lower level domain topology information for advertisement to the next higher level domain.

As shown in Figure 9–6, a peer group may represent a lower level peer group, or stated another way, lower peer groups can be aggregated to a higher peer group. The lower level peer group is called a child peer group, and the upper level group is called a parent peer group. The parent node is a logical group node that represents the containing peer group of a specific node at the next level of the PNNI routing hierarchy.

Notice the relationship of the physical topology in Figures 9–4 and 9–5 to the physical and logical topologies in Figure 9–6, using peer group A as the example.

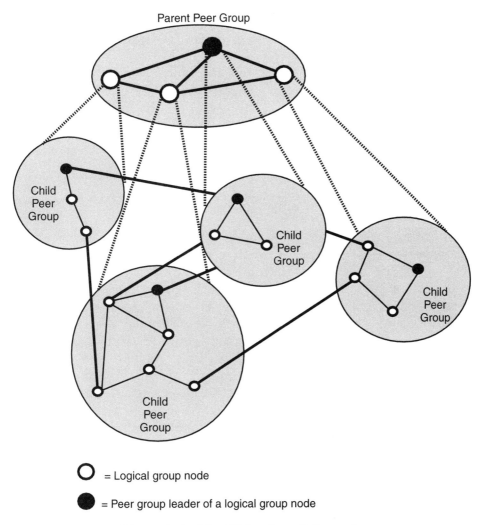

Parent Peer Group

Child Peer Group

Child Peer Group

Child Peer Group

Child Peer Group

○ = Logical group node

● = Peer group leader of a logical group node

**Figure 9–6   The Higher Level Hierarchy**

A group of nodes can be represented by one single node, which we learned earlier is called a logical node. Each child peer group is associated with (represented by) a logical group node inside the parent peer group. This relationship means that a logical group node represents a lower level peer group (the entire peer group). This relationship is depicted in Figure 9–6 with the dashed lines.

Within the peer group, one logical group node is elected to be a peer group leader. This entity is responsible for route advertisements, and topology aggregation for all the nodes in the peer group. The representation of the peer group leader is made available in the parent node.

Another concept needs to be emphasized. The logical node is an abstract representation of a group of physical nodes. Therefore, the aggregated topology information associated with this logical node is actually a representation of the connectivity of the physical nodes.

Figure 9–6 also shows the border node. This node is a logical node in a specified peer group, and is so defined if it has at least one attachment to another peer group across a peer group boundary. No restriction is placed on how many border nodes are configured in a PNNI network.

## METRIC AGGREGATION

Modern routing technology is based on a number of criteria called type of service factors (TOS), an Internet term for quality of service factors (QOS), an OSI term. These factors are defined by the network administrators and users and may include criteria such as delay, throughput, security needs, etc. The path through an internet is chosen based on the ability of the routers and networks to meet a required service.

This technique is also called link state routing, because the TOS values are applied to each communication link in the internet. Like other routing protocols, link metric is defined as the sum of a link state parameter (based on TOS) along a given path from a source address to a destination address. One of the purposes of PNNI is to provide means to advertise these metrics in order for a node to choose a "best" path (known as the shortest path) between two nodes. The length of the shortest path between the nodes is known as the distance between the nodes.

In typical large networks, more than one path will be available from one node to another. Moreover, the various combinations of paths in a network may make the advertisements of all possibilities an onerous task. However, if a node in the network (say, a PNNI logical group node) somehow aggregates these many metrics to a shorter summary, and then advertises this summary, the task becomes feasible.

However, PNNI metric aggregation pays a price for this usefulness. In many situations, it will not lead to the optimum route. In these systems, one must weigh the amount of aggregation vs. the accuracy (and usefulness) of the aggregation.

To illustrate this point, consider Figure 9–7, which is extracted from the topology from the previous figures. Four nodes are connected to each other with four physical links. I change the topology in the bottom part of the figure to a meshed topology to make some points regarding metric ag-

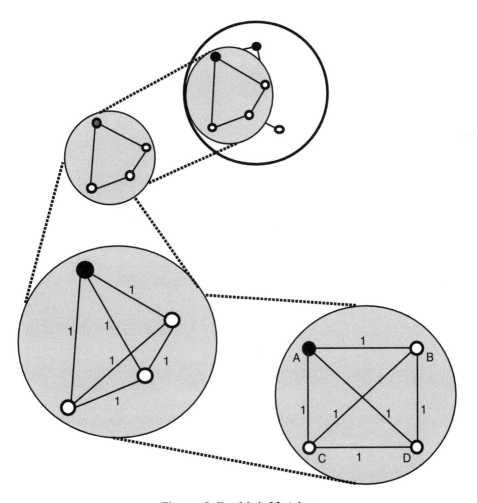

**Figure 9–7  Link Metrics**

gregation. Nodes A, B, C, and D are now fully connected with six links.[2] Link state parameters of 1 are assigned to each link for this simple example.

### Metric Aggregation and the Stretch Factor

The metrics for the fully-meshed 6-links network in Figure 9–8(a) is aggregated to a 5-links network in Figure 9–8(b). The dashed lines in these figures indicate the links have been eliminated from the network logical topology. Stated another way, they have been aggregated out of the graph.

A key goal in metric aggregation is to create a fully-connected subgraph that has small *stretch factor*. The stretch factor is the maximum ratio of the distance in the subgraph to the distance in the original graph. For the 5-links subgraph, the stretch factor is 2, and 5 links are used to maintain the logical full-mesh topology. The compromise from the original graph is that the distance between B and C is now 2, but the aggregation translates to fewer variables in an advertisement. Furthermore, due to costs, it may be preferable not to install a physical link between B and C. Let's assume the links are T1 channels, for example. These links are expensive to lease, and the nature and amount of traffic between B and C may not warrant the cost of the T1 link.

To continue this example, Figure 9–8(c) shows another possibility for aggregating the metrics for this network. The 3-links aggregation still provides full connectivity, with the stretch factor remaining at 2. The compromise is that the distances between nodes A to C, and B to C are now 2. Once again, this compromise may or may not be desirable, depending upon the nature of traffic between these nodes, and the costs to provide direct links between them.

PNNI does not tell the network manager how to make the decisions on the physical topology, but it does provide a tool for advertising the topology, and to use the network effectively.

---

[2]This analysis is based on several papers on the subject. I recommend for the reader who wishes more details: (1) David Peleg and Alejandro A. Schaffer, "Graph Spanners," *Journal of Graph Theory,* Vol. 13, No. 1, 1989. (2) Numerous ATM Forum working papers. See ATM Forum Contributions 94–0606, 95–0153, 94–0449. (3) Whay C. Lee (whay@prospero.dev.cdx.mot.com) is a noted expert in this field, and any of his papers are recommended. Mr. Lee contributed to most of the ATM papers, and (4) Whay C. Lee, "Topology Aggregation for Hierarchical Routing in ATM Networks," *Computer Communication Review,* Vol. 25, Number 2, April, 1995.

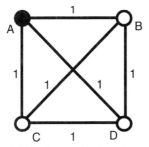

(a) Fully meshed nodes

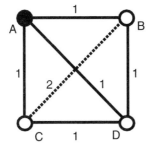

(b) Logically meshed with 5 links & stretch factor = 2

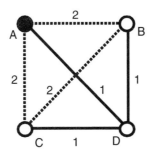

(c) Logically meshed with 2 links & stretch factor = 2

**Figure 9–8     Metric Aggregation**

In ATM and other networks, it is likely that the link attributes may vary from node to node. Even if the links are the same (for example, all OC-48 links), their utilization may vary, with some links carrying more traffic than others. This situation gives rise to different TOS values with regard to delay and throughput.

Figure 9–9 shows examples of metric aggregation with varying link attributes. Figure 9–9(a) shows a fully-meshed network. Figure 9–9(b)

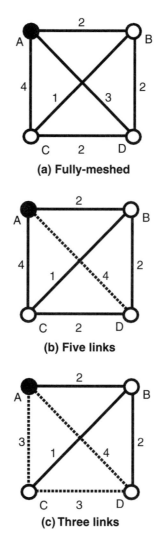

**Figure 9–9    Metric Aggregation with Varying Link Attributes**

shows a 5-link aggregation. Figure 9–9(c) shows a minimum spanning tree with a 3-link aggregation.

This example illustrates that shorter paths may be available between physically adjacent nodes through nonadjacent nodes. The direct, physical path between nodes A and C is 4, yet the aggregated path distance between A and C, through B is 3. This situation can occur if (as examples) (a) node A's link to C is congested, (b) the link is operating at a low bit-rate, (c) the metric represents a high cost in relation to the error rate on the link, and so on. Another example in Figure 9–9(c) is the link aggregation between C and D of 3. Traffic between these nodes goes through B, and this might make sense if a physical link between C and D is too costly, not utilized enough, etc.

## PNNI TOPOLOGY STATE ELEMENTS (PTSEs)

Routing exchange information is advertised in a PNNI system by each node flooding PNNI topology state elements (PTSEs) within a designated part of the overall network (the routing domain), which (one more time) is called a peer group. Figure 9–10 illustrates these concepts. The information includes the node identity, and the status of the node's links to its neighbors.

This information is used to keep a topology database updated at each node in the peer group. In effect, the topology database is a reflection of the information in the PTSEs and contains all the needed information to calculate a route from any node in the peer group to any other node. The PTSEs contain (a) link state parameters (also called topology state parameters), and (b) nodal state parameters. The former describes

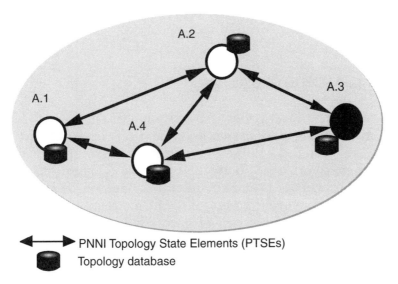

PNNI Topology State Elements (PTSEs)
Topology database

**Figure 9–10   Exchanging Information within a Peer Group (PG)**

the state of each link at a node; the latter describes the state and characteristics of the node.

Remember that the topology state parameters are classified as follows (and they may be static or dynamic; PNNI does not care):

- *Attribute:* A single value, considered individually when making a routing decision (for example, link failure attribute that causes a link not to be selected for a route).
- *Metric:* An accumulation of values along a path (for example, a delay metric on each link that is added-up for the end-to-end path.

The PTSEs are transmitted in a PNNI topology state packet (PTSP), and they must be acknowledged by the receiving node. Upon receiving a PTSP, a node examines its contents and performs the following actions:

- If the PTSE is (a) new or (b) more recent than the current copy that is in the topology database, it is placed in the database.
- This PTSE is sent out on all the node's links except the link from which the information was received.

These operations are an ongoing activity, and a PTSE is sent whenever something changes, or on a periodic basis. At the topology database, entries are removed if they are not refreshed within a specific period. A node can only resend a PTSE that it originated.

## HORIZONTAL AND OUTSIDE LINKS

Between lowest level nodes, connections are made of PNNI *logical links,* which consist of the physical links and ATM virtual path connections (VPCs). Figure 9–11 shows two aspects of these links: logical links inside a peer group are called horizontal links, and logical links that connect two peer groups are called outside links. Links between two lowest level nodes in the same peer group cannot be aggregated. For example, if two physical links connect a pair of lowest level nodes they are represented by two separate logical links.

When a logical link is set up and becomes operational, the neighbor nodes exchange information though a well known VCC (virtual channel connection). This VCC is called a PNNI routing control channel (RCC). A special protocol called the Hello protocol, sends Hello packets across the

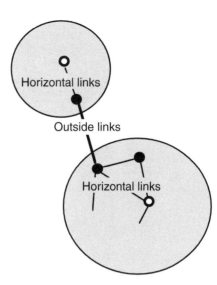

**Figure 9–11    Horizontal Links and Outside Links**

RCC to keep neighbor nodes aware of each other's existence and the state of their communications channels. The PNNI Hello protocol allows a node to determine if it belongs or does not belong to a peer group.

## THE PNNI HIERARCHY IN MORE DETAIL

We have taken a broad overview of PNNI so far; this section delves into more detail. The alphanumerics in Figure 9–12 represent addresses. They are drawn in place of specific addresses for ease of explanation. The highest PNNI hierarchy in this figure is peer group A identified with the address of A. The nodes inside the group are identified as A1, A4, etc., and they are connected with logical links. Within each peer group is a peer group leader whose responsibility is to receive topology information from all nodes in the group and advertise this information to other groups.

The information that is advertised is "filtered" in that summary information is given to the other groups. This idea is central to the design philosophy behind PNNI, and for that matter all the newer routing protocols. The hierarchy concept obviates a flat network topology shown in Figure 9–4. A flat network requires each switching node to maintain a database of the entire topology of a full routing domain. This approach is

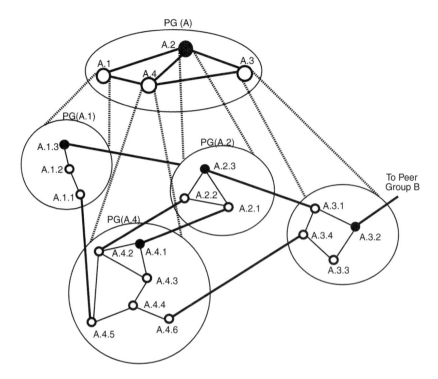

**Figure 9–12    The PNNI Hierarchy**

not feasible for large internets. Thus, the PNNI routing hierarchy is designed to scale well for large internets.

The next level of the PNNI hierarchy is shown with peer groups A.1,
A.2, and so on. Within these peer groups are other nodes labeled as A.1.3,
A.4.1, etc. PNNI establishes rules about how messages can be sent up
and down the hierarchy based on the functions of the nodes in a peer
group. Once again, this concept of packet containment places restrictions
on how many route advertisements can be sent between nodes.

There is no database exchange across outside links. The nodes on
these links exchange Hello packets to stay aware of each other, but they
do not exchange routing information. The Hello packets include information about their respective higher level peer groups, and the logical group
nodes that represent them in these peer groups. For example, in Figure
9–12, nodes A.4.6 and A.3.4 are border nodes because the are connected
to each other, and they belong in different peer groups. These nodes identify that they have peer group A in common.

## THE ESSENCE OF PNNI

Using Figure 9–12, we can now see how PNNI operates.
Feeding information up the hierarchy:

- The logical group node represents the entire underlying peer group. For example, A.4 represents A.4.1 through A.4.6.
- A.4 receives complete topology state information from all these nodes, principally dealing with topology aggregation and reachability.

Feeding information down the hierarchy:

- Each logical group node (say A.4) feeds information down to its underlying peer group.
- This information allows nodes (A.4.1 through A.4.6) in the lower peer groups to reach all destinations in the PNNI routing domain.

Which translates to:

- Each node knows the complete topology within its peer group, as well as complete (yet summarized) information of the higher level parent peer group.
- At the same time, PNNI has also achieved link aggregation by representing some of the links between the same two peer groups by a single logical link. For example in Figure 9–12, a single logical link between A.2 and A.4 is the aggregation of the two links: (a) A.2.1 – A.4.1, and (b) A.2.2 – A.4.2).

## EXAMPLES OF PNNI ROUTE AND ADDRESS SUMMARIZATION OPERATIONS

In this section, we see how PNNI can scale to large networks by reducing the amount of routing information that needs to be distributed in a PNNI routing domain. This example is from [ATMF96], section 3.5. You should be familiar with address prefixes when you read this material (see Appendix B).

Previous figures have been redrawn as shown in Figure 9–13. PG (A.2) is the focus of attention. The nodes A.2.1, A.2.2, and A.2.3 have end

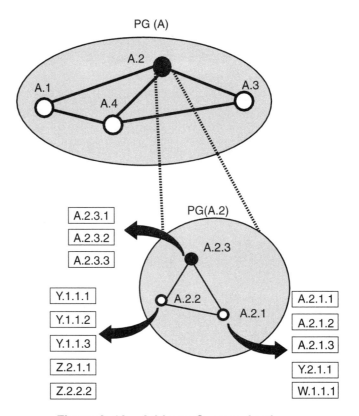

**Figure 9–13    Address Summarization**

systems attached to them. The end systems are shown by their ATM address. For example, end system A.2.3.1 is an end system on node A.3.2. Addresses beginning with Y and W belong to other domains.

The PNNI specification uses the following convention to represent an address prefix. If A.2.2.1 represents an address, then P<A.2.2>, and P<A.2>, and P<A> represent shorter prefixes for that address.

**Table 9–1    Summary Address Configuration for PG A.2 Nodes**

| Summary Addresses at A.2.1 | Summary Addresses at A.2.2 | Summary Addresses at A.2.3 |
| --- | --- | --- |
| P<A.2.1> | P<Y.1> | P<A.2.3> |
| P<Y.2> | P<Z.2> | |

**Table 9–2    Summary Address Configuration LGN A.2**

P<A.2>

P<Y>

Table 9–1 provides an example of how this PNNI routing domain could be configured. This configuration for the summary addresses is not the only possibility. For example, at node A.2.2, the prefix P<Y.1.1> could be used instead of P<Y.1>, because this longer prefix would still aggregate the addresses correctly. Also, at node A.2.1, the address of W.1.1.1 is classified as a foreign address, and does not match any of the summary address entries at node A.2.1. As you can see, this table is the address summarization table, but the absence of W.1.1.1 in the table does not mean node A.2.2 will not advertise this address. This table is a summary address table; it is not a routing table, which is shown shortly.

LGN A.2 also needs a list of summary addresses, and Table 9–2 shows some possibilities. There are alternatives. While P<A.2> is an appropriate summary address, P<Y.1> and P<Y.2> can be summarized further to P<Y>. P<Z.2> is not in this table for reasons explained shortly.

Table 9–3 shows part of the routing tables that reflect the address prefixes advertised by the nodes in peer group A.2. Notice that the foreign addresses (those not in the peer group) are indeed advertised; that is, address prefix P<W.1.1.1>.

After PNNI has created its routing tables, as seen in the example in Table 9–3, it operates like any other address aggregation protocol. For example, LGN A.2 summarizes every reachable prefix advertised in peer group A.2. When it receives advertisements from say, nodes A.2.1 (for prefix A.2.1), and A.2.3 (for prefix A.2.3), it does not redistribute both of these prefixes. Instead it advertises prefix A.2. The prefixes that are advertised by LGN A.2 are shown in Table 9–4.

**Table 9–3    Advertised Reachable Prefixes by PG A.2 Nodes**

| Flooded by A.2.1 | Flooded by A.2.2 | Flooded by A.2.3 |
|---|---|---|
| P<A.2.1> | P<A.2.2> | P<A.2.3> |
| P<Y.2> | P<Y.1> | |
| P<W.1.1.1> | P<Z.2> | |

Table 9–4    Advertised Reachable Prefixes by LGN A.2

P<A.2>

P<Y>

P<Z.2>

P<W.1.1.1>

## PNNI SIGNALING OPERATIONS

PNNI signaling was introduced earlier with a brief description of its functions. The remainder of this chapter is devoted to this subject.[3] Figure 9–14 shows the topology and model for the PNNI signaling interfaces. A calling user is called the *preceding side* and the called user is called the *succeeding side*. PNNI uses the term *forward direction* to connote the calling user to called user and the term *backward direction* to connote the called user to the calling user. In addition, the network that originates the call from the user is called the *preceding network,* and the network that receives the call is called the *succeeding network.*

The basic messages for PNNI signaling are derived from Q.2931 and Table 9–5 lists these messages and their major functions. In turn, the Q.2931 messages are based on the ISDN Q.931 messages.

PNNI uses a subset of the Q.2931 message set. The call establishment messages are used to set up the call, and the call clearing messages are used to tear down the call. The miscellaneous messages are used to check the status of connection (with the STATUS ENQUIRY and STATUS messages), and to provide more information about a call (with the NOTIFY message).

The flow of the messages use the same procedures as the conventional Q.2931 and Q.931 operations.

## EXAMPLES OF PNNI SIGNALING

Figure 9–15 shows how PNNI signaling is used to set up and tear down a connection. PNNI signaling takes advantage of the information

---

[3]An entire book in this series is devoted to the subject of ATM-based signaling. See *ATM,* volume II in this series.

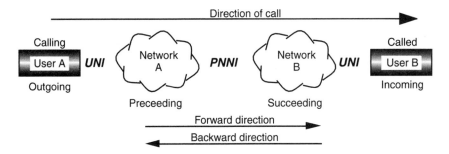

**Figure 9–14    The PNNI Interface and Associated Terms**

gathered in the routing operations explained in the first part of this chapter. It knows of an efficient route from the calling to the called party.

The events in Figure 9–15 are straightforward. The SETUP message is relayed in the forward direction from user A (the preceding user) across three networks to user B (the succeeding user). Each recipient network of this message must return a CALL PROCEEDING message to inform the sending network that the SETUP message has been accepted and that the call is indeed proceeding. Upon user B accepting the connection, it sends the CONNECT message in the backward direction to its network, and this message is relayed back to the calling user. Either party can release the call, as shown at the bottom of the figure.

**Table 9–2    The PNNI Signaling Messages**

| Message | Function |
|---------|----------|
| **Call establishment** | |
| SETUP | Initiate the call establishment |
| CALL PROCEEDING | Call establishment has begun |
| CONNECT | Call has been accepted |
| ALERTING | Called party has been alerted |
| **Call clearing** | |
| RELEASE | Initiate call clearing |
| RELEASE COMPLETE | Call has been cleared |
| **Miscellaneous** | |
| STATUS ENQUIRY (SE) | Sent to solicit a status message |
| STATUS (S) | Sent in response to SE or to report error |
| NOTIFY | Sent to provide additional information about a call |

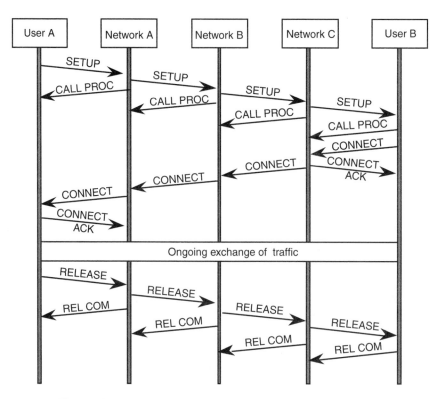

**Figure 9–15    PNNI Connection Set Up and Tear Down**

## DESIGNATED TRANSIT LISTS (DTLs)

During the call setup operations shown in Figure 9–15, PNNI signaling can request a route from PNNI routing. This information is provided in a designated transit list (DTL). This list consists of the complete path across a peer group, and is provided by the DTL originator or an entry border router node to a peer group. More than one DTL can be used to set up a connection from one party to another, which leads to the possibility of alternate routing discussed next.

## CRANKBACK AND ALTERNATE ROUTING

The DTL may not be the most accurate information because of the changing conditions in the routing domain. Consequently, a call being processed according to the DTL information may be blocked. When this situation occurs, the call is cranked back to the creator of the DTL, with an indication of the problem. This node can then choose an alternative path for the call, or may crank back the call further. The alternate path must avoid the paths in the original call of course, and must obey all received higher-level DTLs, in order to support the address aggregation tables in the routing domain.

## SUMMARY

PNNI is an ATM-based protocol. It has the ability to make routing decisions on ATM addresses, and is able to support a call request from a network user, based on that user's ATM quality of service requirements, such as high peak cell rate, and minimum cell burst size. This aspect of PNNI makes it unique among routing protocols.

PNNI is also used for signaling and defines the procedures to establish point-to-point or point-to-multipoint connections through an ATM network. The PNNI signaling operations are quite similar to many of the other protocols, because they are based on the ITU-T Q.2931 signaling specification.

Thus far, PNNI has not seen extensive use in the industry, but then ATM is still finding its way into the marketplace. Time will tell if PINNI becomes as widely used as other routing protocols, such as RIP, OSPF, and BGP.

## FOLLOW-UP READING

There is not a lot of information on PNNI. I refer you to the footnotes in this chapter for some excellent papers on the subject. As I have said before, there is no substitute for reading the actual specification, and for PNNI (383 pages), set aside a lot of time.

# Appendix A

## Layered Protocols

## THE OSI LAYERED MODEL

The Open Systems Interconnection (OSI) Model was developed by several standards organizations and is now a widely used model for the design and implementation of computer networks. The ITU-T and the ISO are the two organizations that have led the effort. The OSI Model has been in development for about ten years. The ITU-T publishes its OSI Model specifications in the X.200–X.290 Recommendations. The X.200 documents contain slightly over 1100 pages. The ISO publishes its OSI Model in several documents, but does not use a common numbering scheme.

The Model is organized into seven layers, shown in Figure A–1. Each layer contains several to many protocols and are invoked based on the specific needs of the user. Each protocol in a layer need not be invoked and the OSI Model provides a means for two users to negotiate the specific protocols that are desired for the session between the users.

### Functions of the Layers

The lowest layer in the model is called the *physical layer*. The functions within the layer are responsible for activating, maintaining, and deactivating a physical circuit between a DTE and a DCE and the communicating DCEs. This layer defines the type of physical signals (electri-

| Application |
| Presentation |
| Session |
| Transport |
| Network |
| Data Link |
| Physical |

**Figure A–1    The OSI Layered Model**

cal, optical, etc.), as well as the type of media (wires, coaxial cable, satellite, etc.).

Many standards are published for the physical layer; for example EIA-232-D, V.22bis and V.35 are physical level protocols.

Physical level protocols are also called physical level interfaces. Either term is acceptable.

The *data link layer* is responsible for the transfer of data across one communications link. It delimits the flow of bits from the physical layer. It also provides for the identity of the bits. It usually ensures that the data arrives safely at the receiving DTE. It often provides for flow control to ensure that the DTE does not become overburdened with too much data at any one time. One of its most important functions is to provide for the detection of transmission errors and provide mechanisms to recover from lost, duplicated, or erroneous data.

Many data link layer protocols exist in the industry, and most vendors market their own proprietary products. However, the trend is toward standardized data link protocols.

Common examples of data link control (DLC) protocols are high level data link control (HDLC), published by the ISO; synchronous data link control (SDLC), used by IBM; binary synchronous control (BSC), used by some vendors, but largely replaced by HDLC.

The *network layer* specifies the network/user interface of the user into a network, as well as the interface of two DTEs with each other through a network. It allows users to negotiate options with the network and each other. For example, the negotiation of throughput, delay (response time), and acceptable error rates are common negotiations.

The network layer also defines switching/routing procedures within a network. It also includes the routing conventions to transfer traffic between networks—a term called internetworking.

Common network layer protocols at this layer are X.25 (a network interface standard), and the connectionless network protocol (CLNP), which provides internetworking operations. CLNP is an OSI standard that was designed based on the widely used Internet Protocol (IP). IP is not part of the OSI Model.

While this layer does include switching/routing operations, many networks use proprietary solutions to this task.

SNA's Path Control is another example of a network layer protocol, although this SNA layer also supports some functions found in the OSI transport layer.

The *transport layer* provides the interface between the data communications network and the upper three layers (generally part of the user's system). This layer gives the user options in obtaining certain levels of quality (and cost) from the network itself (i.e., the network layer). It is designed to keep the user isolated from some of the physical and functional aspects of the network.

It provides for the end-to-end accountability across more than one data link. It also is responsible for end-to-end integrity of users' data in internetworking operations. Therefore, it is a vital layer if a user sends traffic to another user on a different network.

Until the last few years, this layer was implemented in vendors' proprietary products, such as SNA's Transmission Control Layer. Today, the Transmission Control Protocol (TCP), sponsored by the Internet, is a widely used standard. TCP is not part of the OSI Model. Its counterpart in OSI is called the Transport Protocol-Class 4.

The *session layer* serves as a user interface into the transport layer and is responsible for managing an end user application program's exchange of data with another end user application (for example, two COBOL programs).

The layer provides for an organized means to exchange data between user applications, such as simultaneous transmission, alternate transmission, checkpoint procedures, and resynchronization of user data flow between user applications. The users can select the type of synchronization and control needed from the layer.

Until the past few years, this layer was not standardized and each vendor used proprietary approaches to achieving these functions. For example, SNA's Data Flow Control Layer contains session layer functions. The OSI now includes this layer in its architecture.

The *presentation layer* provides services dealing with the syntax of data; that is, the representation of data. It is not concerned with the meaning or semantics of the data. Its principal role is to accept data types (character, integer) from the application layer and then negotiate with its peer layer as to the syntax representation (such as ASCII). The layer consists of many tables of syntax (teletype, ASCII, Videotex, etc.).

This layer also contains a language called Abstract Syntax Negotiation One (ASN.1), which is used to describe the structure and syntax of data. It is similar to a COBOL File Description.

The presentation layer also contains protocols that are used to describe the basic encoding rules (BER) for the transfer of data between computers.

This layer has not been used very much, but is gaining support from vendors and users. Most implementations now use the ITU-T defined standards, X.208, X.209, X.216 and X.226, which are in conformance with the OSI Model.

The *application layer* is concerned with supporting the end user application process. It serves as the end user interface into the OSI Model.

The layer contains service elements to support application processes such as file transfer, job management, financial data exchange, programming languages, electronic mail, directory services, and database management.

This layer is changing as new standards are added to it by the ITU-T and the ISO.

The X.400 Message Handling Services reside in this layer, as well as the File Transfer and Access Management (FTAM). The X.500 Directory Services also reside here.

Among the most widely used standards in this layer are the non-OSI Internet protocols: the File Transfer Protocol, the Simple Mail Transfer Protocol (SMTP) and TELNET, a terminal protocol.

## END-TO-END COMMUNICATIONS

The layers of the OSI Model and the layers of vendor's models (such as IBM's SNA, or the Internet layered model) contain the communications functions at the lower three or four layers. From the OSI perspective, it is intended that the upper four layers reside in the host computers, as depicted in Figure A–2.

This does not mean that the lower three layers reside only in the network. In order to effect complete communications, the hardware and

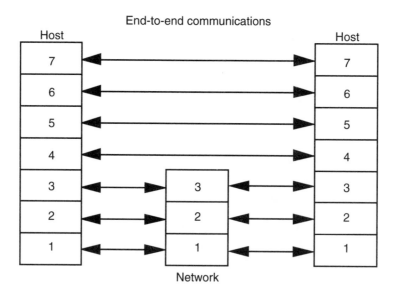

**Figure A–2    End-to-End Operations**

software implemented in the lower three layers also exist at the host machine. End-to-end communications, however, occurs between the hosts by
invoking the upper four layers, and between the hosts and the network
by invoking the lower three layers. This concept is shown in Figure A–2
with the arrows drawn between the layers in the hosts and the network.

The "network" in this figure consists of components such as routers,
ATM switches, and Frame Relay switches. Although this figure shows
only one node, an end-to-end path between two hosts may run between
10 to 20 nodes. Also, while this figure shows that the upper layers of the
model are not running in the network nodes, that is hardly the case. The
point of the figure is to emphasize that the network nodes do not execute
the upper layers for the ongoing processing of user traffic. But for operations such as file exchange, and network management between network
nodes, the network nodes do execute these upper layers.

## A CLOSER LOOK AT THE LAYER OPERATIONS

Layered network protocols allow interaction between functionally
paired layers in different locations without affecting other layers. This
concept aids in distributing the functions to the layers. In the majority of

layered protocols, the data unit, such as a message or packet, passed from one layer to another is usually not altered, although the data unit contents may be examined and used to append additional data (trailers/headers) to the existing unit.

Each layer contains entities that exchange data and provide functions (horizontal communications) with peer entities at other computers. For example, in Figure A–3, layer N in machine A communicates logically with layer N in machine B, and the N+1 layers in the two machines follow the same procedure. Entities in adjacent layers in the same computer interact through the common upper and lower boundaries (vertical communications) by passing parameters to define the interactions.

Typically, each layer at a transmitting station (except the lowest in most systems) adds "header" information to data, as shown in Figure A–4. The headers are used to establish peer-to-peer sessions across nodes, and some layer implementations use headers to invoke functions and services at the N+1 or N adjacent layers. The important point to understand is that, at the receiving site, the layer entities use the headers created by the *peer entity* at the transmitting site to implement actions.

Figure A–5 shows an example of how machine A sends data to machine B. Data is passed from the upper layers or the user application to layer N + 1. This layer adds a header to the data (labeled N + 1 in the figure). It performs actions based on the information in the transaction that accompanied the data from the upper layer.

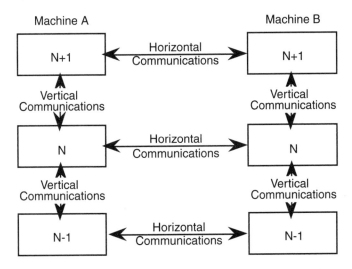

**Figure A–3   Horizontal and Vertical Communications**

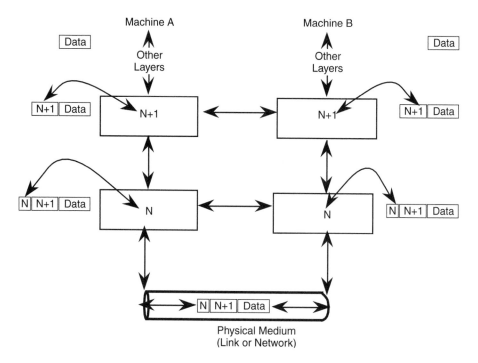

**Figure A–4    The Header Operations**

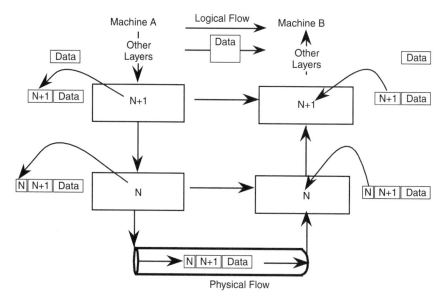

**Figure A–5    Machine A Sends Data to Machine B**

Layer N + 1 passes the data unit and its header to layer N. This layer performs some actions, based on the information in the transaction, and adds its header N to the incoming traffic. This traffic is passed across the communications line (or through a network) to the receiving machine B.

At B, the process is reversed. The headers that were created at A are used by the *peer layers* at B to determine what actions are to be taken. As the traffic is sent up the layers, the respective layer "removes" its header, performs defined actions, and passes the traffic on up to the next layer.

At the user application, it is presented only with user data—which was created by the sending user application. These user applications are unaware (one hopes) of the many operations in each OSI layer that were invoked to support the end user data transfer.

The headers created and used at peer layers are not to be altered by any nonpeer layer. As a general rule, the headers from one layer are treated as transparent "data" by any other layer. This idea is shown in Figure A–6.

There are some necessary exceptions to this rule. As examples, data may be altered by a nonpeer layer for the purposes of compression, encryption, or other forms of syntax changing. This type of operation is per-

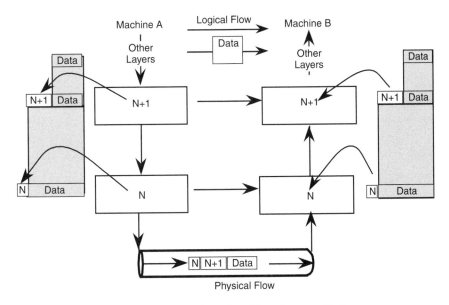

**Figure A–6   Treating Headers as Data**

missible, as long as the data are restored to the original syntax when presented to the receiving peer layer.

As an exception to the exception, the presentation layer may alter the syntax of the data permanently, because the receiving application layer has requested the data in a different syntax (such as ASCII instead of BIT STRING).

Figure A–7 shows the full seven-layer stack of the OSI Model and the effect of sending and receiving traffic through all the layers. On the left side of the figure, the traffic is sent down the layers where each protocol data unit (PDU) at each layer is encapsulated into the PDU at the next layer.

The arrows in between the stacks show that the headers are exchanged logically (not physically) between peer layer entities.

At the receiving site (on the right side of the figure), the data is decapsulated as it traverses up the layers.

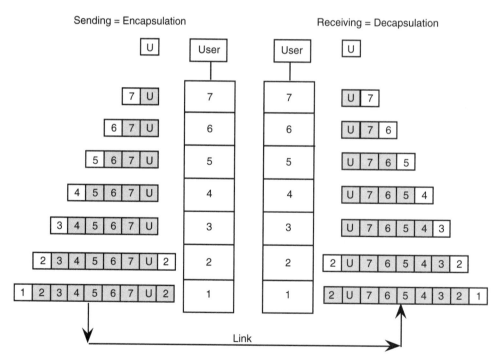

Figure A–7   Seven-Layer Sending/Receiving Process

## SERVICE ACCESS POINTS (SAPs)

Service access points (SAPs) are OSI addresses and identifiers of OSI entities, such as an application that resides in layer 7, or a protocol that resides in layer 3. Figure A–8 illustrates these concepts.

The identifier idea is straight forward; it simply identifies something in a machine. Unfortunately, SAPs can be confusing because they can be used in more than one way. Just keep in mind that they are used to identify a process (in practice, a software module) in a layer.

We must defer to the OSI Model in its description of the SAP. The Model states that: *an (N + 1)-entity requests (N)-services via an (N)-service access point (SAP) which permits the (N + 1)-entity to interact with an (N)-entity.*

This paragraph cites the details of the SAP options. The (N)-service access point [or (N)-address] can identify a one-to-one connection between an (N + 1)-entity and (N)-entity through a one-to-one relationship between the (N + 1)-SAP and the (N)-SAP. It is also possible to use an (N)-connection endpoint identifier to identify the corresponding (N)-connection at an (N)-SAP.

The SAP scheme also allows a many-to-one relationship between (N)-addresses and (N - 1)-addresses. OSI also permits this type of connection.

The following points summarize the most important properties of SAPs:

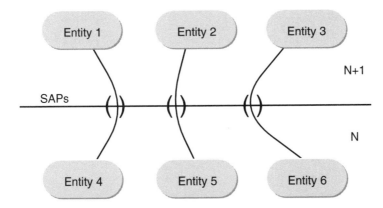

**Figure A–8    OSI Service Access Points (SAPs)**

- An (N + 1)-entity may concurrently be attached to one or more (N)-SAPs attached to the same or different (N)-entities.
- An (N)-entity may concurrently be attached to one or more (N + 1)-entities through (N)-SAPs.
- An (N)-SAP is attached to only one (N)-entity and to only one (N + 1)-entity at a time.

The services invoked at a layer are dictated by the upper layers' passing primitives (transactions) to the lower layer. In Figure A–9, users A and B communicate with each other through a lower layer.

Services are provided from the lower layer to the upper layer through a SAP. The SAP is an identifier. It identifies the entity in N + 1 that is receiving the service(s) for layer N.

An entity in machine A can invoke some services in machine B through the use of SAPs. For example, a user that sends traffic can identify itself with a source SAP ID (SSAP). It identifies the recipient of the traffic with a destination SAP value (DSAP).

It is the responsibility of the receiving lower layer N (in concert of course with the operating system in the receiving machine) to pass the

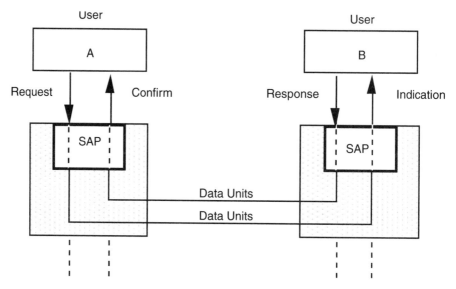

Where:
  SAP   Service access point

**Figure A–9   Communications Between Adjacent Layers**

traffic to the proper destination SAP in layer N + 1. If multiple entities (e.g., processes) exist in the machine, the DSAP serves to properly identify the process.

Some people view the SAP as a software "port." It is akin to the socket concept found in the UNIX operating system environment.

The primitive is used by the layer to invoke the service entities and create any headers that will be used by the peer layer in the remote station. This point is quite important. The primitives are received by adjacent layers in the local site and are used to create the headers used by peer layers at the remote site.

At the receiving site, the primitive is used to convey the data to the next and adjacent upper layer, and to inform this layer about the actions of the lower layer.

The OSI Model uses four types of primitives to perform the actions between the layers, and their functions are summarized in Table A–1. The manner in which they are invoked varies. Not all four primitives must be invoked with each operation. For example, if the remote machine has no need to respond to the local machine, it need not return a response primitive. In this situation, a request primitive would be invoked at the local site to get the operation started. At the remote site, the indication primitive would be invoked to complete the process.

Of course, if the remote station were to send traffic back, it would invoke the operation with a response primitive, which would be mapped to the confirm primitive at the local machine.

One method of assuring that the primitives are related to the same operation is through the use of SAPs, although the OSI Model allows other forms of identification that are discussed later in this course.

One might question why the primitives are so abstract. Indeed, why are they not specific to a language, or at least to a convention, such as a subroutine call-by-value or a subroutine call-by-address? The abstract nature of the primitives make good sense for the reasons cited in this figure.

**Table A–1   The Functions of the Service Definitions (Primitives)**

At user A:
- *Request*. Initiated by a user to invoke a function
- *Confirm*. Invoked by the request

At user B:
- *Indication*. Indicates a function is being invoked
- *Response*. Response to an indication primitive

The OSI Model assumes the parameters in the primitives are used to determine the values in the fields in the PDUs that are transported between the machines. So, the primitives are a means to an end—the exchange of compatible PDUs between two systems.

It should be noted that the use of common PDUs is quite important in achieving compatibility between different architectures. For example, imposing a common tongue "encourages" the individual to think in that tongue and use a common syntax. Common PDUs are to machines what common linguistics are to humans.

## PROTOCOL DATA UNITS (PDUs): FRAMES, PACKETS, AND SUCH

We have learned that most communications systems today are designed around the concept of layered protocols. We also learned that these protocols transmit and receive units of traffic called protocol data units (PDUs).

The term PDU, while useful and applicable to all layers, is often replaced by more common terms. The use of these terms *vis-à-vis* the layers are depicted in Figure A–10. The PDUs created and used at the application layer are known by various names. The term message is used for PDUs and is usually created by electronic mail (email) systems. The terms file and record are generally associated with traffic created and used by file transfer systems and data management systems. This traffic is sent to the lower layers and as discussed earlier, encapsulated into headers at these lower layers which create larger PDUs. Some systems associate the term segment with PDUs created and used at the transport layer. This term is commonly used with the widely used transmission control protocol (TCP). However, some literature uses the term packet at this layer.

The segment or packet is sent to the network layer where it is further encapsulated. The term packet is normally associated with connection-oriented protocols such as X.25, the term datagram is normally associated with connectionless protocols such as OSI's connectionless network protocol (CLNP) and the widely used Internet Protocol (IP). But packet has now assumed almost a generic meaning, and some vendors and service providers use it to describe any type of PDU.

Anyway, this traffic is encapsulated into the frame at the data link layer. Some vendors and designers associate the frame also with the physical layer as well. Another term used at the lower layers is cell. This term connotes a small, fixed-length PDU, in contrast to the terms frame,

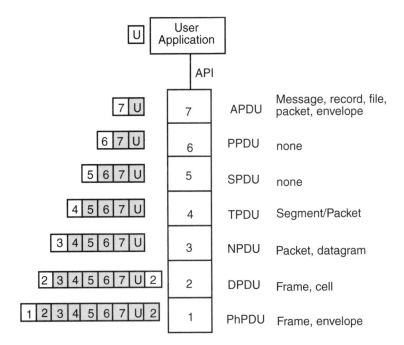

**Figure A–10   Layered Protocols and Protocol Data Units (PDUs)**

datagram and packet, which usually describe a larger, variable-length PDU.

## THE OSI AND INTERNET PROTOCOL STACKS

Figure A–11 and Table A–2 compare the OSI Model protocol stacks and the Internet protocol stacks. The Internet designers did not intend the Internet architecture to be a model. Rather, the protocols were designed and written to solve specific problems. On the other hand, OSI has developed to serve as a model for the development of communications systems. In addition, several of the layers contain protocols as well.

Strictly speaking, most of the systems and protocols shown in the OSI stack are not part of OSI per se. In fact, the seminar delegate can identify an OSI standard (at least those published by the ITU-T) by its document number. They are part of the X Series Recommendations and are published in the X.200 to X.299 publications.

Comparision of OSI and Internet Protocol Stacks

| The OSI Stack | | | | | | | | The Internet Stack | | | | | | |
|---|---|---|---|---|---|---|---|---|---|---|---|---|---|---|

Note: Q.93B specifications are now Q.2xxx (e.g.: Q.2931)

**Figure A–11   The OSI and Internet Layers**

## Table A–2(a)   Comparision of the Upper Layers

| OSI Term | Spelled-out | Int Term | Spelled-out |
|---|---|---|---|
| FTAM | File transfer and access management | FTP | File transfer protocol |
| VT | Virtual terminal | TELNET | |
| IPM | Interpersonal messaging | SMTP | Simple mail transfer protocol |
| EDI | Electronic data interchange | | |
| CMIP | Common management information protocol | SNMP | Simple network management protocol |
| | | DNS | Domain name service |
| X.500 | | | |
| ROSE | Remote operations service element | RPC | Remote procedure call |
| ASN.1 | Abstract notation number 1 | | |
| BER | Basic encoding rules | | |
| TP | Transport protocol | TCP | Transmission control protocol |
| TP CL | TP, connectionless | UDP | User datagram protocol |

**Table A–2(b)   Comparison of the Lower Layers**

| OSI Term | Spelled-out | Int Term | Spelled-out |
|----------|-------------|----------|-------------|
| CLNP | Connectionless layer network protocol | IP | Internet protocol |
| CLNP | Connectionless layer network protocol | ICMP | Internet control message protocol |
| IDRP | Interdomain routing protocol | BGP | Border gateway protocol |
| IS-IS | Intermediate system to intermediate system | OSPF | Open shortest path first |
| ES-IS | End system to intermediate system | ARP | Address resolution protocol |
| GSM | Global system for mobile communications | | |
| LAPD | Link access procedure for the D channel | PPP | Point-to-point protocol |
| BRI | Basic rate interface | | |
| PRI | Primary rate interface | | |
| PLP | Packet layer procedures | | |
| LAPB | Link access procedure, balanced | | |
| LLC | Logical link control | | |
| MAC | Media access control | | |
| LAPF | Link access for frame relay | | |
| AAL | ATM adaptation layer | | |
| ATM | Asynchronous transfer mode | | |
| SONET | Synchronous optical network | | |

The Internet standards do not define seven layers of protocols, and as a general rule, the lower two layers of a conventional 7-layered model are not defined in the Internet standards. Likewise, layers 5 and 6 are not defined either, although a limited number of Internet protocols (like SNMP) use ASN.1, which is considered to reside in layer 6.

# Appendix B

## Names, Addresses, Subnetting, Address Masks, and Prefixes

A newcomer to data networks is often perplexed when the subject of naming and addressing arises. Addresses in data networks are similar to postal addresses and telephone numbering schemes. Indeed, many of the networks that exist today have derived some of their addressing structures from the concepts of the telephone numbering plan.

It should prove useful to clarify the meaning of names, addresses, and routes. And Table B–1 provides a summary of these ideas. A *name* is an identification of an entity (independent of its physical location), such as a person, an applications program, or even a computer. An *address* is also an identification but it reveals additional information about the entity, principally information about its physical or logical placement in a network. A *route* is information on how to relay traffic to a physical location (address).

A network usually provides a service which allows a network user to furnish the network with a name of something (another user, an application, etc.) that is to receive traffic. A network *name server* then uses this name to determine the address of the receiving entity. This address is then used by a routing protocol to determine the physical route to the receiver.

With this approach, a network user does not become involved and is not aware of physical addresses and the physical location of other users and network resources. This practice allows the network administrator

**Table B–1    Names, Addresses, and Routes**

Name: An ID of an entity, independent of physical location
  e.g.: JBrown@acme.com

Address: An ID that reveals a location of an entity
  e.g.: Network = 12.3, Subnetwork = 456, Host = 14

Route: How to reach the entity at the address
  e.g.: Next node is: Subnet 456

Practice is: Name and address are correlated:
  12.3.456.14 is acme.com

---

to relocate, and reconfigure network resources without affecting end users. Likewise, users can move to other physical locations but their names remain the same. The network changes its naming/routing tables to reflect the relocation.

## PRINCIPAL ADDRESSES USED IN INTERNET AND INTRANETS

Communications between users through a data network requires several forms of addressing. Typically, two addresses are required: (a) a physical address, also called a data link address, or a media access control (MAC) address on a LAN, and (b) a network address. Other identifiers are needed for unambiguous end-to-end communications between two users, such as upper layer names and/or port addresses.

Each device (such as a computer or workstation) on a communications link or network is identified with a physical address. This address is also called the hardware address. Many manufacturers place the physical address on a logic board within the device or in an interface unit connected directly to the device. Two physical addresses are employed in a communications dialogue, one address identifies the sender (source) and the other address identifies the receiver (destination). The length of the physical address varies, and most implementations use two 48-bit addresses.

The address detection operation on a LAN is illustrated in Figure B–1. Device A transmits a frame onto the channel. It is broadcast to all other stations attached to the channel, namely stations B, C, and D. We assume that the destination physical address (DPA) contains the value C. Consequently, stations B and D ignore the frame. Station C accepts it, performs several tasks associated with the physical layer, strips away the physical layer headers and trailers, and passes the remainder of the protocol data unit (PDU) (it is no longer called a frame) to the next upper layer.

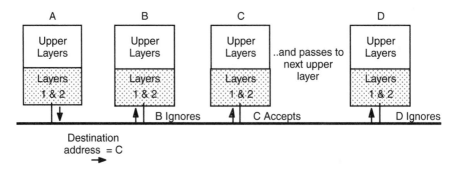

Notes:

For LANs, address is called a MAC address

For non-LAN links, address is called a link address, or some variation of an "HDLC" address

Where:
HDLC    High level data link control
MAC     Media access control

**Figure B–1    Link Address Detection on a LAN**

## The MAC Address

The IEEE assigns LAN addresses and universal protocol identifiers. Previously this work was performed by the Xerox Corporation by administering what were known as block identifiers (Block IDs) for Ethernet addresses. The Xerox Ethernet Administration Office assigned these values, which were three octets (24 bits) in length. The organization that received this address was free to use the remaining 24 bits of the Ethernet address in any way it chose.

Due to the progress made in the IEEE 802 project, it was decided that the IEEE would assume the task of assigning these universal identifiers for all LANs, not just CSMA/CD types of networks. However, the IEEE continues to honor the assignments made by the Ethernet administration office although it now calls the block ID an *organization unique identifier (OUI)*.

The format for the OUI is shown in Figure B–2. The least significant bit of the address space corresponds to the individual/group (I/G) address bit. The I/G address bit, if set to a zero, means that the address field identifies an individual address. If the value is set to a one, the address field identifies a group address which is used to identify more than one

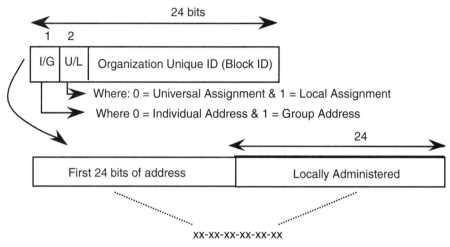

Note: Format of xx represents an octet, with each x 4 bits: A2-59-ED-18-F5-7C

Where:
  MAC    Media access control

**Figure B–2    The MAC Address**

station connected to the LAN. If the entire OUI is set to all ones, it signifies a broadcast address which identifies all stations on the network.

The second bit of the address space is the local or universal bit (U/L). When this bit is set to a zero, it has universal assignment significance—for example, from the IEEE. If it is set to a one it is an address that is locally assigned. Bit position number two must always be set to a zero if it is administered by the IEEE.

The OUI is extended to include a 48-bit universal LAN address (which is designated as the *media access control [MAC]* address). The 24 bits of the address space is the same as the OUI assigned by the IEEE. The one exception is that the I/G bit may be set to a one or a zero to identify group or individual addresses. The second part of the address space consisting of the remaining 24 bits is locally administered and can be set to any values an organization chooses.

### The Network Address

A network address identifies a network or networks. Part of the network address may also designate a computer, a terminal, or anything that a private network administrator wishes to identify within a network (or attached to a network), although the Internet standards place very strict rules on what an IP address identifies.

A network address is a "higher level" address than the physical address. The components in an internet that deal with network addresses need not be concerned with physical addresses until the data has arrived at the network link to which the physical device is attached.

This important concept is illustrated in Figure B–3. Assume that a user (host computer) in Los Angeles transmits packets to a packet network for relaying to a workstation on a LAN in London. The network in London has a network address of XYZ (this address scheme is explained shortly).

The packets are passed through the packet network (using the network's internal routing mechanisms) to the packet switch in New York. The packet switch in New York routes the packet to the gateway located in London. This gateway examines the destination network address in the packet and determines that the packet is to be routed to network XYZ. It then transmits the packet onto the appropriate communications channel (link) to the node on the LAN that is responsible for communicating with the London gateway.

Notice that this operation did not use any physical addresses in these routing operations. The packet switches and gateway were only concerned with the destination network address of XYZ.

The reader might question how the London LAN is able to pass the packet to the correct device (host). As we learned earlier, a physical ad-

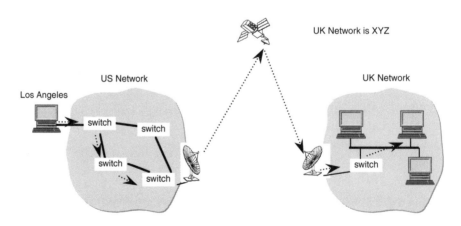

**Figure B–3   Network Layer Addressing**

dress is needed to prevent every packet from being processed by the upper layer network layer protocols residing in every host attached to the network. Therefore, the answer is that the target network (or gateway) must be able to translate a higher layer network destination address to a lower layer physical destination address.

In Figure B–4, a node on the LAN is a server that is tasked with address resolution. Let us assume that the destination address contains a network address, such as 128.1 *and* a host address, say 3.2. Therefore, the two addresses could be joined (concatenated) to create a full internet network address, which would appear as 128.1.3.2 in the destination address field of the IP datagram.

Once the LAN node receives the datagram from the gateway, it must examine the host address, and either (a) perform a look-up into a table that contains the local physical address and its associated network address, or (b) query the station for its physical address. Then, it encapsulates the user data into the LAN frame, places the appropriate LAN physical layer address in the destination address of the frame, and transmits the frame onto the LAN channel. All devices on the network examine the physical address. If this address matches the device's address, the PDU is passed to the next upper layer; otherwise, it is ignored.

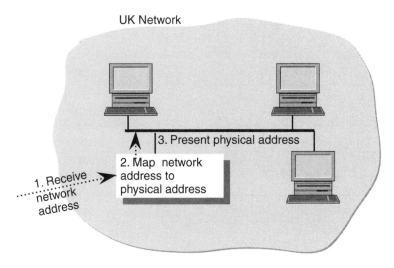

**Figure B–4  Mapping  Network  Addresses  to  Physical Addresses**

## The IP Address

IP networks use a 32-bit layer 3 address to identify a host computer and the network to which the host is attached. The structure of the IP address is depicted in Figure B–5. Its format is:

IP Address = Network Address + Host Address.

The IP address identifies a host's connection to its network. Consequently, if a host machine is moved to another network, its address must be changed.

IP addresses are classified by their formats. Four formats are permitted: class A, class B, class C, or class D formats. As illustrated in this figure, the first bits of the address specify the format of the remainder of the address field in relation to the network and host subfields. The host address is also called the local address (also called the REST field).

The *class A* addresses provide for networks that have a large number of hosts. The host ID field is 24 bits. Therefore, $2^{24}$ hosts can be identified. Seven bits are devoted to the network ID, which supports an identification scheme for as many as 127 networks (bit values of 1 to 127).

Note: Internet Network Information Center (InterNIC) assigns addresses:
Contact: rs.internic.net

**Figure B–5    Internet Protocol (IP) Address Formats**

*Class B* addresses are used for networks of intermediate size. Fourteen bits are assigned for the network ID, and 16 bits are assigned for the host ID. *Class C* networks contain fewer than 256 hosts ($2^8$). Twenty-one bits are assigned to the network ID. Finally, *class D* addresses are reserved for multicasting, which is a form of broadcasting but within a limited area.

The IP address space can take the following forms as shown in Table B–2, and the maximum network and host addresses that are available for the class A, B, and C addresses are also shown.

There are instances when an organization has no need to connect into the Internet or another private intranet. Therefore, it is not necessary to adhere to the IP addressing registration conventions, and the organization can use the addresses it chooses. It is important that it is certain that connections to other networks will not occur, since the use of addresses that are allocated elsewhere could create problems.

In RFC 1597, several IP addresses have been allocated for private addresses, and it is a good idea to use these addresses if an organization

**Table B–2 IP Addresses**

| | Network Address Space Values | |
|---|---|---|
| A | from: 0.0.0.0 | to: 127.255.255.255* |
| B | from: 128 .0.0.0 | to: 191.255.255.255 |
| C | from: 192.0.0.0 | to: 223.255.255.255 |
| D | from: 224.0.0.0 | to: 239.255.255.255 |
| E | from: 240.0.0.0 | to: 247.255.255.255** |

\* Numbers 0 and 127 are reserved

\*\* Reserved for future use

| | Maximum Network Numbers | Maximum Host Numbers |
|---|---|---|
| A | 126* | 16,777,124 |
| B | 16,384 | 65,534 |
| C | 2,097,152 | 254 |

\* Numbers 0 and 127 are reserved

The addresses set aside for private allocations:

Class A addresses: 10.x.x.x - 10.x.x.x (1)

Class B addresses: 172.16.x.x - 172.31.x.x (16)

Class C addresses: 192.168.0.x - 192.168.255.x (256)

chooses not to register with the Internet. Systems are available that will translate private, unregistered addresses to public, registered addresses if connections to global systems are needed.

Figure B–6 shows examples of the assignment of IP address in more detail (examples use IP class B addresses). A common backbone (Common Net) connects three subnetworks: 176.16.2, 176.16.3, and 176.16.4. Routers act as the interworking units between the legacy (conventional) LANs and the backbone. The backbone could be a conventional Ethernet, but in most situations, the backbone is a Fiber Distributed Data Interface (FDDI), a Fast Ethernet node, or an ATM hub.

The routers are also configured as subnet nodes and access servers are installed in the network to support address and naming information services.

The IP datagram contains the source address and the destination address of the sender and receiver respectively. These two addresses do not change. They remain intact end-to-end. The destination address is used at each IP module to determine which "next node" is to receive the

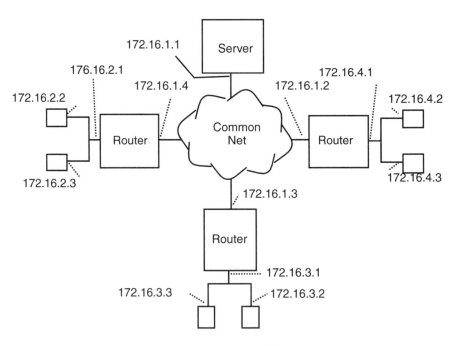

**Figure B–6    Examples of IP Addressing**

datagram. It is matched against the IP routing table to find the outgoing link to reach this next node.

In contrast, the MAC source and destination addresses change as the frame is sent across each link. After all, MAC addresses have only significance at the link layer.

In Figure B–7, the IP source address of A.1 and destination address of C.2 stay the same throughout the journey through the internet. The MAC addresses change at each link. It is necessary for the destination MAC address to contain the MAC address of the machine on the respective LAN that is to receive the frame. Otherwise, the frame cannot be delivered.

At first glance, it might appear that the IP addressing scheme is flexible enough to accommodate the identification of a sufficient number of networks and hosts to service almost any user or organization. But this is not the case. The Internet designers were not shortsighted; they simply failed to account for the explosive growth of the Internet as well as the rapid growth of the IPs in private networks.

The problem arises when a network administrator attempts to identify a large number of networks and/or computers (such as personal computers) attached to these networks. The problem becomes onerous

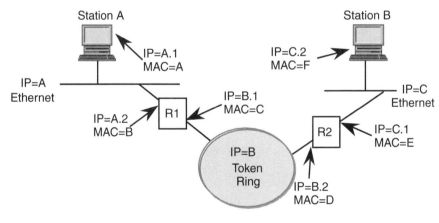

| From | To | Source IP Address | Destination IP Address | Source MAC Address | Destination MAC Address |
|------|-----|------------------|------------------------|--------------------|-------------------------|
| Station A | Router 1 | A.1 | C.2 | A | B |
| Router 1 | Router 2 | A.1 | C.2 | C | D |
| Router 2 | Station B | A.1 | C.2 | E | F |

**Figure B–7    Relationship of IP and MAC Addresses**

because of the need to store and maintain many network addresses and the associated requirement to access these addresses through large routing tables. The use of the address advertising to exchange routing information requires immense resources if they must access and maintain big addressing tables.

The problem is compounded when networks are added to an internet. The addition requires the reorganization of routing tables and perhaps the assignment of additional addresses to identify the new networks.

To deal with this problem, the Internet establishes a scheme whereby multiple networks are identified by one address entry in the routing table. Obviously, this approach reduces the number of network addresses needed in an internet. It also requires a modification to the routing algorithms, but the change is minor in comparison to the benefits derived. For example, in Figure B–8, three networks are identified with one address: 128.11.0.0. Each of these networks is then identified with: (a) 128.11.1.0, (b) 128.11.2.0 and (c) 128.11.3.0.

Figure B–9 shows the structure of the slightly modified internet address. All that has taken place is the division of the local address, heretofore called the host address, into the subnet address and the host address.

It is evident that both the initial internet address and the subnet address take advantage of hierarchical addressing and hierarchical rout-

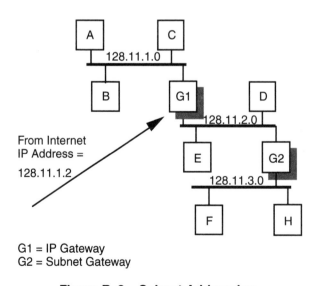

G1 = IP Gateway
G2 = Subnet Gateway

**Figure B–8   Subnet Addressing**

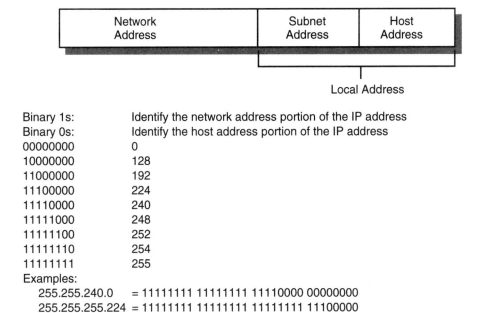

| Network Address | Subnet Address | Host Address |
|---|---|---|

Local Address

Binary 1s:          Identify the network address portion of the IP address
Binary 0s:          Identify the host address portion of the IP address
00000000            0
10000000            128
11000000            192
11100000            224
11110000            240
11111000            248
11111100            252
11111110            254
11111111            255
Examples:
    255.255.240.0    = 11111111 11111111 11110000 00000000
    255.255.255.224  = 11111111 11111111 11111111 11100000

**Figure B–9    The Subnet Address Structure**

ing. This concept fits well with the basic gateway functions inherent in the Internet.

The choice of the assignments of the "local address" is left to the individual network implementors. There are many choices in the definition of the local address. As we mentioned before, it is a local matter, but it does require considerable thought. It requires following the same theme of the overall internet address of how many subnets must be identified in relation to how many hosts must be identified that reside on each subnet.

In order to support subnet addressing, the IP routing algorithm is modified to support a subnet mask. The purpose of the mask is to determine which part of the IP address pertains to the subnetwork and which part pertains to the host.

The convention used for subnet masking is to use a 32-bit field in addition to the IP address. The contents of the field (the mask) are set as shown in this figure.

Table B–3 is provided to the reader to aid in correlating the IP binary subnet mask to hexadecimal and decimal equivalents. The table is self-descriptive.

Table B–4 should be helpful if you are trying to determine how many subnets and hosts can be derived from different combinations of

**Table B–3   IP Subnet Mask Values**

| Binary Values | | | | Hex Values | | | | Decimal Values | | | |
|---|---|---|---|---|---|---|---|---|---|---|---|
| 1111 1111 | 1111 1111 | 1111 1111 | 1111 1111 | FF | FF | FF | FF | 255 | 255 | 255 | 255 |
| 1111 1111 | 1111 1111 | 1111 1111 | 1111 1110 | FF | FF | FF | FE | 255 | 255 | 255 | 254 |
| 1111 1111 | 1111 1111 | 1111 1111 | 1111 1100 | FF | FF | FF | FC | 255 | 255 | 255 | 252 |
| 1111 1111 | 1111 1111 | 1111 1111 | 1111 1000 | FF | FF | FF | F8 | 255 | 255 | 255 | 248 |
| 1111 1111 | 1111 1111 | 1111 1111 | 1111 0000 | FF | FF | FF | F0 | 255 | 255 | 255 | 240 |
| 1111 1111 | 1111 1111 | 1111 1111 | 1110 0000 | FF | FF | FF | E0 | 255 | 255 | 255 | 224 |
| 1111 1111 | 1111 1111 | 1111 1111 | 1100 0000 | FF | FF | FF | C0 | 255 | 255 | 255 | 192 |
| 1111 1111 | 1111 1111 | 1111 1111 | 1000 0000 | FF | FF | FF | 80 | 255 | 255 | 255 | 128 |
| 1111 1111 | 1111 1111 | 1111 1111 | 0000 0000 | FF | FF | FF | 00 | 255 | 255 | 255 | 00 |
| 1111 1111 | 1111 1111 | 1111 1110 | 0000 0000 | FF | FF | FE | 00 | 255 | 255 | 254 | 00 |
| 1111 1111 | 1111 1111 | 1111 1100 | 0000 0000 | FF | FF | FC | 00 | 255 | 255 | 252 | 00 |
| 1111 1111 | 1111 1111 | 1111 1000 | 0000 0000 | FF | FF | F8 | 00 | 255 | 255 | 248 | 00 |
| 1111 1111 | 1111 1111 | 1111 0000 | 0000 0000 | FF | FF | F0 | 00 | 255 | 255 | 240 | 00 |
| 1111 1111 | 1111 1111 | 1110 0000 | 0000 0000 | FF | FF | E0 | 00 | 255 | 255 | 224 | 00 |
| 1111 1111 | 1111 1111 | 1100 0000 | 0000 0000 | FF | FF | C0 | 00 | 255 | 255 | 192 | 00 |
| 1111 1111 | 1111 1111 | 1000 0000 | 0000 0000 | FF | FF | 80 | 00 | 255 | 255 | 128 | 00 |
| 1111 1111 | 1111 1111 | 0000 0000 | 0000 0000 | FF | FF | 00 | 00 | 255 | 255 | 00 | 00 |
| 1111 1111 | 1111 1110 | 0000 0000 | 0000 0000 | FF | FE | 00 | 00 | 255 | 254 | 00 | 00 |
| 1111 1111 | 1111 1100 | 0000 0000 | 0000 0000 | FF | FC | 00 | 00 | 255 | 252 | 00 | 00 |
| 1111 1111 | 1111 1000 | 0000 0000 | 0000 0000 | FF | F8 | 00 | 00 | 255 | 248 | 00 | 00 |
| 1111 1111 | 1111 0000 | 0000 0000 | 0000 0000 | FF | F0 | 00 | 00 | 255 | 240 | 00 | 00 |
| 1111 1111 | 1110 0000 | 0000 0000 | 0000 0000 | FF | E0 | 00 | 00 | 255 | 224 | 00 | 00 |
| 1111 1111 | 1100 0000 | 0000 0000 | 0000 0000 | FF | C0 | 00 | 00 | 255 | 192 | 00 | 00 |
| 1111 1111 | 1000 0000 | 0000 0000 | 0000 0000 | FF | 80 | 00 | 00 | 255 | 128 | 00 | 00 |
| 1111 1111 | 0000 0000 | 0000 0000 | 0000 0000 | FF | 00 | 00 | 00 | 255 | 00 | 00 | 00 |
| 1111 1110 | 0000 0000 | 0000 0000 | 0000 0000 | FE | 00 | 00 | 00 | 254 | 00 | 00 | 00 |
| 1111 1100 | 0000 0000 | 0000 0000 | 0000 0000 | FC | 00 | 00 | 00 | 252 | 00 | 00 | 00 |
| 1111 1000 | 0000 0000 | 0000 0000 | 0000 0000 | F8 | 00 | 00 | 00 | 248 | 00 | 00 | 00 |
| 1111 0000 | 0000 0000 | 0000 0000 | 0000 0000 | F0 | 00 | 00 | 00 | 240 | 00 | 00 | 00 |
| 1110 0000 | 0000 0000 | 0000 0000 | 0000 0000 | E0 | 00 | 00 | 00 | 224 | 00 | 00 | 00 |
| 1100 0000 | 0000 0000 | 0000 0000 | 0000 0000 | C0 | 00 | 00 | 00 | 192 | 00 | 00 | 00 |
| 1000 0000 | 0000 0000 | 0000 0000 | 0000 0000 | 80 | 00 | 00 | 00 | 128 | 00 | 00 | 00 |
| 0000 0000 | 0000 0000 | 0000 0000 | 0000 0000 | 00 | 00 | 00 | 00 | 00 | 00 | 00 | 00 |

**Table B–4    Class B and C Subnet Masks and Resultant Subnets and Hosts**

| *For Class B:* Number of Bits | Subnet Mask | Resultant Subnets | Resultant Hosts |
|---|---|---|---|
| 2 | 255.255.192.0 | 2 | 16392 |
| 3 | 255.255.224.0 | 6 | 8190 |
| 4 | 255.255.240.0 | 14 | 4094 |
| 5 | 255.255.248.0 | 30 | 2046 |
| 6 | 255.255.252.0 | 62 | 1022 |
| 7 | 255.255.254.0 | 126 | 510 |
| 8 | 255.255.225.0 | 254 | 254 |
| 9 | 255.255.225.128 | 510 | 126 |
| 10 | 255.255.225.192 | 1022 | 62 |
| 11 | 255.255.225.224 | 2046 | 30 |
| 12 | 255.255.225.240 | 4094 | 14 |
| 13 | 255.255.225.248 | 8190 | 6 |
| 14 | 255.255.225.252 | 16382 | 2 |

| *For Class C:* Number of Bits | Subnet Mask | Resultant Subnets | Resultant Hosts |
|---|---|---|---|
| 2 | 255.255.225.192 | 2 | 62 |
| 3 | 255.255.225.224 | 6 | 30 |
| 4 | 255.255.225.240 | 14 | 14 |
| 5 | 255.255.225.248 | 30 | 6 |
| 6 | 255.255.225.252 | 62 | 2 |

subnet masks. The tables are for class B and class C networks. One rule should be remembered: the first and last address of a host or subnet range of numbers cannot be used. They are reserved. So, if the range of the value is 3 bits (0–7), the values permit 6 addresses. The first bit is used to identify the actual subnet number, and the last bit is used as the broadcast address for that subnet.

Here is an example from the Chris Lewis reference (and the tables as well[1]):

---

[1]The table in Chris Lewis's book on class C subnet mask is in error (Mr. Lewis leaves out one iteration of 255; see page 38). It is not a big deal, and does not distract from the overall quality of the book . . . and I have notified the publisher.

| | |
|---|---|
| IP address | 210.222.5.121 |
| Subnet mask | 255.255.255.248 |
| Subnet address | 201.222.5.120 |
| Usable subnet host addresses | 201.222.5.121–201.222.5.126 |
| Subnet broadcast address | 201.222.5.127 |

## ADDRESS AGGREGATION AND SUBNET MASKS AND PREFIXES

Address aggregation is introduced in Chapter 1. It is the method used today to reduce the size of the routing tables. It is quite similar to the use of subnet masks, with the following exceptions: (a) the net and subnet bits are contiguous, and begin in the high-order (most significant) part of the address space, (b) a 32-bit submask is not used, rather (c) a prefix value is appended to the end of an address to describe how many bits are to be used as the mask. In most routers, addresses can be configured with a conventional decimal doted notation, or a prefix.

Figure B–10 shows how address aggregation is used. The three subnets 172.16.1.0, 172.16.2.0, and 172.16.3.0 use a prefix of 24. This value

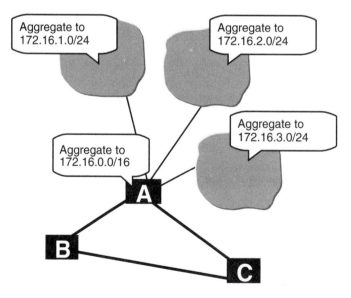

**Figure B–10    Reducing Routing Table Sizes**

means the net/subnet (actually, net/subnet lose their meaning now) span across the first 24 bits of the address, leaving the last 8 bits to identify the hosts.

However, router A does not have to advertise all three addresses. It "aggregates" these addresses into: 172.16.0.0/16. The /16 means the first 16 bits of the advertised address pertains to networks (actually prefixes) at router A.

As a consequence of this approach, routers B and C do not have to store three addresses in their routing tables. They need only to store one address with its prefix. Whenever routers B and C receive an IP datagram with 172.16.x.x in the destination address, the use of a stored prefix value in the routing table enables the routers to know that the datagram is to be sent to router A.

Routers B and C are not concerned with knowing about any more details of the bit contents of the address beyond the prefix. It is router A's job to know that the three networks are directly attached to router A's interfaces. Router A knows this fact, because it has a special table containing the addresses of directly attached networks, and it consults this information before it accesses the long routing table.

Figure B–11 is a more detailed view of address aggregation. The arrows depict route advertising packets, more commonly known as routing packets. The small arrows are advertisements being sent from hosts, and are conveyed to an assigned router on each of the three subnets. These routers are not shown in this figure. In this simple example, seven hosts are sending routing packets. Each subnet is aggregated with the prefix of 24, resulting in three packets being sent to router A.

Router A aggregates these advertisements to a prefix of 16, and sends routing packets to its neighbor routers, B and C.

These routers send this same advertisement to each other. Consequently, routers B and C know of two routes to 176.16.0/16. Under most conditions, the most direct route would be chosen to these subnets; that is, directly through A. However, we will see that circumstances exists where B's packets to A might go through C first, and C's packets to A might go through B first. The obvious circumstance is a link failure between A and either B or C, but other circumstances are possible, and are explained later.

One other situation needs explaining in this example. Routers A, B, and C are connected together in a loop. It is therefore conceptually possible for the routing packets to loop around over-and-over. Of course, measures are taken to preclude the looping of advertisements, and are also explained later.

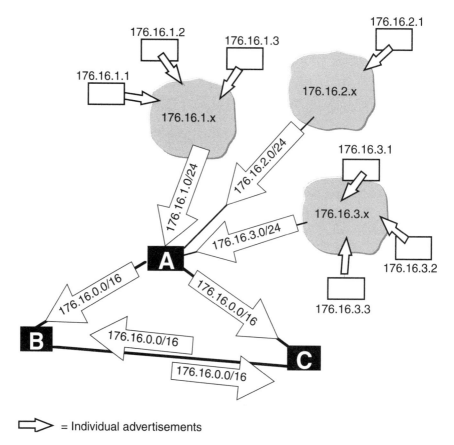

= Individual advertisements

**Figure B–11    The Routing Messages**

Figure B–12 shows how a subnet mask is interpreted. Assume a class B IP address of 128.1.17.1, with a mask of 255.255.240.0. At a router, to discover the subnet address value, the mask has a bitwise Boolean *and* operation performed on the address as shown in the figure (this address is in a routing table). The mask is also applied to the destination address in the datagram.

By the notation "don't care," it means that the router is not concerned at this point with the host address. It is concerned with getting the datagram to the proper subnetwork. So, in this example, it uses the mask to discover that the first 4 bits of the host address are to be used for the subnet address. Further, it discovers that the subnet address is 1.

As this example shows, when the subnet mask is split across octets, the results can be a bit confusing if you are "octet-aligned." In this case,

|              | 128.                | 1.       | 1.       | 1          |
|--------------|---------------------|----------|----------|------------|
| IP address   | 10000000  00000001  | 0001     | 0001     | 00000001   |
| Mask         | 11111111  11111111  | 1111     | 0000     | 00000000   |
| Result       | 10000000  00000001  | 0001     | don't care |          |
| Logical address | 128      1       | 1        | don't care |          |
|              | network             | sub net  | host     |            |

Note: "don't care" means router doesn't care at this time (the router is looking for subnet matches)

**Figure B–12    Example of Address Masking Operations**

the actual value for the subnet address is $0001_2$ or $1_{10}$, even though the decimal address of the "host" space is 17.1. However, the software does not care about octet alignment. It is looking for a match of the destination address in the IP datagram to an address in a routing table, based on the mask that is stored in the routing table.

The class address scheme (A, B, C) has proved to be too inflexible to meet the needs of the growing Internet. For example, the class address of 47 means that 3 bytes are allocated to identify hosts attached to network 47, resulting in $2^{24}$ hosts on the single network—clearly not realistic! Moreover, the network.host address does not allow more than a two-level hierarchical view of the address. Multiple levels of hierarchy are preferable, because it permits using fewer entries in routing tables, and the aggregation of lower-level addresses to a higher-level address.

The introduction of subnets in the IP address opened the way to better utilize the IP address space by implementing a multilevel-level hierarchy. This approach allows the aggregation of networks to reduce the size of routing tables.

Figure B–13 is derived from the Halabi text (cited in the preface), and shows the advertising operations that occur without route aggregation [without Classless Interdomain Routing (CIDR), discussed next]. The ISPs are ultimately advertising all their addresses to the Internet to a NAP. Four addresses are shown here, but in an actual situation, thousands of addresses might be advertised.

In contrast to the above example where each address is advertised to the Internet, the use of masks allows fewer addresses to be advertised.

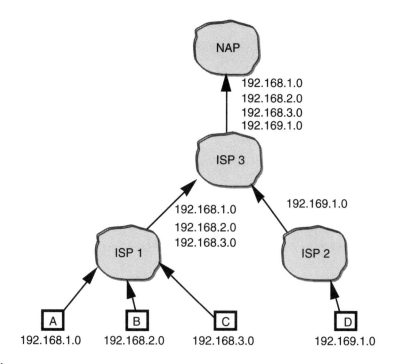

Where:
  NAP   Network access point
  ISP    Internet service provider

**Figure B–13   Without Aggregation**

In Figure B–14, ISP1 and ISP2 are using masks of 16 bits in length (255.255.0.0), and ISP1 need only advertise address 192.168.0.0 with the 16 bit mask to inform all interested nodes that all addresses behind this mask can be found at 192.168.x.x. ISP1 uses the same mask to achieve the same goal.

ISP3 uses a mask of 8 bits (255.0.0.0) which effectively aggregates the addresses of ISP1 and ISP2 under the aggregation domain of ISP3. Thus, in this simple example, one address is advertised to the NAP instead of four.

In order to extend the limited address space of an IP address, Classless Interdomain Routing (CIDR) is now used in many systems and is required for operations between autonomous systems. It permits networks to be grouped together logically, and to use one entry in a routing table for multiple class C networks.

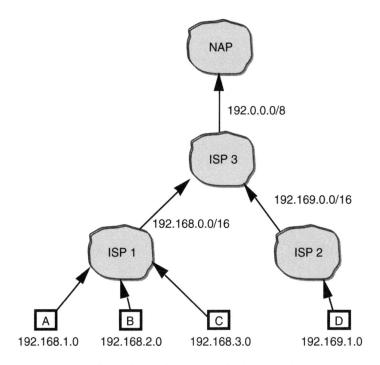

Note: The notations /16 and /8 refer to the lengths of masks

Where:
  NAP   Network access point
  ISP   Internet service provider

**Figure B–14    With Aggregation**

This example shows how the concept works. The first requirement for CIDR is for multiple networks to share a certain number of bits in the high-order part of the IP address. In this example, the first 7 bits in the address are the same. Thus, by using the mask of 254.0.0.0 (11111110.00000000.00000000.00000000), all addresses between 194.0.0.0 and 195.255.255.255 can be identified by a single entry in the routing table.

Once the point in the network has been reached, the remainder of the address space can be used for hierarchical routing. For example, a mask of say 255.255.240.0 could be used to group networks together. This concept, if carried out on all IP addresses (and not just class C addresses) would result in the reduction of an Internet routing table from about 10,000 entries to 200 entries.

Additional information on CIDR is available in RFCs 1518, 1519, 1466, and 1447.

## VARIABLE LENGTH SUBMASKS

Subnet masks are useful in internetworking operations, especially the variable length subnet mask (VLSM). This figure (which is a summary of a more detailed example from the Halabi reference) shows the idea of VLSM.

We assume an organization is using a class C address of 192.168.1.x. The organization needs to set up three networks (subnets) as shown in Figure B–15. Subnet A has 100 hosts attached to it, and subnets B and C support 50 hosts each.

Recall from our previous discussions that the subnet mask is used to determine how many bits are set aside for the subnet and host addresses. This figure shows the possibilities for the class C address. (The resultant numbers in the table assume that the IP address reserved numbers are used, which is possible, since 192.168.1.x is from a pool of private addresses, and can be used as the organization chooses).

The use of one mask for the three subnets will not work. A mask of 255.255.255.128 yields only two subnets, and a mask of 255.255.255.192 yields only 64 hosts.

**Table B–5    Classless Interdomain Routing (CIDR) ("Supernetting")**

- Reduces the size of routing tables
- Requirements:
  - Multiple IP addresses must share a specific number of high-order bits of an address
  - Masks must be used
  - Routing protocols must support the masks
- Example (from RFC 1466):
  - Addresses from 194.0.0.0 through 195.255.255.255
  - 65536 different class C addresses, but the first 7 bits are the same: 1100001x (they show the same high-order 7 bits)
  - One entry in a routing table of 194.0.0.0 with a mask of 254.0.0.0 suffices of all addresses (to a single point)
- A longer mask can be used to route to addresses beyond first mask

Class C Address of 192.168.1.x is used by an organization
Organization needs the following topology:

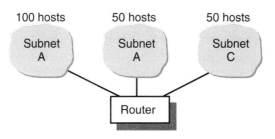

Possible Masks:

| Subnet Mask | Resultant Subnets* | Resultant Hosts* |
|---|---|---|
| 255.255.255.128 | 2 | 128 |
| 255.255.255.192 | 4 | 64 |
| 255.255.255.224 | 8 | 32 |
| 255.255.255.240 | 16 | 16 |
| 255.255.255.248 | 32 | 8 |
| 255.255.255.252 | 64 | 4 |

* Assumes use of reserved bits
Use .128 yields 2 subnets with 128 hosts each: Won't work
Use .192 yields 4 subnets with 64 hosts each: Won't work
Answer? Use both (Variable length subnet mask):

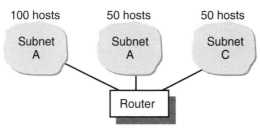

Subnet A mask = 255.255.255.128
Subnet B mask = 255.255.255.192
Subnet C mask = 255.255.255.192

**Figure B–15    Managing the IP Addresses**

Fortunately, different subnetwork masks can be used on each sub-net. As the figure shows, subnet A uses subnet mask 255.255.255.128, and subnets B and C use subnet mask 255.255.255.192.

Not all route discovery protocols support subnetwork masks. So, check your product before you delve into this operation.

# Appendix C
## Address Resolution, Translation, and Configuration

**ADDRESS RESOLUTION**

As explained in Appendix B, each device attached to a single physical LAN is identified by a specific MAC address. We also learned that other addresses are assigned, such as network addresses. The vast majority of MAC addresses are assigned by the manufacturer before the product is shipped to the customer or when the product is installed at the customer's site.

We find ourselves with an interesting problem which we began to address in previous discussions: how to relate the MAC address to a network address and vice-versa. As an example on a LAN (and see Figure C–1), if host A wishes to send a datagram to host D, it may not know the MAC of host D. To compound the problem, the higher layer network address may also be unknown to host A. Therefore, some means must be devised to relate different addresses to each other.

Our focus in this part of the appendix is on address resolution or mapping protocols. They are so-named, because they map (correlate or translate) one form of an address to another form. This operation is quite important because networks often employ different addresses. Therefore, when sending traffic from one network to another, a destination address must be understandable to the receiving network.

One could reasonably ask, "Why do we have different addresses? Why can't we have one 'universal identifier'?" Technically speaking, we

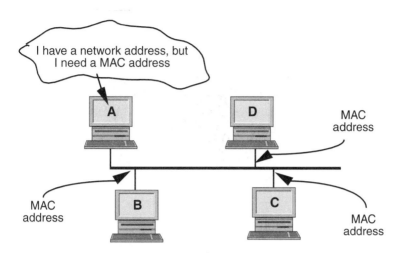

Figure C–1    Addressing Problems

can. But our world is not so perfect. Different organizations have developed a variety of addressing schemes. The telephone companies developed the telephone number; the Internet task forces developed the IP address; the IEEE committees developed the MAC address; the U.S. government developed the social security number, and so on.

(It is accepted that different addresses/identifiers are needed because they serve different purposes. Notwithstanding, the industry could benefit if fewer address plans were implemented, which is beyond the focus of this seminar.)

The most common operations performed with address mapping protocols are: the (a) correlation of a MAC address to an IP address, and (b) the correlation of an IP address to a MAC address. Recent implementations in Asynchronous Transfer Mode systems (ATM) also correlate MAC/IP addresses to ATM addresses with a version of ARP, called AT-MARP.

## THE ADDRESS RESOLUTION PROTOCOL (ARP)

The IP stack provides a protocol for resolving addresses. The Address Resolution Protocol (ARP) is used to take care of the translation of IP addresses to physical addresses and hide these physical addresses from the upper layers.

Generally, ARP works with mapping tables (referred to as the ARP cache). The table provides the mapping between an IP address and a physical address. In a LAN (like Ethernet or an IEEE 802 network), ARP takes the target IP address and searches for a corresponding physical address in a mapping table. If it finds the address, it returns the 48-bit address back to the requester, such as a device driver or server on a LAN. However, if the needed address is not found in the ARP cache, the ARP module sends a broadcast onto the network.

The broadcast is called the *ARP request*. The ARP request contains an IP address. Consequently, if one of the machines receiving the broadcast recognizes its IP address in the ARP request, it will return an ARP reply back to the inquiring host. This datagram contains the physical hardware address of the queried host. Upon receiving this datagram, the inquiring host places this address into the ARP cache. Thereafter, datagrams sent to this particular IP address can be translated to the physical address.

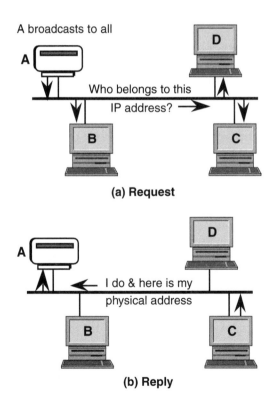

**Figure C–2    The ARP Request and Reply**

The ARP system thus allows an inquiring host to find the physical address of another host by using the IP address.

The concepts of ARP requests and replies are shown in Figure C–2. Host A wishes to determine C's physical address. It broadcasts datagrams to B, C, and D. Only C responds because it recognizes its IP address in the incoming ARP request datagram. Host C places its address into an IP datagram in the form of the ARP reply. The other hosts, B and D, do not respond.

The format for the ARP message is shown in Figure C–3. The first part of the message is the header of the Ethernet frame, consisting of the MAC addresses and the Ethertype field. Thereafter, the hardware type and protocol type describe the types of addresses that are to be "resolved." The term *hardware* refers to a physical, link layer address, and the term protocol refers to an upper layer address, typically an L_3 address, such as IP, X.25, IPX, etc.

The length fields explain how long the address fields are, and for Ethernet and IP addresses, they are 6 and 4 octets respectively. The sending address fields identify the addresses of the sending entity. The target addresses are those that need resolving. In a typical ARP request,

Octets

| | |
|---|---|
| Destination Address | 6 |
| Source Address | 6 |
| Ethertype | 2 |
| Hardware type | 2 |
| Protocol type | 2 |
| Hardware length | 1 |
| Protocol length | 1 |
| Op code | 2 |
| Sending hardware address | 6 |
| Sending protocol address | 4 |
| Target hardware address | 6 |
| Target protocol address | 4 |

**Figure C–3   The ARP Message Format**

the target hardware address is left blank, and in the reply, it is filled-in by the responding station.

## PROXY ARP

Another protocol, called proxy ARP or promiscuous ARP allows the learning of other routes (RFC 1027). The concept is illustrated in Figure C–4. The router hides the two networks from each other. For example, if host A wishes to send traffic to host D, host A might first form an ARP message in order to obtain the physical address of host D on network Y. However, the ARP message does not reach host D. The gateway intercepts the message, performs the address resolution, and sends an ARP reply back to host A with the gateway's physical address in the ARP target hardware address field. Host A then uses the ARP response to update its ARP table and the ARP operation is complete. The example in this figure can be reversed. The hosts on network X can be serviced by the gateway in a similar manner just discussed for host A.

Proxy ARP is quite flexible and nothing precludes mapping different IP address prefixes to the same physical address. However, some ARP implementations have diagnostic procedures that will display alarms to network control if multiple addresses are mapped to the same physical address. This problem is called "spoofing" and serves to alert network control of possible problems.

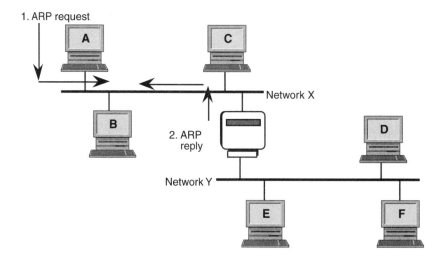

**Figure C–4    Proxy ARP**

## REVERSE ARP (RARP)

The ARP protocol is a useful technique for determining physical addresses from network addresses. However, some workstations do not know their own IP address. For example, diskless workstations do not have any IP address knowledge when they are booted to a system. The diskless workstations know only their hardware address.

The reverse address resolution protocol (RARP) works in a manner similar to ARP except, as the name suggests, it works in reverse order.

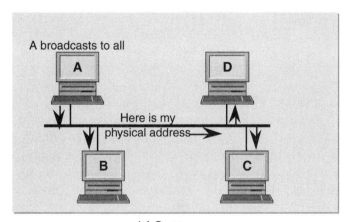

**(a) Query**

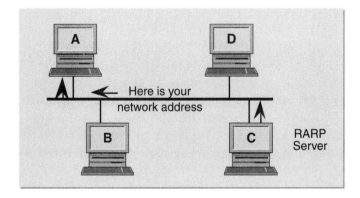

**(b) Response**

**Figure C–5    RARP Operations**

The process is illustrated in Figure C–5. The inquiring machine (for example, a diskless workstation) broadcasts a RARP request. This request specifies that machine A is the target machine in contrast to the ARP protocol, which would identify the receiving machine as the target machine. The RARP datagram contains the physical address of the sending machine. This transmission is sent out as a broadcast. Therefore, all machines on this physical network receive this request. However, only the RARP servers are allowed to reply.

The servers reply by filling in the target protocol address field, and they change the operation code in the RARP message from a request to a reply (3 = a request, 4 = a reply). The packet is sent back to the inquiring station, which then is able to use the information in the frame to derive its IP address. The Ethertype field in the frame is coded as $8035_{16}$ ($32821_{10}$) to identify the I field as an RARP packet.

## BOOTP

RARP is used to obtain an IP address from a MAC address. Although widely used, RARP has some disadvantages. Since it is intended to operate at the hardware level, it is cumbersome to obtain and manage the routine from an applications program. It also contains limited information. Its purpose is to obtain an IP address, but not much other information is provided. It would be useful to have the reply of a message contain information about other protocols supported by the machine, such as the gateway address, server host names, etc. Due to these problems, the Internet now supports the Bootstrap Protocol, also known as BOOTP.

BOOTP utilizes UDP at the transport layer. Consequently, the operation is connectionless. The UDP uses a checksum to check for corruption of data. BOOTP performs some transport layer functions by sending a request to the server, then a timer is started and if no reply is received within a defined period, BOOTP attempts a retransmission.

Figure C–6 shows the format for the BOOTP message. All BOOTP fields are of fixed length and the replies and requests have the same format. The field labeled *operation* is set to 1 to denote a request and 2 to denote a reply. The next two fields are identical to the ARP protocol. The *hops* field must be set to a 0 in a request message. The server is allowed to pass a BOOTP message to another machine, perhaps in another network, if so it must increment the hop count by one. The *transaction ID* field is used to coordinate requests and response messages. The *seconds*

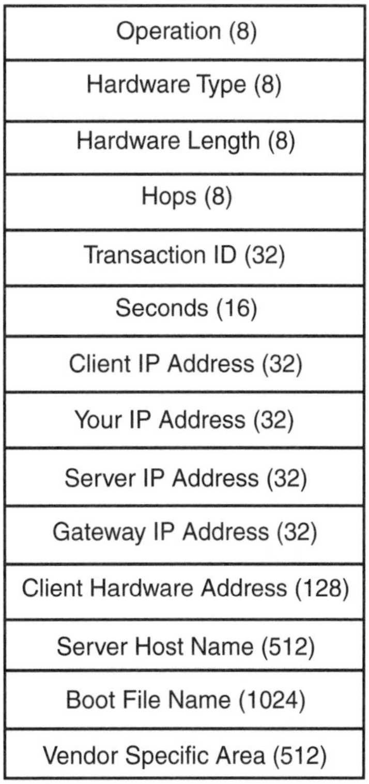

| |
|---|
| Operation (8) |
| Hardware Type (8) |
| Hardware Length (8) |
| Hops (8) |
| Transaction ID (32) |
| Seconds (16) |
| Client IP Address (32) |
| Your IP Address (32) |
| Server IP Address (32) |
| Gateway IP Address (32) |
| Client Hardware Address (128) |
| Server Host Name (512) |
| Boot File Name (1024) |
| Vendor Specific Area (512) |

**Figure C–6    BOOTP Message Format**

field is used to determine (in seconds) the time since the machine has started to establish the BOOTP procedure. The next four fields contain the IP addresses of the *client address,* as well as the *requester's address, server address,* and *gateway address.* The *client hardware address* is also available. The message also contains the *client server* and the *boot file* names. The *vendor specific area* is not defined in the standard.

## THE DYNAMIC HOST CONFIGURATION PROTOCOL (DHCP)

The Dynamic Host Configuration Protocol (DHCP) provides a framework for passing configuration information to hosts on a TCPIP-based network. DHCP is based on the BOOTP, and adds the capability of automatic allocation of reusable network addresses and additional configuration options. DHCP is published in RFC 2131, from which the following information is extracted.

DHCP is built on a client-server model. A designated DHCP server dynamically allocates network addresses and delivers configuration parameters to hosts.

DHCP supports three mechanisms for IP address allocation: (a) automatic allocation, (b) dynamic allocation, and (c) manual allocation. With automatic allocation, DHCP assigns a permanent IP address to a client. With dynamic allocation, DHCP assigns an IP address to a client for a limited period of time. With manual allocation, a client's IP address is assigned by the network administrator, and DHCP is used to convey the assigned address to the client. An internet can use one or more of these mechanisms, depending on the policies of the network administrator. Dynamic allocation is the only one of these mechanisms that allows automatic reuse of an address that is no longer needed by the client to which it was assigned.

### The DHCP Messages

The format of DHCP messages is based on the format of BOOTP messages, to capture the BOOTP relay agent behavior described as part of the BOOTP specification. This format was shown earlier in this appendix in Figure C–6. Figure C–7 shows the DHCP format. The messages and their functions are summarized in Table C–1.

To begin the DHCP operations, the client broadcasts a DHCPDIS-COVER message onto its subnet. This message may include options that

| 0 | 9–15 | 1 5 | 1 6 | 17–22 | 2 3 | 2 4 | 25–30 | 3 1 |
|---|---|---|---|---|---|---|---|---|
| op (1) | htype (1) | | hlen (1) | | | hops (1) | |  |
| xid (4) | | | | | | | | |
| secs (2) | | | flags (2) | | | | | |
| ciaddr (4) | | | | | | | | |
| yiaddr (4) | | | | | | | | |
| siaddr (4) | | | | | | | | |
| giaddr (4) | | | | | | | | |
| chaddr (16) | | | | | | | | |
| sname (64) | | | | | | | | |
| file (128) | | | | | | | | |
| options (variable) | | | | | | | | |

**Figure C–7   The DHCP Message Format**

**Table C–1    The DHCP Messages**

DHCPDISCOVER: Client broadcast onto subnet to locate available servers

DHCPOFFER: Message from server to client in response to DHCPDISCOVER with offer of configuration parameters

DHCPREQUEST: Client message to servers either (a) requesting offered parameters from one server and implicitly declining offers from all others, (b) confirming correctness of previously allocated address after, e.g., system reboot, or (c) extending the lease (time-of-use) for a particular network address.

DHCPACK: Server message to client with configuration parameters, including committed network address

DHCPNAK: Server message to client indicating client's notion of network address is incorrect (e.g., client has moved to new subnet) or client's lease has expired

DHCPDECLINE: Client message to server indicating network address is already in use

DHCPRELEASE: Client message to server relinquishing network address and cancelling remaining lease

DHCPINFORM: Client message to server, asking only for local configuration parameters; client already has externally configured network address

suggest values for the network address and lease duration. BOOTP relay agents may pass the message on to DHCP servers that are not on the same subnet.

Each server may respond with a DHCPOFFER message that includes an available network address in the "yiaddr" field of the message. Other configuration parameters are coded in the in DHCP options. The servers need not reserve the offered network address, although the protocol will work more efficiently if the server avoids allocating the offered network address to another client. When allocating a new address, servers check that the offered network address is not already in use; e.g., the server may probe the offered address with an ICMP echo request message. The server transmits the DHCPOFFER message to the client, using the BOOTP relay agent, if necessary.

## THE NETWORK ADDRESS TRANSLATION PROTOCOL

The Network Address Translation (NAT) allows an organization to use private, nonregistered IP addresses (nonglobally routable addresses) within its own routing domain. If traffic is to be sent out of this domain, NAT translates these addresses to globally routable addresses. The reverse process occurs at the router for traffic received by the domain. NAT thus allows an organization to use its own private addresses. It also supports a process called the TCP load distribution feature that allows the mapping of a single global address to multiple nonglobal addresses. This feature is used to conserve addresses, and is explained shortly. NAT is described in RFC 1631, and examples used in this discussion are sourced from this RFC and [CISC98].

Figure C–8 is used to introduce the basic concepts of NAT. First, a couple of definitions are in order. An *inside local IP address* is a nonglobal address that is assigned to a host. This host resides on an inside

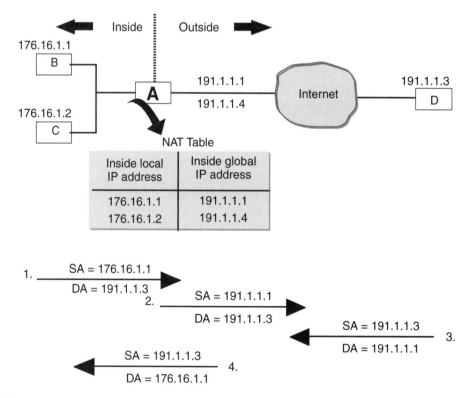

**Figure C–8   Network Address Translation (NAT)**

network—one that uses nonglobal addresses. An *inside global IP address* is a global address and represents the inside address to the outside networks (global addressing networks). Router A in this figure houses a NAT table that correlates these addresses.

The bottom part of Figure C–8 shows how NAT is used to map addresses between the inside and outside networks. In event 1, host B sends an IP datagram to Host D, through router A. Router A checks the address in the datagram and knows that source address (SA) 176.16.1.1 is an inside address. If an entry in the NAT table does not exist, the router dynamically selects an available global address from a pool of addresses, and creates an entry in the table. In event 2, the router replaces the inside SA with the corresponding outside SA, and forwards the datagram.

In event 3, host D replies, and uses its SA of 191.1.1.3, and the NAT global address for the destination address (DA) of 191.1.1.1. This datagram is received by router A, which performs the mapping of the global DA of 191.1.1.1 to the inside DA of 176.16.1.1, depicted as event 4 in the figure.

NAT is a straightforward configuration; essentially the local IP and global IP addresses are entered into the table during the configuration, along with the inside and outside interfaces on the router.

NAT allows the reuse of inside global addresses by mapping one of these addresses to more than one local address. This operation is called *overloading an inside global address.* The ability to maintain unambiguous identification of all user sessions is through the inside local address, the inside global address, plus the port numbers that are carried in the TCP or UDP segment header.

NAT defines another address; it is called the *outside global IP address,* and it is a conventional IP address assigned to a host on the globally addressable outside network.

Figure C–9 shows how this part of NAT works. In event 1, host B sends a datagram to host D, through router A. The figure shows the source address (SA), source port (SP), destination address (DA), and destination port (DP). The router intercepts the datagram, and performs either static or dynamic translation of the inside local IP address (176.16.1.1) to a shared inside global IP address (191.1.1.1).

In event 2, the router forwards the datagram toward the destination host D. In event 3, host D replies. The host simply exchanges the destination address and port number with the source address and port number.

Router A receives this datagram, and looks at the NAT table to determine what it is to do. It uses the socket pair shown in event 3 as a key to the table.

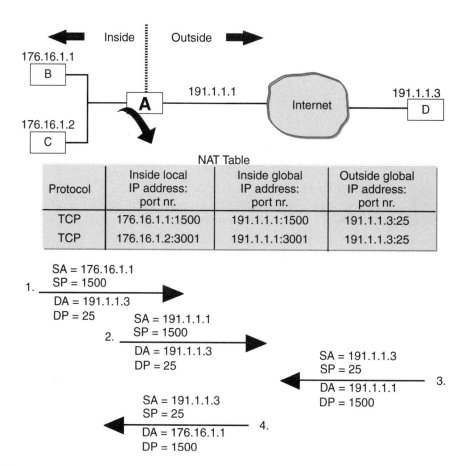

Where:
  DA   Destination IP address
  DP   Destination port number
  SA   Source IP address
  SP   Source port number

**Figure C–9    Overloading Inside Global Addresses**

In event 4, the translation is made back to host B's inside local IP address and the datagram is delivered to host B in the inside network.

The same operation can be performed for host C, using the second entry in the NAT table.

The configuration at the router entails the allocation of a pool of global addresses as needed, and then correlating them with the inside addresses and the associated input and output interfaces.

NAT has several other useful features, and one of them merits a description here. It has nothing to do with IP address management, but is concerned with the distribution of workload across multiple hosts. The operation can be useful in a situation where a host is overloaded with work. For example, a name server may be heavily used, and it is a relatively simple matter to down load a Domain Name System (DNS) file from the authoritative name server to one or more hosts, and use them to absorb the extra work. Figure C–10 shows how NAT is used to support *TCP load distribution*.

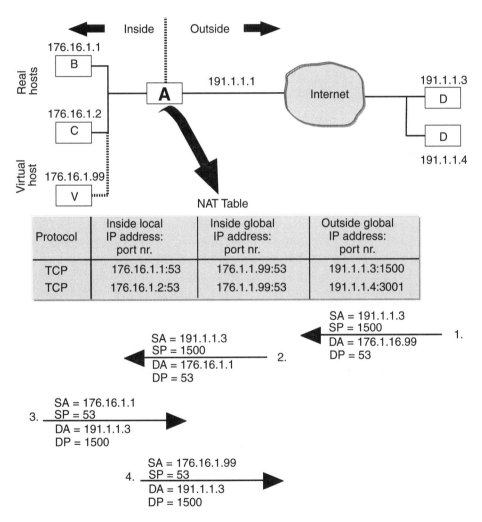

**Figure C–10   TCP Load Distribution**

The key to this operation is to configure the router with the IP addresses of the hosts that will share the workload (they are called *real hosts*), and to indicate that these hosts belong to a rotary pool. Another IP address is set up to identify a *virtual host*. This "host" does not exist, and its address is used by the router to identify the rotary group; it is shown as host V in this figure. Once the system is configured, the operations are similar to the examples covered earlier.

The second entry in the table is not explained in this text. Its operations are like the operations for the first entry, except the NAT table identifies host C (instead of host B, in the first entry) to receive the datagram.

The NAT TCP load distribution operation in this example could distribute the workload between hosts B and C, and each new connection could be shifted between these machines.

## INTERNET CONTROL MANAGEMENT PROTOCOL (ICMP)

A relatively new ICMP operation is the router discovery feature (RFC 1256). It entails a host, upon being installed and bootstrapped onto a network, sending an ICMP router solicitation message. The concept is shown in Figure C–11. It is sent as a broadcast or multicast message.

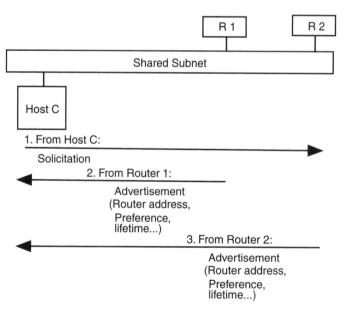

**Figure C–11    Router Discovery Operations**

Any router on the same subnet responds with a router advertisement message. This message contains the router's IP address (or addresses) and a preference level for which address the host should when sending traffic to that router. The preference level field can be set to x80000000 to indicate that an address is not to be used as a default router address. The lifetime field in the advertisement informs the receivers how long (in seconds), the addresses are valid. If an interface is down, the advertisement's lifetime field is set to 0.

Obviously, this ICMP operation allows the host to discover the routers on its subnet. And when the host is first brought-up on the subnet, it usually sends solicitation messages three seconds apart. When it receives an advertisement, it stops sending the solicitations.

A router transmits router advertisements on all its interfaces that are configured as broadcast or multicast. These advertisements are sent by the router every 450 to 500 seconds.

Since some systems have multiple routers on a subnet, the messages must be set up such that the preference levels are indicative of the network administrator's intents with regard to primary routers, backup routers, etc.

# Appendix D

## The Next Hop Resolution Protocol (NHRP)

### PURPOSE OF NHRP

The purpose of NHRP is to discover and correlate a layer 3 (network layer address) and the NBMA subnetwork address of the NBMA *next hop* *to* a destination station. The term NBMA subnetwork address refers to the underlying layer beneath the internetworking layer. Examples of NBMA subnetwork addresses are X.25 addresses, ATM addresses, and SMDS addresses.[1]

If the L_3 destination address is connected to the NBMA subnetwork, then the next hop is directly to the destination station. If the destination is not connected to the NBMA subnetwork, then the next hop must be to an egress router that can reach the destination station. Ideally, this router is the best path to the destination, but NHRP is not designed to resolve address mappings or path analysis beyond the NBMA subnetwork. Of course, for a system to function properly, conventional route discovery protocols should be employed between NBMA subnet-

---

[1]Strictly speaking, this definition of an NBMA subnetwork address is not correct, although it is used throughout the NHRP specifications. X.25 is a internetwork layer operation but the idea behind the NHRP is to define the conventional internetworking layer (layer 3) to operate over the NBMA subnetwork. So, for X.25 we could have two layer 3 protocols involved in the process with, say, IP running on top of X.25.

works to find these paths. Notwithstanding, NHRP can find an egress router by its own operations, and does not have to rely on other discovery protocols, even though ARP can co-exist with NHRP.

## EXAMPLES OF NHRP OPERATIONS

In Figure D–1, the source IP node is sending packets to the destination IP node. The packets are traversing routers 1, 2, and 3 to reach the destination. This example assumes ATM is operating in this network, and the connections between these switches are ATM links.

In Figure D–2 a server residing in Network 1 is responsible for the support of the client's users ability to reach destination nodes. The sources and sinks of the traffic are IP nodes, using conventional IP addresses.

The client is not responsible for route discovery. This task is assumed by an egress router, running an external gateway protocol, such as the Border Gateway Protocol (BGP). The addresses discovered by the egress router are conveyed to the server.

Later, when user A sends traffic to user B, user A's datagram is intercepted by the client. The client's responsibility is to send this traffic to the most efficient egress point in the network. It may have this information stored locally. If not, it sends a request to the server.

The server knows about the destination IP address, courtesy of the egress router's keeping the server informed through the Open Shortest Path First (OSPF), BGP, or some other routing protocol. The server will

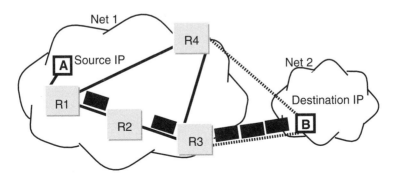

**Figure D–1   Operations without NHRP**

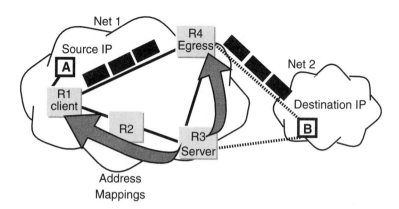

**Figure D–2    Route Server-based Relaying with NHRP**

respond to the client's request by sending it a message containing the address of the egress router. The client then forwards this traffic for user B to the egress router, typically over an established ATM connection. The server could also send a label that is to be used for this particular flow.

The next example in Figure D–3 is an example of the contents of the NHRP Next Hop Resolution Request and Reply messages. The job of NHRP in this example is to map IP addresses to ATM addresses. To keep matters simple, I use the letters ABC, DEF, and KLM to represent ATM addresses, which are based on the ITU-T Network Service Access Point (NSAP) standard.

Referring to Figure D–3, we assume the NHC with addresses DEF/192.168.3.3 receives a datagram destined for station 192.168.2.3 that is located in NBMA 2.[2] NHC DEF sends an NHRP request message to the NHS whose address is HIJ/192.168.3.4. Notice that the request message has the destination protocol address coded as the target protocol address of 192.168.2.3.

The NHS NHRP tables reveal that subnet 192.168.2 is reachable through NHC KLM/192.168.3.2. Therefore, the NHS sends back the NHRP response message with the next hop fields coded to identify the egress router to NBMA 2. This router is identified with addresses KLM/192.168.3.2.

---

[2]NMBA is the initials for a nonbroadcast multiple access network, such as X.25, ATM, SMDS, or Frame Relay. That is, a switched network.

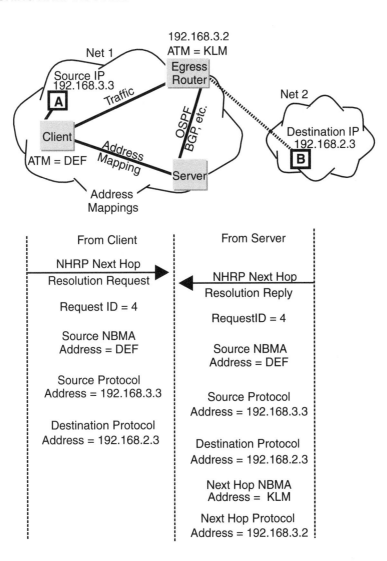

**Figure D–3    Example of the NHRP Packet Exchanges**

## CONFIGURING NHRP ROUTING

To configure NHRP routing, the routers must be configured to per-form the tasks summarized in Table D–1. This section provides an overview of each of these tasks. The specific rules for each of these tasks are documented in the router's user's manuals.

**Table D–1   NHRP Configuration Tasks**

Enabling NHRP on an interface

Configuring a station's static IP-to-NBMA address mapping

Statically configuring a next hop server

Configuring NHRP authentication

Controlling NHRP rate

Suppressing forward and reverse record options

Specifying the NHRP responder address

Changing the time period NBMA addresses are advertised as valid

Some of these tasks are straightforward; others need more explanation. Some are somewhat tertiary to the operation of the routing domain, and others are of primary importance. For each task explained, if I have already discussed the operations pertaining to the task in the chapter, I refer you to that discussion with an identification of the section header title.

- Enabling NHRP on an interface: This task sets up NHRP for execution on the router. A unique identifier is entered with this command. All NHRP nodes within a logical NBMA network must be configured with the same identifier.

- Configuring a station's static IP-to-NBMA address mapping: Each node in the network must also be configured with an ATM address. This command is used to enter this address and correlate it to the node's IP address.

- Statically configuring a next hop server: This command establishes a designated node as the next hop server.

- Configuring NHRP authentication: This task entails the entry of a "string," which is an identifier. All NHRP nodes use this string to authenticate each other.

- Controlling NHRP rate: This task is used to control which IP packets trigger the sending of NHRP requests. It also provides a parameter that sets a limit on how many NHRP packets are emitted by a node.

- Suppressing forward and reverse record options: The NHRP router automatically records the routes of the NHRP packets in order to detect possible loops among next hop servers. This command suppresses this operation.

- Specifying the NHRP responder address: If a NHRP wants to know which NHRP server generates a response, this command is configured.
- Changing the time period NBMA addresses are advertised as valid: This command controls the length of time that NBMA addresses are considered valid.

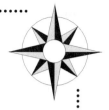

# Abbreviations

A    application layer
ACK    acknowledgment
ARP    Address Resolution Protocol
AS    autonomous systems
ASN.1    Abstract Syntax Negotiation One
ATM    automated teller machines
B    bandwidth
BER    basic encoding rules
BGP    Border Gateway Protocol
BPDU    bridge message or protocol data unit
BSC    binary synchronous control
BVI    bridge-group virtual interface
C bit    Cost bit
C/R    command/response bit
CIDR    Classless Interdomain Routing
CIX    Commercial Internet Exchange
CLNP    connectionless network protocol
CM    configuration message
CSMA/CD    Carrier Sense Multiple Access/Collision Detect
D bit    delay bit
D    delay

DA    destination address
DF    Don't Fragment
DHCP    Dynamic Host Configuration Protocol
DLC    data link control
DLS    Data Link Switching
DP    destination port
DSAP    destination service access point address
DSP    domain specific part
DTL    designated transit list
EBGP    external border gateway protocol
EGP    external gateway protocol
EIGRP    Enhanced IGRP
ESI    end system identifier
FDDI    Fiber Distributed Data Interface
FIX    Federal Internet Exchange
FTAM    File Transfer and Access Management
GGP    gateway-to-gateway protocol
HDLC    high level data link control
I/G    individual/group bit
IBGP    internal BGP

ICMP   Internet Control Management Protocol
IDP   initial domain port
IDRP   interdomain routing protocol
IEEE   Institute of Electrical and Electronics Engineering
IGP   internal gateway protocol
IGRP   Inter-Gateway Routing Protocol
IP   Internet Protocol
IS-IS   intermediate system to intermediate system
ISP   Internet Service Provider
IWU   internetworking unit
LLC   logical link control
LSA   link state metric advertisement
LSAP   link service access point
MAC   media access control
MAE   Metropolitan Area Exchange
MAN   metropolitan area network
MAXage   maximum age
MED   Multiple Exit Discriminator
MTU   maximum transmission unit
N   network layer
NAP   Network Access Point
NAT   Network Address Translation
NHRP   Next Hop Resolution Protocol
NSAP   Network Service Access Point
NSSA   not so stubby areas
NW   network
ODR   On Demand Routing
OID   object ID
OSI   Open Systems Interconnection
OSPF   open shortest path first
OUI   organization unique identifier
P   physical layer
P/F   poll/final bit
PARC   Palo Alto Research Center
PDU   protocol data unit
PG   peer group
PNNI   private network-to-network interface
PPP   point-to-point protocol
PTSE   PNNI topology state elements
PTSP   PNNI topology state packet

PU   physical unit
QOS   quality of service
R bit   reliability bit
RARP   reverse address resolution protocol
RCC   routing control channel
RD   Routing Domains
RIF   routing information field
RIP   Routing Information Protocol
RIU   ring interface unit
RNR   receive not ready
RR   receive ready
SA   Source address
SAAL   Signaling ATM Adaptation Layer
SABME   Set asynchronous balanced mode extended
SAP   service access point
SDLC   synchronous data link control
SEL   selector
SMTP   Simple Mail Transfer Protocol
SP   source port
SPF   shortest path protocol
SRT   source rate transparent bridging
SSAP   source service access point address
SSCF   Service Specific Coordination Function
SSCOP   service specific connection oriented protocol
SSP   switch-to-switch protocol
T bit   throughput bit
T   transport layer
TCP   Transmission Control Protocol
TOS   type of service
TTL   time-to-live
U/L   local or universal bit
UA   unnumbered acknowledgment
UCB   University of California at Berkeley
UI   Unnumbered information
VLSM   variable length subnet mask
VPC   virtual path connections
WAN   Wide Area Network

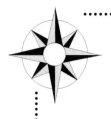

# Index